Chicago Católico

LATINOS IN CHICAGO AND THE MIDWEST

Series Editor
Frances R. Aparicio, Northwestern University

A list of books in the series appears at the end of this book.

Chicago Católico

Making Catholic Parishes Mexican

DEBORAH E. KANTER

1 2 3 4 5 C P 5 4 3 2 1
♾ This book is printed on acid-free paper.

Library of Congress Cataloging-in-Publication Data
Names: Kanter, Deborah E, 1961– author.
Title: Chicago católico: making Catholic parishes Mexican / Deborah E Kanter.
Description: Urbana: University of Illinois Press, 2020. | Series: Latinos in Chicago and the Midwest | Includes bibliographical references and index.
Identifiers: LCCN 2019040151 (print) | LCCN 2019040152 (ebook) | ISBN 9780252042973 (cloth) | ISBN 9780252084843 (paperback) | ISBN 9780252051845 (ebook)
Subjects: LCSH: Hispanic American Catholics—Religious life. | Catholic Church—Illinois—Chicago—Membership. | Church work with Hispanic Americans—Catholic Church. | United States—Emigration and immigration. | Mexico—Emigration and immigration.
Classification: LCC BX1407.H55 K36 2020 (print) | LCC BX1407.H55 (ebook) | DDC 282/.773110896872—dc23
LC record available at https://lccn.loc.gov/2019040151
LC ebook record available at https://lccn.loc.gov/2019040152

To the very generous people—del pasado, del presente—of St. Francis of Assisi, St. Adalbert, St. Ann, St. Paul, St. Pius V, St. Procopius, and Providence of God. To the generations of Chicagoans to come, from Mexico and around the world.

Contents

Acknowledgments

IT TOOK A LEAP OF FAITH to go from work on colonial Mexican ethnohistory to twentieth-century Chicago, Mexican, and Catholic history. I basically started at square one in the fields of U.S. urban and Catholic history. Fortunately I found good counsel from many scholars along the way. I considered the possibilities of a Mexican Chicago project while in residence at the Newberry Library: essentially sneaking out to other archives. Jim Grossman sensed promise in the topic and urged me to read John McGreevy's *Parish Boundaries*. That crucial book made me rethink essential questions about urban life, history, and the black-white binary that so characterized the Chicago of my childhood.

On my first day at the archive, I met Malachy McCarthy, then completing his dissertation on Catholic and Protestant outreach to Mexicans before 1940. Malachy welcomed my explorations, generously offered leads and introductions, and patiently answered my ignorant questions about Catholic history. Over the eighteen years it took me to complete this project, he has offered support and encouragement. When my ambitions lagged, he helped jumpstart my vision of the research. I treasure our travels from Pittsburgh to Austin, from Momence to Mundelein.

In 2001 my father mailed me an article from the *Chicago Tribune* Magazine: Patrick Reardon's thoughtful "The Americanization of the Lunas." I contacted Luna family historian Cesar Garza. Soon Cesar shared family photos and introduced me to people from St. Francis of Assisi (who, in turn, opened up a network of fabulous people). Cesar generously invited me to the Luna family reunion in Chicago and, another year, in Monterrey, Mexico. I learned a great deal from spending time with this warm, transnational family who made me feel included on both sides of the border.

When I read Tim Matovina's *Guadalupe and Her Faithful*, I found the kind of work I aspired to. Still I questioned my ability to pull off the deep research of place, multiple perspectives, and evolving identities that Tim had masterfully pulled together. A decade later, Tim asked me if "my book" was ready. His question made me realize that my scattered papers and articles were the makings of a book. Tim has been a wise, generous colleague in the ups and downs of writing this book.

I received much early encouragement from Peter Alter, the late Peter D'Agostino, Robert Devens, Leon Fink, Rita Arias Jirasek, the late Arturo Rosales, and Carlos Tortolero. Visits to the National Museum of Mexican Art offer steady inspiration. I am ever grateful for sustained connections with Chicago scholars Rima Lumin Schultz and Ellen Skerrett: together, we share a passion to reframe the history of the Near West Side. I owe a great deal to the communities of scholars I have worked with at the Newberry Library Latino/Borderlands Seminar, the American Catholic Historical Association, and the Chicago Urban History Seminar. I can hardly express my appreciation for the CEHILA-USA members with whom I share work, conversations, and fellowship.

From conferences and seminars, to Facebook and email, I feel supported by fellow researchers René Alvarez, Gerry Cadava, Sergio González, Felipe Hinojosa, Cheryl Ganz, Myrna García, Cristina Heisser, Tim Hernandez, Michael Innis-Jiménez, Benjamin Johnson, Nicole Marroquin, Kristen McCleary, Michael McCoyer, Eduardo Moralez, Tim Neary, Elaine Peña, and Bob Wright. Thanks to my friends, many of whom read or talked about pieces of this book, including Marcos Alcaine-Soto, Chris Blaker, Carrie Booth-Walling, Chris Burgess, Laura Day, Wes Dick, Mike Elliott, Riva Feshbach, Ann Davis Garvin, Liz Goetz, Anne Heise, Joe Ho, JaShong King, Amy Lesemann, AJ Mattson, Marcy Sacks, and John Thiels, Extra thanks to my "it takes a village," final proof readers! Laura Brade provided Czech language translations. I love a good walk around Pilsen and learned much by doing so in the company of John Brady, Michael McCoyer, the late Francisco Mendoza, David Diego Rodríguez, and the historians that took part in my "Churches of Pilsen" tour.

Archivists and librarians have helped at many places. I owe a special thanks to Héctor Hernandez at the Rudy Lozano branch of the Chicago Public Library; Julie Satzik and Megan Romero Hall at the Joseph Cardinal Bernardin Archives & Records Center; Fr. James Flint OSB of the St. Procopius Abbey Archives; Sr. Margaret Zalot SSC of the Sisters of St. Casimir Archive; the Sisters of St. Francis in Joliet; Paul Nemecek and volunteers at the Czech & Slovak American Genealogy Society of Illinois; and Steve Balkin and Lori

Grove of the Maxwell Street Preservation Society. At the Claretian Missionaries Archive, Malachy McCarthy and Doris Cardenas have been true collaborators and always make me feel at home on Monroe Street.

Fiction writers including Sandra Cisneros, Stuart Dybek, Philip Kolin, Hugo Martínez-Serros, Alice McDermott, and Salvatore Scibona inspire me with their musings on neighborhoods, families, and being Catholic in past times. This book took a fundamental pivot because of a conversation I had at the Providence of God School reunion. One alumna asked me if my book would be like one he had loved, Luis Alberto Urrea's *The Hummingbird's Daughter*. That question made me re-think the end product. Could I write a book that was more story driven? Could I write a history that people might enjoy reading? Carol Spindel's creative non-fiction workshop at the Iowa Summer Writing Festival gave me the boost to think of myself as a writer and to break out, somewhat, from academic conventions. Students in my Mexican American history classes at Albion College read drafts, offered comments, and suggested I was on the right track.

I am grateful to Chicago clergy who met with me, providing context and often fruitful leads: Fr. Chuck Dahm, OP, Fr. Don Nevins, Fr. Arturo Pérez-Rodríguez, Fr. Dan Reim SJ, Fr. Tim Howe SJ, Bishop John Manz, Fr. Rosendo Urrrabazo, CMF, and Fr. Esequiel Sánchez. It was a special treat to conduct research at religious communities: at abbeys and motherhouses, I gained a sense of the distinct charism of orders including the Sisters of St. Francis, the Sisters of St. Casimir, the Benedictines, and the Claretians. Secretaries at the Pilsen rectories answered questions and pulled out old photos.

What makes this book special are the stories of Chicago's Mexican laypeople. All of the people I interviewed helped me to recreate, to the best of my ability, the world of historic parishes from multiple perspectives. Early in the research I met Loretta Jaimes. Every single chapter in this book connects to Loretta, from her aunt Elidia to an evolving Pilsen. Much thanks to the entire the Jaimes and Cabrera families! Ever the organizer, Loretta introduced me to The Cobras. I was tickled to tag along for their reunions. I am inspired by these spunky women, including Lupe Almendarez, Grace Gonzalez, Lee Lopez, Blaze Pérez, and Flora Soto-Ortega. Rich interviews with members of the Galvan family, so involved with St. Francis, proved vital. Thanks to the St. Francis Wildcats and the Santo Nombre at St. Francis. The vital Mexican neighborhood of Near West Side—gone since my birth—lives on in the memories of all the Mexican American people who grew up at St. Francis. I hope this book preserves a sense of this past community.

Todo respeto al St. Francis Preservation Committee. Their story is just mentioned in this book, but I hope to write soon about their herculean efforts to keep their church open in the 1990s. Margarita and Carlos Villaseñor have long supported my research; I treasure their warmth and *pláticas*.

It has been a wonder to get to know many long-time Pilsen families. At first, St. Procopius or St. Ann's were just church buildings to me. Over time, I gained a sense of each parish as a community. At St. Procopius, I thank the late Julia Rodriguez and her children Concha and Gelacio; Silvia Juarez; the Paz family; and the St. Procopius Guadalupanas. At Providence of God, the school alumni graciously allowed me to tag along at their reunion and to ask questions in their on-line group. Special thanks to Marietta Rotman Torres, Daniel Jiménez, and Sal Medina. Richard Olszewski and Blanca Torres shared thoughts about their inspired struggle to preserve St. Adalbert Church. At St. Ann's, thanks to María Elena Arciniega and Beto Montaño. I am ever indebted to the Almendarez family who spilled out their hearts. Lisa Almendarez has become a dedicated collaborator and a dear friend.

I received valuable support from Lori Duff, Joan Skinner Eagen, Yvonne Spence, Linda Wooden, and my student researcher Christian Márquez. The baristas at Mighty Good Coffee support me with good chats and cortados. Without Brady Mikusko, I would not have completed my first book. She helped me clarify my goal of publishing this book and instilled the skills to execute that vision. Albion College generously supported this research with the Hewlettt-Mellon Fund for Faculty Development and the Julian S. Rammelkamp Endowed Chair. As the book nears publication, I am glad for incisive comments from readers at the University of Illinois Press, Dawn Durante, and Frances Aparicio. Kris Kopek created tables and a much-improved timeline. Cartographer Molly O'Halloran has worked with me to research and draw the maps. Many thanks to copy editor Mary Hill and indexer Heather Dubnick for their great attention to detail.

As I finished this book, I reconnected with my graduate advisor William B. Taylor. My first semester at the University of Virginia, we did a wonderful directed study on colonial Mexican churches. In grad school, I wanted to make the connection between the *hijos del pueblo* I chose to study in Tenango del Valle and the Mexican immigration I was witnessing in 1980s Chicago. That seemed improbable at the time. At last, I am tying things together on my winding scholarly path from *colonialista* to *Chicago Católico*. Bill's prodigious scholarship on Mexican religious history dovetails with many of the questions that surfaced in this book. Bill generously read and commented on several chapters. I appreciate the mentoring I received thirty years ago and the collegiality I found more recently.

I think of my late parents (both children of immigrants) often as I completed this book. Early on they instilled a lively interest in Chicago and its changing neighborhoods. My mother, Madelyne, organized my first visit to Pilsen: Mexican Independence Day in 1974. My father, Manuel, was game to visit South Chicago. With delight, I watched him eat *pan dulce* and kibbitz with the *guadalupanas* in the church basement. Thanks to my siblings, their spouses, and my nieces and nephews for their interest in my project over many years.

León Pescador was along for much of the ride in the early years of this project. As a preschooler, I bundled him up at 4 a.m., drove in a blizzard, and we attended *misa de gallo* at Saint Francis. A couple years later he walked the length of 18th Street in a cold drizzle for the Via Crucis and endured the heat of a Grand Rapids procession. Older, León listened with patience and often with interest as I wrote this book. Raising a child while writing a book has its challenges, but my son has been easy-going, understanding, and joyful during the long haul.

How fortunate am I to have Dan Freidus with me in the home stretch of completing this book! He has supported me through the challenges of securing publication and the tedium of revisions. He enthusiastically chased after books and theses; provided frank comments on troublesome aspects of manuscript preparation; and suggested a better book title. Dan has fed me and brought me joy. When I can no longer see the forest for the trees, he helps me clarify essential questions about my research. At moments I wonder why I spent so many years delving into Catholic history. The answer in Dan's words: because I care about Mexican people and many of them care about Catholicism.

A word about names:

Many people mentioned in this book used accent marks variably in their names. For example, Charles Galvan versus Charles Galván. I have followed each person's preferred spelling whenever their preference is clear.

Unless otherwise noted, all translations are my own.

Introduction

My story, your story, the Church's story
continue as *nuestra historia*.
—José López, "The Liturgical Year"

WHEN I ATTEND parish picnics and Mexican family reunions, people occasionally ask what motivated me to pursue the history of Mexican Catholics in Chicago. Thirty-five years ago I began to spend considerable time in Mexico, leading to my PhD in colonial Mexican history. I always marveled at the grand, glowing sanctuaries of Mexican churches, where the faithful offered *milagros* (metal charms) and *trenzas* (braids) to their favorite saints. These demonstrations of devotion—in processions, barrio shrines, and stores and on dashboards—fascinated me. Catholicism in the United States, as I knew it growing up post–Vatican II, seemed so restrained by comparison. Religious devotion in Mexico appeared omnipresent.

I often visited Pilsen and other Mexican barrios in Chicago in the same years. On December 12, 1985, I attended the feast day of the Virgin of Guadalupe at St. Jerome's in the emerging Mexican outpost of Rogers Park. The evening Mass was poorly attended, ministered by a priest who muddled through in Spanish and conveyed little enthusiasm for the patroness of Mexico. An earnest, if lifeless, folk guitar trio played in the dark sanctuary. To me, it seemed a sad and not very Mexican night for the *mexicanos* of San Gerónimo. I wondered how they could ever feel at home in Chicago. I vaguely pondered why the archdiocese could not do better by the immigrants.

Fast forward to a Sunday in 2000 when I stepped into Blessed Agnes Church in Chicago's bustling Little Village neighborhood. The Mass, in Spanish, and the sanctuary here felt much more Mexican. Was it the various statues of saints, the rows of lit votive candles? The Virgin of Guadalupe to the main altar's left, vases of roses on a shelf just below? Maybe it felt more like Mexico due to the lively presence of so many families with young children.

Or possibly Blessed Agnes, with the sunlight streaming through the colored panes, reminded me of Mexico. There I stood, in Chicago, entranced by this undeniably Mexican church.

Yet looking up at the stained-glass windows with their angels and crosses, I was surprised to find that each panel listed the donors' names in Czech. The neighborhood had been Czech and Polish just three decades earlier. What had it been like, I mused, to be the first mexicana to attend Mass in an all-Czech parish? Had she been stared at? Shooed away? How had the first mexicanos managed to transform Blessed Agnes into Santa Inés? Pondering Chicago's demography and neighborhoods, I soon realized that this transformation must have occurred in dozens of churches throughout the city. I went to the archives to see whether there was any documentation of how these parishes became Mexican.[1]

I would soon learn that Chicago's most populous Mexican neighborhood had been demolished in the early 1960s to make way for the construction of the University of Illinois Chicago campus. Italian American remnants of the Near West Side still existed (known today as "Taylor Street"). Of the vanquished Mexican neighborhood, only St. Francis of Assisi Church remained. On weekdays in 2000 the ruddy brick church stood quietly, with only a smattering of decaying Maxwell Street shops, their customers, and the homeless for company. But stepping inside St. Francis's high-vaulted sanctuary, aglow with jewel-like stained-glass windows, I was astonished to find that here the faithful brought milagros and trenzas to their favorite saints. More precisely, during that first visit I watched a young immigrant couple place their baby's sonogram at the bloodied Jesús Nazareno statue in the church's back corner. They lit a red votive candle, adding to dozens already flickering. Side altars featured the Virgin of San Juan de los Lagos and the Santo Niño de Atocha. The Virgin of Guadalupe and her devotee, Juan Diego, filled a massive canvas looming over the main altar. My recent visit to Blessed Agnes paled. I felt then that I had never visited such a Mexican church outside of Mexico. On Sundays the sidewalks around St. Francis filled with Mexican parishioners, young and old, visiting and snacking from a dozen stands that offered tamales, mangos, atole, and sweet corn. How had Mexico re-created itself so faithfully every weekend at St. Francis? This book tells the story of how Mexicans have made a home in Chicago and its churches. Further, Mexicans and other Latinos are transforming the archdiocese into Chicago *católico* in ways that past generations of German and Irish bishops, priests, and sisters could not imagine.

I use the Catholic parish to view Mexican immigration and transformation in the United States.[2] For individuals arriving from Mexico, these parishes

FIGURE 1. Window, St. Agnes of Bohemia Church, "Darovel Spolek Ziveho Ruzence Marianska Druzina" (Given by the Society of the Living Rosary and the Blessed Virgin Mary Daycare). Translation by Laura Brade. Photo by the author.

served as a *refugio* (refuge). Mexicans fiercely attached themselves to specific parishes, much like European ethnic groups in days gone by. These parishes also had an Americanizing influence on Mexican members. Men and women took part in regular devotions and parish activities in ways quite similar to Polish, Italian, or Irish Catholics elsewhere in Chicago. Their children participated in May crownings of the Virgin Mary and played baseball on parish teams. At the same time, many Mexican American laypeople gained a sense of *mexicanidad* by participating in the parish's religious and social events. The parish acted as a glue that connected immigrant parents and their US-reared children. This process of building a Mexican identity and community well beyond the Southwest began at two Chicago parishes in the 1920s. *Chicago Católico: Making Catholic Parishes Mexican* tells intimate stories of immigrants, their children, and the communities they encountered, reshaped, and made anew in Chicago.

My research stretches and expands Chicano history narratives that often minimize religion's role in everyday lives. Chicano history, with its activist and secular bent, has often marginalized the place of religion for Mexican people in the United States.[3] Mexican immigrants to Chicago were more than "hog butchers to the world," mill hands, and factory workers. They had families, built communities, formed sports teams, and went to the movies. And Mexicans certainly went to Mass. Religious life countered their (often racialized) subordination as workers.

Even within cultural and social history, some Chicano scholars have claimed that settling in the United States meant secularization for immigrants and their children. George Sánchez, for example, asserts that "with so many other things to do in a metropolis such as Los Angeles, more and more Chicanos drifted from formal religious practices." He surmises that "Catholic religious practice . . . increasingly narrowed to the province of women, and became less a community function and more a set of rituals performed at home."[4] Early twentieth-century social scientists, including Manuel Gamio, Ernest Burgess, Robert Redfield, and their protégés, had a modernizing and/or anti-Catholic bent. For example, in 1934 a Burgess student described new arrivals from Mexico in this way: "All of them are Catholic in their religious background, and it is a highly superstitious, fanatical religious belief."[5] These social scientists produced reams of notes and theses on the first wave of Mexican immigrants, but their influential work underestimates and distorts what being Catholic meant to immigrants. These primary sources must be read carefully and in conjunction with religious archival sources.[6]

Some Chicano scholars characterize the institutional Catholic Church as ethnocentric and unwelcoming. Discussing a small city in California, Martha

Menchaca writes, "Thus, by 1929 the not-so-subliminal message to Mexican Catholics was: 'We are all God's children, but some races are superior to others, so stay on your side of town.'"[7] Some scholars of Mexican Chicago have generalized that "before the 1960s, local clergy ordered Mexican Catholics to the basement for worship."[8] In fact, this was seldom true. Early Chicana feminist writers criticized the Catholic Church as a patriarchal and racist institution that oppressed Spanish speakers and Chicanas.[9] This vein of *mujerista* scholarship positions genuine religious life not in the institutional, formal spaces of church but in the more intimate, informal spaces of home, reframing religious belief and practice toward the "popular," the "folk," or the "traditional." For Roberto Treviño, Mexican "ethno-Catholicism" was nurturing in contrast to the institutional US church, which tended to marginalize Mexicans in Houston.[10]

Of course, religion is lived in multiple spaces. While this book includes home *altarcitos* and rosary-chanting mothers (and fathers), much of the action takes place at the parishes. Being Catholic in the United States meant interacting with priests, teaching sisters, and the power structures of a diocese. *Chicago Católico* shows that Catholic devotion and church participation proved central for most Mexicans and the communities that they built, especially in a Catholic city like Chicago.

This book beats the drum for scholars—and Americans generally—to recognize the century-old presence of Mexican people in Chicago and other midwestern cities.[11] Chicano historiography emphasizes the "lost land" and racial subjugation of the historic Mexican populations of Texas, the Southwest, and California. By contrast, Mexicans in Chicago and throughout the Midwest were not colonized people. They arrived as immigrants and fortunately found themselves in a city of diverse immigrant populations and without entrenched anti-Mexican feelings in the early twentieth century.[12] Their neighbors, coworkers, and coreligionists came from Poland, Italy, Lithuania, and elsewhere. Each of these immigrant groups had, in time, integrated into the city's workplaces, neighborhoods, and parishes. Mexicans benefited from the fact that early twentieth-century Chicago was endowed with schools, settlement houses, and churches accustomed to the foreign-born. Accepted as Catholics, Mexicans undoubtedly had a much easier time entering many Chicago neighborhoods and parishes than African Americans. But European American congregations slighted Mexican newcomers in small ways, motivated less by racism than by a strong desire to preserve their ethnic identity and their aging national parishes.

John T. McGreevy posits that "how these Catholic ideas and institutions at once inhibited and facilitated assimilation into U.S. society is the central drama of twentieth-century U.S. Catholic history."[13] How did Mexicans intersect with US Catholic institutions? Did joining a US parish or sending children to parochial school lead to assimilation? Did it nurture mexicanidad? *Chicago Católico* shows that both currents were, in many instances, simultaneously possible. This book underlines religion's critical role in immigrants' urban adjustment and racial politics while recasting the Eurocentric assumptions of immigration history narratives. The field of US Catholic history truly needs more work on Latino communities and religious life, especially research that foregrounds the experiences of laymen and laywomen. Beyond a rich and suggestive theological literature, scholarship that explores Mexicans' engagement with the US Catholic Church in historic settings remains limited.[14] Given the rapidly shifting composition of the American Catholic Church, soon with a majority Latino laity, uncovering these Latino narratives is crucial.

What developed almost a century ago in just two Chicago parishes, St. Francis of Assisi and Our Lady of Guadalupe (in South Chicago), impacts the entire archdiocese. Today Latinos comprise 17 percent of the US population and nearly 40 percent of US Catholics. The Mexican-descent population (63 percent of US Latinos) has settled in every state. In 2017 Latinos became Chicago's second largest ethnic group, surpassing the city's African American population.[15] Chicago's century-old Mexican population offers historic lessons for myriad communities currently undergoing ethnic integration and succession around the nation.

A quick word especially to readers from Chicago about my scope and focus. If your family hails from South Chicago, Back of the Yards, or Little Village, you will not find much about these specific barrios here. You will find a new take on Chicago's history, one that will certainly connect to your parents, grandparents, or great-grandparents who arrived from Mexico, Bohemia, or Poland. My first chapters focus on the Near West Side and St. Francis of Assisi Church, and the rest of the book explores the many parishes of Pilsen. Taken together, the two neighborhoods reflect a century of Mexican and Mexican American life in Chicago. Because of my geographic focus, Puerto Ricans appear only tangentially. Mexican people were the city's Latino pioneers. While Puerto Ricans crossed paths with Mexicans, reaching equal numbers around 1960, they generally did not settle in Pilsen. My title alludes to a larger story of Latino Catholics, but only occasionally does the book get beyond the stories of Mexican people and their parishes.

This book reflects my expertise in Mexican history, as well as my native understanding of Chicago's intricate ethnic geography. I studied and worked in Mexico for four years conducting research in ecclesiastical archives, and I had countless participant-observer experiences in popular religious rituals. In Michoacán I watched people set up chairs for the night in front of their homes on December 11. What were they doing? The terse and mysterious answer: "Velando a la Virgen" (Accompanying the Virgin). I hopped off a bus near Malinalco and joined a stream of pilgrims walking the last miles to the sanctuary of El Señor de Chalma. I saw the matachines dance at Zapopan and took in the Cristero martyrs' relics in San Juan de los Lagos. With Mexico as my backdrop, I follow evolving forms of Latino/a popular piety in the United States. Over the past two decades, I marched in many religious processions, mingled at parochial school reunions, served up enchiladas with the *guadalupanas* at a church fair, and attended Polish-language Mass, all in Chicago. At 5:00 a.m. on December 12, I made my way in the dark and sometimes in the snow to churches in Detroit, Ann Arbor, Riverside, California, and Chicago to join others in singing my favorite hymn, "La Guadalupana" ("Desde el cielo una hermosa mañana . . ."). In recent years, I have observed the hard decisions and deep emotions that accompany parish closings. Along the way I have gained a palpable sense of the interplay of past changes and present-day challenges for Mexican and other parishes in the United States.

This book draws on a rich array of sources: parish bulletins and anniversary albums, archdiocesan correspondence, social science scholarship on Mexico and Chicago, school records, photos, parish newspapers, teaching sisters' convent annals, records of social service and community organizations, and Spanish-language newspapers. People have generously shared a 1924 diary, 1940s trophies, and family photos. I recorded dozens of oral histories. These chapters highlight memories from laity and clergy, Mexican American schoolchildren and their female religious teachers, parish athletes and coaches, European American social workers and neighbors, and the immigrant women who organized as guadalupanas and their husbands who took part in the Holy Name Society. All of these historical actors played a role in making parishes Mexican.

1. Paths to Chicago

Early Mexican Immigration and Catholicism, 1920–1939

Adiós estado de Texas con toda tu plantación.
Me despido de tus tierras por no pizcar algodón.

Good-bye, state of Texas with all your growing crops.
I bid farewell to your fields so I won't have to pick cotton.
—Ignacio M. Valle, "Corrido de Texas"

At the Church St. Francis on Roosevelt Road the predominant Catholic background of these immigrants reveals itself. There at a special Mass conducted for the Mexicans nearly a thousand worshippers often kneel and are comforted by the beauty and upreach of the prayers offered in the universal language of the Church of Rome. There at a shrine at one side of the church their own national patron saint, Our Lady of Guadalupe, gazes upon them.
—Robert C. Jones and Louis R. Wilson, *The Mexican in Chicago*

ELIDIA BARROSO THOUGHT BACK upon the events that preceded leaving her homeland of Mexico and the prolonged path that had brought her north. On October 20, 1924, Elidia put pen to paper, first jotting her new location—Chicago, Illinois—and humbly began in Spanish: "I have decided to write a little today. I wish that I could be a poet in order to tell a story, but I can't even spell." She wanted to weave together scattered writings from the past with thoughts on her current life. Sitting at a table in her new home in Chicago, twenty-six-year-old Elidia filled lined pages with memories of family members and homes, forever lost.[1]

"I will speak of my childhood," Elidia wrote, chronicling her earliest years in Guanajuato. She was born in 1897 on a ranch overseen by her grandfather don Nicolás Barroso, a man much respected by local notables. She grew up amid a multitude of family members. Her grandmother dressed in Spanish style and rode elegantly on horseback, while her well-dressed aunts preferred carriage rides. Elidia's grandparents hosted big parties for weddings and their grandchildren's baptisms. And every year they opened their house on Christmas, New Year's, June 24 and 29, September 10, and October 4. Notwithstanding the passage of twenty years, Elidia remembered these dates, which celebrate St. John the Baptist, St. Peter and St. Paul, St. Nicholas Tolentino, and St. Francis of Assisi. Her diary reminds us that the calendar of saints' days was widely known. Scattered rural places may not have had churches, but Catholic belief and practices greatly colored the Bajío in those years.

The family summoned a priest to her grandfather's deathbed. Elidia's father, Pedro Barroso, received his dying father's blessing there. After the patriarch's death, the family's fortunes became tenuous. Pedro and his wife, Savina, moved to a small *rancho* that Elidia warmly recalled for its "very good neighbors and furthermore a chapel featuring a Holy Cross venerated by those good people. We were very happy there." Due to financial insecurity, Pedro moved his family about Guanajuato several times in the waning years of the Porfirio Díaz regime. The revolution erupted, bringing greater financial troubles. Motivated by fears of the *revolucionarios*' "scandal" and "disorder," the family's internal migrations continued throughout Elidia's adolescence. While living in the city of Silao, Elidia often visited the temple of the Virgin of Loretito, including on her feast days.[2]

In the fall of 1916, when Elidia was eighteen, an epidemic struck Guanajuato. It killed her father, then her mother within weeks. Elidia and her three siblings found themselves orphaned. Within a year, "we resolved to emigrate." In the fall of 1917 they traveled, accompanied by relatives, to Laredo, Tamaulipas. They crossed apparently to Laredo, Texas, where an aunt lived. Elidia provided no details about their entry, which was likely a simple process, as it was for literate, middle-class Mexicans at that time.[3]

While a considerable family network had sheltered the Barroso children in Mexico, such protection proved impossible for the first years in the United States. The older sisters left the younger siblings in Laredo. As Elidia wrote, "We girls, now alone," pursued work in a remote Texas town. This is the first time that she mentions working; her middle-class upbringing likely precluded wage work in Mexico. Employed on a ranch in Frio County, Elidia felt vulnerable. Looking back on those first months in Texas, she noted, "We were well respected; I don't complain, despite the fact that we were entirely alone and young [solas y chicas todas]."[4] Imagine these young, middle-class Barroso women, thick braids down their back, speaking no English, not a Catholic church in sight, still mourning their parents, and working for strangers. In the Texas countryside they were very alone indeed.

The three Barroso sisters managed to reunite a year later in Fort Worth and established ties with kindly *mexicanos* in their boardinghouse. Elidia recalled a "gentleman" who helped her locate her older sister and a *señora* who looked out for her. In Fort Worth, they lived among good people who took them under their wing.[5] With this attention, Elidia was surprised to feel "some happiness. Since my parents left me, I hadn't had such a feeling." The señora even introduced Elidia to a respectable young man, and a romance soon developed in the fall of 1918. Elidia was especially touched that when she fell ill with the often fatal Spanish influenza, he continued to visit her. Without her older sister's approval, the courtship proceeded in secret. Learning of the couple's intent to marry, the older sister (acting as the family's patriarch) packed off Elidia to an aunt in San Antonio. Elidia quickly found work at one of the city's cigar factories, where "I met many girls, including two from my village."[6] Her sister sternly prohibited contact with the *novio*, yet Elidia maintained a secret correspondence with him, aided by her supportive younger sister. Eventually, she won her elder sister's consent for their engagement. He gave Elidia a ring and a watch. (Years later, she recorded its price of $32.50.) While Elidia steadily worked for five years in San Antonio, her fiancé apparently moved for work, even returning to Mexico for a job. Their courtship, similar to that of many young, highly mobile Mexican immigrants, did not involve parental approval.[7]

Elidia integrated into San Antonio's vibrant Mexican Catholic community. She began to reference the Catholic calendar, familiar since her earliest years on the rancho. Perhaps invited by her female coworkers, "on Easter Saturday, I went to a church." Soon after, she found her way to San Fernando Cathedral, where "I often went to Mass, to fiestas and rosaries."[8] With the active Claretian missionary order at its helm, San Fernando served the city's large Spanish-speaking population. Historian Timothy Matovina details the missionaries' attention to the growing numbers of Mexican immigrants. The order promoted public, communal devotions, including outdoor processions, and expanded Masses to celebrate the Virgin of Guadalupe. Elidia may well have participated in these very public celebrations. Perhaps she joined one of the eighteen lay societies, which functioned as minicommunities in the large parish.[9] This kind of Mexican public piety certainly eased the sting of exile from Mexico. Elidia reported being happy with her factory job, surrounded by mexicanas who respected her character; she seemed buoyed with occasional visits and letters in her long-distance courtship. Yet after five years, she quit her job in 1924. The next day ("blessed June 13") she bade farewell to her girlfriends, some of whom accompanied her to the *dipo*.[10] Then she boarded a train bound for Joliet, Illinois.

Elidia rode that coach with a heady mix of excitement and trepidation. She had grown up in a culture that questioned a lone woman's decency.[11] Despite six years in the United States, she spoke little English. Living and working among the Mexican exile community in Texas offered few chances to do so.[12] Heading to Illinois, she might have been giving up that linguistic and cultural cushion. That may explain why, on the busy day of her departure, she paid a final visit to confess with the *padres claretianos* at San Fernando: Would a confession in Spanish be possible up north? Any fears about venturing to distant Illinois were tempered by the reasons for her trip: she was visiting her younger sister Sofía, now married and awaiting her first child, and brother-in-law in Rockdale, Illinois. Furthermore, Elidia's fiancé now lived in "Chicago, Ill., a big city in that state."[13]

The train eventually rolled into Joliet. Elidia anxiously made her way into Union Station's grand lobby, awed by its vaulted ceiling and arched windows. The place bustled with hundreds of people, none of whom seemed to speak Spanish. Suddenly, she spied her beloved sister Sofía and relaxed. The following Sunday, after a quiet week in Rockdale, Elidia's fiancé came to visit her—with the older sister's permission. Three months later, at age twenty-six, Elidia finally married in a modest civil ceremony, witnessed by two *padrinos de casamiento*, at Sofía's house on a Saturday. The newlyweds left for Chicago the next day.

Within a few weeks, in the fall of 1924, Elidia began to keep her diary. She reflected much on the on-again, off-again six-year courtship, which finally brought her to Chicago and their marriage. She nostalgically remembered saints' days and romantic *serenatas* in Mexico. She grieved for her lost parents. Her notes about living in the United States are punctuated by train rides, correspondence, hard-earned dollars, separations and joyful reunions with her loved ones, and gratitude to divine Providence. Overall, Elidia experienced many episodes of dislocation tempered by connections to kinsfolk and a deeply Catholic piety. Chicago and her marriage, I believe, allowed her the leisure to consider all this in writing. While she wrote of her employment in Texas, she never mentions wage work in Chicago. Her husband apparently earned enough that, for the first time since leaving Mexico, Elidia did not have to work outside the home. (She proudly tallied how much cash her husband had given her during their courtship and after their marriage.) Her husband's wages seemed bountiful compared to Mexicans' earnings in Texas;

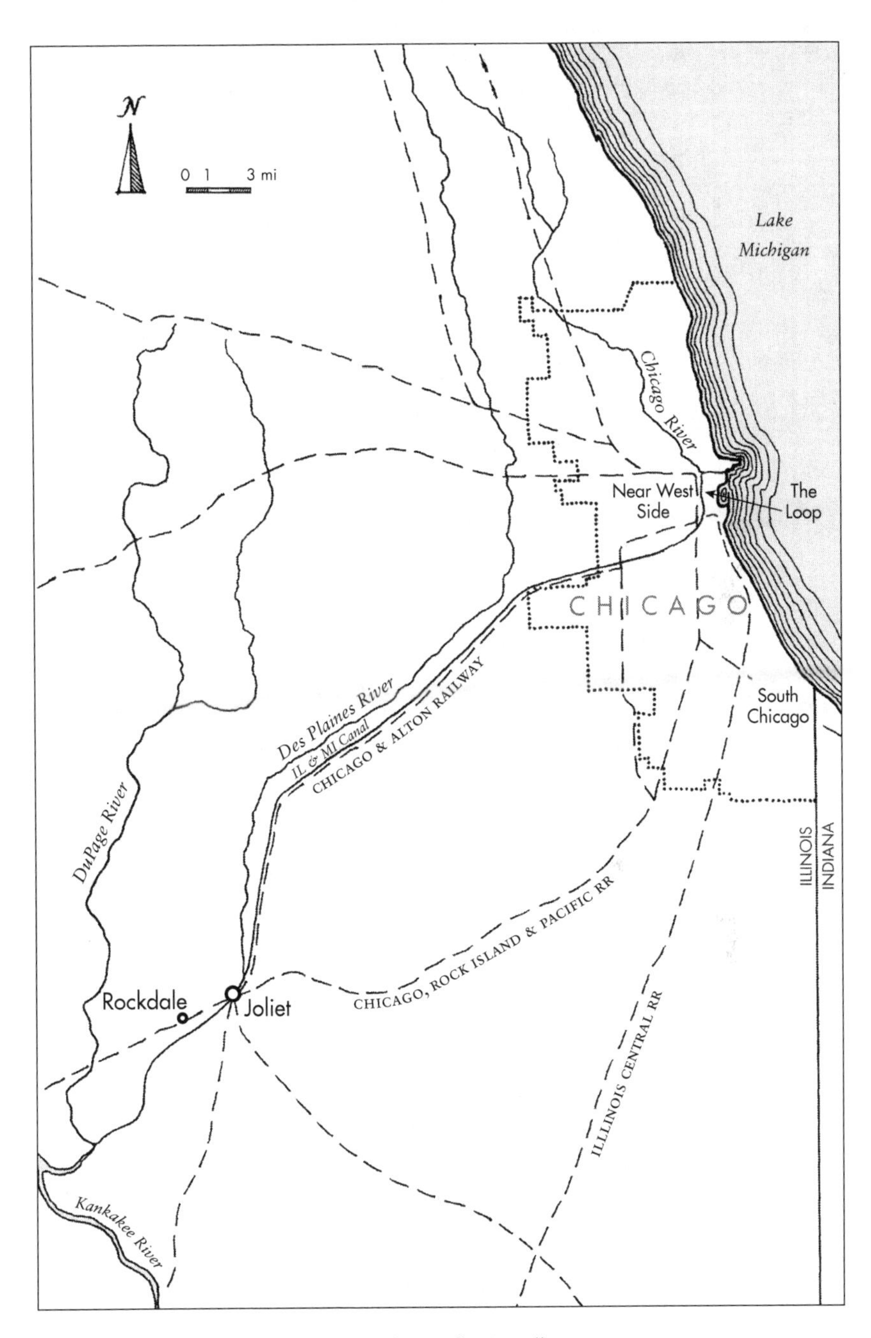

MAP 1. Elidia Barroso's Illinois. Map by Molly O'Halloran.

not only did he provide for them both, but Elidia could even send funds to her younger brother in Texas.

The newlyweds likely settled in the Near West Side, which would soon become the largest Mexican enclave in Chicago, close to work in the Loop and the vast train yards. Mexicans moved into dilapidated frame houses and cold-water flats alongside Italians, eastern European Jews, Greeks, and smaller numbers of African Americans. Outsiders saw the Near West Side as a slum. Elidia, while not very descriptive, recorded a largely positive view of her first months there. During her first Chicago winter, she noted on Christmas Eve, "The day is lovely. It had snowed heavily before, but today the sun has been so clear and beautiful that it truly lifts the heart. The ground all carpeted with white snow and with the golden sun, it gives an appearance of grace and virtue. So I sent my little brother out to do the shopping, and he had the luck to find $10. Thanks to God."[14]

Best of all, Chicago proved to be a place where Elidia could strengthen family ties and practice her Catholic faith as part of a larger community. She rejoiced that her first niece, born in Rockdale, was named for the Virgin of Loretito. With nostalgia and affection, she recalled the Virgin in Silao and the fiestas there; the child's birth and naming brought back memories of faith and place in her homeland. Train service enabled visits with her sister and new niece, who lived some thirty miles away. Northern wages allowed the two Barroso sisters in Illinois to send tickets to their two siblings who remained in Texas. In December 1924 the family reunited.

Elidia also started to connect with her faith in more formal ways in Chicago. When she first arrived, the only Catholic church that served Spanish speakers was the recently established Our Lady of Guadalupe in distant South Chicago. Just weeks after their civil ceremony, the couple ventured to that remote Mexican parish. Fr. Miguel García, CMF, an exiled priest from Guadalajara, officiated at the wedding. They married in a makeshift wooden church (a former army barracks) that temporarily housed the parish.[15] Regular Mass attendance at that time required a train trip for the thousands living in the Near West Side.

Yet opportunities for Mexican Catholic worship in the Near West Side soon emerged. In June 1925 Elidia joyfully wrote about going to Mass with her husband. Perhaps they were among the Mexican faithful who attended Mass at a storefront church, probably within walking distance from their home, with Fr. James Tort, CMF, presiding. Finally, after many years of migrations and uncertainty, Elidia was sufficiently settled that she could fulfill a long-standing desire in Chicago: she requested a Mass for her parents' souls for later that summer. She could communicate her desire to the Spanish-speaking

FIGURE 2. Elidia Barroso and her niece Loretta Cabrera, Rockdale, Illinois, ca. 1926. From the collection of the Jaimes family.

Claretian priests. With the date set, certainly her siblings in Rockdale and Chicago would join her at the Mass. Five months later, the Claretians began to minister at St. Francis of Assisi, an old German church in the Near West Side.[16] There Loretta Cabrera, the first Barroso grandchild, celebrated her first communion; her siblings were also baptized there, followed by weddings and more baptisms until the present. Nine decades later, St. Francis persists as a center of Mexican piety and community. This Catholic parish became a place for the Barroso family to pay homage to past generations and to establish new Mexican American lives. After a sad departure from Mexico and long periods of uncertainty in this country, going to church meant Elidia Barroso was finally home in Chicago.

▪ ▪ ▪

Ignacio Valle, after comparably winding paths, also made a home for himself in Chicago. In 1929 the bespectacled twenty-eight-year-old had his own music store, stocked with an array of ukuleles, guitars, violins, and bins of records. As most of his customers worked long days, Ignacio had some quiet on weekdays. He watched the fall light come through the plate-glass window, etched with the *tienda*'s name, El Arte Mexicano, with 837 S. Halsted St. above the entry. He prominently displayed the recordings of the four songs that he had composed and recorded at the Victor Studio on Michigan Avenue. His favorite was "El Bombaso" (The Bombastic), a foxtrot. His new record, "Soy puro Michoacán" (I am pure Michoacán), sold quite well. But with a wife, three kids, and a baby on the way, Ignacio needed more income.[17]

He pondered a recent big seller at his shop, "El Corrido de Pensilvania," that so captivated the young workingmen who stopped in on the weekends. Perhaps he could rewrite this train ballad. He placed the record on the gramophone and listened again to the lyrics. Yes, this was a story familiar to most every *paisano* who had made it to Chicago. Ignacio picked up a pencil and quickly refashioned the lyrics to fit the midwestern scene; in fact, he copied as much as he rewrote. In November he found musicians—regulars at his shop—to record his new "Corrido de Texas." He excitedly contracted Silvano Ramos, a strong tenor who had recently recorded dozens of Mexican songs in New York and Chicago, along with Daniel Ramírez.[18] Sure enough, the *corrido* (ballad) began to sell. Mexicanos living all over Chicago bought records from Valle's store. These records made "their way to the portable phonographs in the box-car homes of Mexican railroad workers all over the United States, or even the little far-away shacks which house the migratory laborers in the sugar-beet fields."[19] Corridos, while age-old folk expressions, were also a novelty: the first recording of a corrido in the United States was made in 1926. The ever-adaptable corridos also reflected immigrants' new challenges: labor recruiters, sugar beet work, automobiles, *pelonas* (flappers), and *el sistema americano*.[20]

Valle's "Corrido de Texas" told of a young couple parting ways in Texas as the husband headed north, solo, for work. The husband plaintively bid Texas farewell, singing,

> Adiós estado de Texas con todo tu plantación . . .
> Esos trenes del T.P. que cruzan por la Louisiana,
> Se llevan los mexicanos para el estado de Indiana.
>
> Good-bye state of Texas with all your growing crops . . .
> Those Texas & Pacific Railroad trains that cross Louisiana
> Carry the Mexicans to the state of Indiana.[21]

The workingman boarded the train with his *reganche*, a bunch of contracted men who had been warned not to take their wives with them so they could return easily. The singer did not know his exact destination: "Adiós Fort Worth y Dallas, poblaciones sin un lago. / Nos veremos cuando vuelva de por Indiana y Chicago" (Good-bye, Fort Worth and Dallas, cities without a lake. / We'll see each other when I return from Indiana and Chicago). The corrido also gave voice to the stranded wife, who wanted to join him up north ("pasearme por el norte") and care for him. She understood that she could not go, yet the wife begged, "Wherever you may be, write to me, don't be ungrateful; / And in reply I'll send you my picture as a forget-me-not."[22] This corrido's sentiments rang true for thousands who had made their way from Texas, gradually and often without much of a plan, to Chicago and other midwestern locales in the 1920s. The men usually ventured north first, leaving behind families or sweethearts.

"Corrido de Texas" in many ways mirrored Ignacio Valle's own winding trajectory. The Jalisco native escaped service in the revolutionary army and easily entered the United States in 1916. After several years employed by the railroads in Texas, he worked his way north on the rails and landed a steady job at an Illinois zinc mill. Surveying his early years, Valle commented, "All time I got better jobs—you know, I was smart, looked all right, they gave me better jobs."[23] By 1925 he had established himself in Chicago along with his wife, Louisa Soto, and their children. Ignacio worked at the Rialto Music House in the Loop; the store drew a significant foreign clientele, including Mexicans eager for corridos and dance music.[24] Within a few years, he launched his own business in the fast growing Mexican *colonia* on the Near West Side. He leased a shop across the street from Hull House in an area that many called Little Italy, a label that masked the influx of Mexicans. Valle advocated for entrepreneurs and artists in the growing Mexican community.[25] Just a few blocks south, Spanish-language Mass had started at St. Francis Church.

In the 1920s Mexicans came to Chicago in heretofore unimaginable numbers, but few had planned this destination. Fleeing the revolution, many Mexicans crossed the border never having heard of Illinois.[26] Most immigrants first established themselves in Texas, but low pay, seasonal labor, and discrimination kept many in poverty. Northern industries and farmers faced labor shortages, initially occasioned by World War I and then due to immigration restrictions (1921–24), and sent labor recruiters to Texas. Mexicans, fed up with harvesting cotton, took a chance and were "hooked" by the *enganchista* (contractor). They boarded the train and mouthed, if not sang, "Adiós estado de Texas con toda tu plantación." Initially, most went north to work on the railroads from Kansas to New York or on sugar beet farms from Nebraska to Michigan. These jobs required much moving around and entailed rough living conditions. Elida Barroso fortunately never had to keep house in a boxcar, a common story among pioneering Mexican families in the Midwest.[27] In 1919 the steel industry in Chicago and northern Indiana began sending enganchistas to Texas as well. In sum, few mexicanos came straight to Chicago.

After 1923 greater numbers of new arrivals from Mexico intentionally sought Chicago as a place to establish themselves. One recruiter used to hire cotton pickers in Laredo, but then he realized, "All they have in their heads is Chicago or Detroit; they won't stop in Texas for a $10 job."[28] Letters to family and friends increased the flow of Chicago-bound emigrants. By 1927 Illinois had become the fourth most common destination of Mexicans entering the United States. The typically winding path to Chicago certainly deserved its own song.

When sugar beet harvests finished or a stint on the *traque* ended, many mexicanos came to Chicago seeking work or looking for a compadre, or maybe they wanted to see the big city before heading back to Texas. For a newcomer, finding one's way in Chicago could be daunting. In 1920 a young man named Gómez arrived in Chicago; he anxiously stood "on the corner of Wabash and Harrison looking for Mexicans." He spied a brown-skinned man with familiar indigenous features and stopped him. Much to his relief, the kind paisano guided the young man to the Near West Side and quite possibly offered a floor on which he could sleep for the night.[29] An overalls-clad Matías Lara arrived in Chicago on a chilly November day in 1918. The unceasing traffic unnerved him. Lara found himself so lost in Chicago that he entrusted himself to the Virgin of San Juan de los Lagos, "asking that She illuminate the road that I sought." When the Virgin granted his petition, he then found his way. Lara never shook that feeling of absolute helplessness that enveloped him upon arrival in Chicago.[30] A first winter in Chicago proved difficult for many: getting (and holding on to) a job, finding decent housing, paying for coal, keeping clean in a cold-water flat, and contending with the *polacos* and *italianos* at jobsites, in a new neighborhood, or at church.[31] Many struggled for years before settling in. Others gave up on their Chicago sojourn, returning to Texas or Mexico.

■ ■ ■

When Elidia Barroso and her husband set up housekeeping in the mid-1920s, the Near West Side had emerged as one of Chicago's two hubs of Mexican life largely because it offered proximity to many jobs. Many men found work

FIGURE 3. Matías Lara and the Virgin of San Juan de los Lagos, retablo, 1918. From the collection of Jorge Durand and Douglas Massey, *Miracles on the Border.*

at the Illinois Central Freight House, less than a mile away, or elsewhere in Chicago's sprawling railway yards and stations, which ringed downtown. Mexicans comprised 42.9 percent of track maintenance workers in the Chicago vicinity in 1928. Some worked at the bedding factories on Roosevelt Road. The city's many candy factories, including the nearby Cracker Jack manufactory, hired Mexican women. Some downtown hotels also employed Mexicans.[32] The other large Mexican enclave took form in South Chicago, with its steel mills, on the city's border with Indiana.[33]

The Near West Side, one of Chicago's oldest and most densely populated neighborhoods, had drawn newly arrived immigrants since the 1850s. The Germans, Irish, and Bohemians arrived first, then the Italians, Jews, and Greeks. In tandem great migrations after 1917, Mexicans and African Americans settled there as well. Workingmen and workingwomen bought new and used goods from the outdoor stands and shops that crowded Maxwell Street, tended almost entirely by Jewish owners. For people of all ethnic groups, this "was where the bargains were." Mexicans would call the market *la pulga* (the flea) or *la garra* (the claw). Budget-conscious shoppers did not venture into the Loop's high-end stores. Instead, they patronized neighborhood department stores such as the Twelfth Street Store and L. Klein's.[34]

Essential to immigrants' well-being were the small shops and restaurants that catered to their dietary needs and palates. Alongside the kosher poultry markets and Italian shops with their baskets of snails and *baccalà*, beginning in 1920 one Mexican business after another opened along Halsted, Roosevelt, and smaller streets. By 1928 mexicanos ran five groceries, four bakeries, and a meat market. The Hernández family ran a small grocery a couple blocks from St. Francis Church in the 1920s. Its cheerful Spanish name, El Gardenia, signaled to new Mexicans that they could shop easily for their daily needs: eggs, a bag of sugar, a stack of *tortillas de maíz*, or flour to make *tortillas de harina*. Two light bulbs dangling from the pressed tin ceiling illuminated wooden shelves stocked high with cans of tomatoes, corn, and evaporated milk. Paula Hernández kept an eye on her son while she chatted politely with her customers, perhaps suggesting that they try a box of cornflakes, and made change. A new customer might purchase a broom or shyly ask doña Paula if she sold *veladoras* (votive candles) for an *altarcito* recently assembled in a dingy apartment up the street.[35]

Mexicans also owned five pool halls and fourteen restaurants in the Near West Side, catering to the high number of *solos* (solo men). El Puerto de Veracruz restaurant served up *bistec* or chicken in *mole poblano* for fifty cents; customers could enjoy a side of *frijoles refritos* for a quarter or *chocolate con pan* for two dimes. Neighborhood banks eagerly accommodated Spanish-speaking customers. In 1926 the Atlas State Bank opened a Spanish Department, headed by a *michoacano*. In 1928 the bank boasted six hundred Mexican depositors plus hundreds more who sent drafts to Mexico.[36]

With some twenty-five hundred Mexicans living nearby, Ignacio Valle bet on a steady and growing clientele and joined other Mexican entrepreneurs who set up shop along a mile-long strip of Halsted, from Harrison to 16th Street.[37] Valle may well have sought out the location across from Hull House, the renowned settlement house where the Mexican vogue was astir in the 1920s. El Arte Mexicano attracted American artists and intellectuals who took part in Hull House's ongoing interest in things Mexican: the revolution and its arts and artists. This passion for Mexican "color" increased in the 1930s with the Good Neighbor Policy and the Century of Progress Exposition, held in Chicago.[38]

At the same time, cramped living quarters, abusive working conditions, and squalor drew myriad social scientists and reformers to chronicle and map the eastern European Jews and Italians who dominated the Near West

Side into the 1920s. Outsiders condemned the area as "blighted."[39] Yet this ramshackle neighborhood provided certain benefits to its immigrant residents. The Jews had established over forty synagogues. Six Catholic churches stood in the area, catering to the established ethnic groups. The largest, the territorial parish of Holy Family, served English speakers, including its founding Irish. The "national" parishes included Our Lady of Pompeii and Holy Guardian Angel, serving Italian immigrants; Notre Dame for the French speakers; and Holy Trinity Church and St. Francis of Assisi Church, home to the Germans since the 1870s.[40] Six Protestant mission churches aimed their outreach at Mexicans. The Mennonites, for example, established their Mexican mission on Roosevelt Road in the 1930s and soon had fifty attendees at the Spanish-language Sunday school.[41]

Immigrants took advantage of the array of social service centers established to assist and educate the neighborhood's poor. Hull House, Chicago's first settlement house, established in 1889 by Jane Addams and Ellen Gates Starr, had grown to comprise thirteen buildings filling two city blocks. Hull House sat straight across Halsted Street from Ignacio Valle's music store. All day Valle saw people passing in and out of the settlement house's arched brick entryway. In the morning, mothers with young children went to the nursery, and unemployed men headed to the craft workshops, including many mexicanos who fashioned pots and small sculptures for the Hull House kilns. After school, groups of children made their way to classes and clubs. In the evening, adults—Greeks, Italians, and Mexicans—came for meetings, concerts, and classes. Hull House fully opened its doors to Mexicans and established programs specifically for the Mexican newcomers.[42] By contrast, the liberal-minded settlement house struggled over inclusion of its African American neighbors.

In 1931, six blocks to the south, the Newberry Center, a new Methodist-run settlement house, reached out to the neighborhood's changing population, which was "largely Mexican and negro at that time, a very few Jewish families remaining."[43] The three-story building housed the Iglesia Metodista del Buen Pastor and Centro Social Mexicano, with overlapping cultural, religious, and social work, although the social center claimed to be nondenominational. On a Friday evening, various Mexican artists performed at the Centro Social Mexicano's inaugural party. Silvano Ramos, the tenor who recorded "Corrido de Texas" two years earlier, headlined the event.[44]

The Newberry Center offered space for diverse activities. The yard, a former dumping place for Maxwell Street market people, now offered a sanitary playground for local children. Mexican American girls learned *baile folklórico* here; their troupe even danced at the Century of Progress Exposition in

1934.[45] Mexican young adults met two evenings each week to play games, put on plays, and socialize as members of the Nezahualcoyotl Club. The center's European American directors considered the Mexicans "a most interesting group, with many talented members." The positive, if ethnocentric assessment, continued that Mexicans had "a very fine appreciation of music, art, and literature," which "they seem to have inherited from their Indian ancestors, whose culture is older than that of the Egyptians. . . . [E]ven two generations of tenement life has not killed [it]." Social workers tended to needy families. Describing this work for potential donors in Chicago's wealthy North Shore, a Newberry Center staffer took readers for a virtual tour: "Let us call on one of the families. . . . [A] pleasant Mexican woman opens the door and motions for us to come in. She does not speak English so she calls for her daughter to come and translate." The fourteen-person family had an unemployed father. The staffer praised the cleanliness of the family's six small rooms but added, "Many of the homes, however, are very dirty and some have no gas or light, because they cannot pay their bills."[46]

The Newberry Center exemplifies why the Near West Side, blight notwithstanding, offered Mexicans a good spot to land in Chicago. The multiethnic area had an immigrant-ready infrastructure comprised of public and parochial schools, businesses, places of worship, and an array of settlement houses. Mexicans and their children participated in programs at the Old Town Boys Club and Henry Booth House, as well as at Hull House and the Newberry Center.

Crucially, just as the Mexicans rented rooms and opened stores in the 1920s, the neighborhood was changing, especially around Maxwell Street. The Jews who once dominated the area were moving their families and institutions to newer, more middle-class areas farther west. While many Jewish-owned businesses remained, families packed up their belongings and left behind empty apartments with only a telltale mezuzah on the door post.[47] Other European Americans, not only Jews, departed the dilapidated Near West Side. Of the Germans who had made St. Francis their parish since 1853, just a dozen or so families remained. In a rapidly depopulating neighborhood, tenants were in demand regardless of race or religion.[48]

Federal immigration policies (culminating in the restrictive Johnson-Reed Act of 1924) greatly reduced immigration of southern and eastern Europeans. The pipeline of new workers from Europe reduced to a trickle. Chicago employers still needed mill workers, factory hands, and freight loaders, and they considered hiring new migrants. African Americans from the South migrated north and found jobs in some industries, but white Chicagoans refused to include them in most neighborhoods and churches. The area just south and east of Halsted and Roosevelt saw more African American residents and came to be known as Black Bottom; this zone was 44 percent black in 1930.[49] The new immigration laws, importantly, included no quota for people of the Western Hemisphere. Mexicans, if they could pass the literacy test and pay the eight-dollar head tax, easily entered the United States legally.[50] In Chicago they found employment in a range of industries and more options for inclusion than their black counterparts.

Mexicans made up a minuscule percentage of immigrants to Chicago prior to 1920, but a number of observers saw those numbers climbing and responded. In 1913 Presbyterians organized the first mission work aimed at Mexicans in the area, tending especially to people who lived in the boxcar camps dispersed throughout the city. The Baptists and Methodists made concerted efforts to engage Mexicans on the Near West Side. Newcomers took advantage of missionary-sponsored health clinics and attended classes and events at the Baptists' Aiken Institute and the Methodists' Marcy Center, but few joined the Protestant churches.[51]

Following the Protestants' efforts, the Spanish-speaking Claretian order ministered to Chicago's growing Mexican population. This missionary order, founded in Spain in 1849, arrived in the United States in 1902 via Mexico to tend to Spanish speakers in Texas and soon established several mission churches there and elsewhere in the Southwest. The Claretian priests, as they too migrated, had an unusual awareness of the movements and needs of new arrivals from Mexico. They watched a stream of their parishioners leave Texas, including Elidia Barroso, and work their way north.[52] When the Claretians heard that three thousand Mexicans now lived in Chicago, they considered how to reach the mexicanos up north. In 1918 Fr. Domingo Saldívar, CMF, the Claretians' provincial superior, wrote to the archbishop of Chicago, George Mundelein, and offered his order's services.[53] The Claretians' query bore no fruit for five years but surely reminded the archbishop of this new and growing addition to Chicago's Catholic population. As historian Malachy McCarthy details, Catholic lay leaders, spurred on by the persistent Protestant missionary work, began their own outreach to Mexicans in Chicago. These European American Catholics, many of whom were Irish, taught catechism and sponsored Christmas parties in boxcars or any available spaces. The Claretians kept their eye on the Chicago situation and, with Mundelein's approval, traveled to Chicago in 1924. That fall they took over the newly established Our Lady of Guadalupe Church in South Chicago, housed then in a modest wood-frame building.[54]

On the Near West Side, meanwhile, Mexicans tiptoed around the nearby Catholic churches. The extant parishes did not reach out to their newly arrived coreligionists. The devout faced linguistic challenges: while the Mass itself was in Latin, the homily, confession, and novenas were carried out in the vernacular. A newcomer such as Elidia Barroso was hardly drawn to Catholic worship that included portions in Italian, German, or English. Some Mexicans attended Mass and baptized their children at local Italian churches and at the Germans' St. Francis. Socially, the Mexican Catholics almost certainly felt unease in these parishes. Settlement house workers and social scientists made much of Italian-Mexican hostilities. Would a Mexican man who had been jumped and beaten by a gang of Italians on Halsted Street in broad daylight *choose* to attend Mass at the Italians' Holy Guardian Angel Church?[55] Just weeks after the Claretians arrived in South Chicago, Mexicans requested that the missionary fathers provide Catholic services in the Near West Side.

Without a proper church but undeterred, Father Tort leased a Near West Side storefront and started celebrating Mass there in the summer of 1925. Needing chairs for the makeshift chapel, Tort borrowed them from nearby Hull House; apparently, Tort was unperturbed by Chicago Catholics' wariness of the freethinking settlement house.[56] Over that summer and fall, Mexicans gathered for Mass on Sundays and days of obligation. Elidia Barroso and her husband likely attended here. Mexican men soon organized a Sociedad *del Santo Nombre* (Holy Name Society). In January 1926 the first Mass for Spanish speakers took place at the old German church, St. Francis of Assisi. On July 2, 1927, the Claretians became the parish's administrators; on December 13 of that year, the sanctuary added a shrine to Nuestra Señora de Guadalupe.[57] A Mexican Catholic presence was taking root on Chicago's Near West Side.

▪ ▪ ▪

Paul Taylor walked west on Roosevelt Road, away from the bustling Maxwell Street market, one Sunday morning in June 1928. The energetic and perceptive native Iowan and Berkeley PhD was on a quest to document Mexican laborers in different regions of the United States. Cars cruised down the wide thoroughfare. A streetcar came to a stop at the island midstreet, and half a dozen Mexicans disembarked. Like him, they too headed to St. Francis Church. The large red-brick building, capped with its tall steeple, stood oddly on the busy commercial strip of restaurants, dry goods stores, and barbershops. At the church's corner, Taylor peered down Newberry Avenue and took in the St. Francis rectory, the parish school, and a small convent, each marked with a small cross. Three-flat buildings lined the treeless street's east side. A horse-drawn wagon plodded up the block, laden with fresh produce.

Taylor entered the church for the ten o'clock Mexican Mass and slipped into a pew. Scanning the sanctuary, he noted the front altar and several altars lining the sides, including one dedicated to the Virgin of Guadalupe, aglow with votive candles. The windows vividly depicted European saints clothed in rich purple, azure, and ruby red; many panels bore the German names of their individual and group donors. He soon realized, with surprise, that the churchgoers divided themselves by sex. With women and girls on his side, Taylor changed his seat. The men's side was so crowded that many stood up in the back. The Mexican men came to church in a variety of dress, "from tailor-made suits to denim pants and overalls. A few came with no coats, just with their shirts." The sizeable Sociedad Mutualista de Obreros Católicos Mexicanos filled several reserved pews at the front.[58] The worshippers listened quietly as the priest delivered his sermon in the lispy peninsular version of Spanish that Taylor never heard from the Mexicans he interviewed. Parish announcements, again shared in Spanish, revealed a total of five Mexican religious societies. Taylor found the Mexicans' sacrifice considerable, from the lame making their way to church to the steady contributions to the collection ("for a people so proverbially poor"). The ushers extended a basket on a long pole down each pew; they waited patiently for the many people who dropped in a dollar bill but then fished for change, since they could only spare fifteen cents or so. "The thing to notice," Taylor remarked, "all gave something." All present were Mexican and included "pure Indians," mestizos, and whites.[59] Overall, the faithful at St. Francis impressed the researcher with their sizeable attendance and palpable devotion.

Taylor returned to St. Francis later that week to speak with the priest, Father Saldívar—the same one who had queried the archbishop of Chicago a decade earlier, offering to minister to the resident but then unchurched Mexicans. Born in Spain, the priest was himself an immigrant.[60] When the Claretians took over St. Francis, Saldívar became the pastor at this newest (and potentially very important) parish for their order. The priest considered his Mexican flock in Chicago "very good people to work with"; nevertheless, he faulted their difficulties with English, their residential instability, and their lack of group solidarity. As the priest complained to Taylor about the Mexicans' shortcomings, all of which certainly made running a parish difficult, he seemed to perceive these qualities as almost innate to the Mexicans. Instead, one could attribute all these challenges as rooted in the laity's situation as new immigrants in low-paying jobs.

The Mexican Catholics of Chicago's Near West Side went from a storefront church with borrowed chairs to a full-blown parish of their own within just two years. Varied players can take credit for making this parish into San

Francisco de Asís. The arrival of Mexican Catholics in the 1920s presented a conundrum for the archdiocese. Chicago's past archbishops had sanctioned the creation of national parishes for Germans, Poles, Italians, Lithuanians, and many other linguistic-ethnic groups. In 1916, when George Mundelein was installed as the archbishop of Chicago, the nation's largest diocese, his jurisdiction encompassed 211 parishes; 118 were "national," or served a specific ethnic group. Although the archbishop himself was a product of a German national parish in New York, he strongly advocated the Americanization and unification of Catholics. At the same time, he understood that the older, first-generation immigrants needed their own parishes, where they could worship in Polish or Italian and maintain devotions from the homeland. Mundelein did not undo extant national parishes, but as historian Charles Shanabruch stresses, he "did nothing to encourage erection of new national parishes." Yet Mundelein was moved by the Mexicans and wanted to act on behalf of "these strangers in our midst."[61] The rising anticlerical and anti-Catholic tide in revolutionary Mexico also stirred Mundelein's sympathies. Local Protestant missionaries and the Claretian clergy competed with each other and certainly gained Cardinal Mundelein's ear. Fr. Sebastian Ripero, CMF, warned the archbishop, "If you don't resolve this problem soon, you'll be faced with thousands of Mexican Protestants in Chicago."[62]

Meanwhile, Fr. Charles Epstein, St. Francis's pastor, bemoaned the emptying pews at the old German parish. He watched the neighborhood change around his church, where the influx of non-Catholics—apparently the African Americans of Black Bottom—seemed to seal St. Francis's fate. Epstein complained to the Jesuit fathers at nearby Holy Family: "Today there's nothing but poor people and foreigners around." The parochial school became tuition-free with the goal of raising flagging enrollment.[63] Father Epstein and Father Tort, the Claretian, proposed moving the storefront congregation into the German church, where two dozen Mexicans were members. Mexican altar boys already assisted Father Epstein at the Mass. With cautious approval and a two-year transition of power, the archdiocese quietly established Chicago's second Mexican parish but, crucially, via subsidiarity, or entrusting the parish to a religious order responsible for its finances. Cardinal Mundelein raised the profile of both Mexican Catholics and the newly arrived Claretian fathers by hosting events of the 1926 international Eucharistic Congress at St. Francis. After the Claretians took on St. Francis parish, McCarthy found that "Mexicans' attraction to Protestantism diminished."[64]

The Claretians gained a complete parish—with its church, rectory, and school and the convent of the Sisters of St. Francis, who long taught there. The Claretians named the experienced Domingo Saldívar to head the parish, ministering to both the small number of remaining Germans and a growing Mexican laity. Mexican attendance and participation at St. Francis quickly rose. St. Francis drew Mexican Catholics from across the city.

Severna González, for example, longed for Catholic rituals like the *posadas* of her native Jaripo, Michoacán. This wife and mother lived in Back of the Yards; she "attended the Polish-Catholic church near her home twice but does not care to go there." As she told a visitor in 1929, "When she has car fare, she attends St. Francis Church."[65] After the Claretians assumed responsibility for the parish, the number of annual baptisms performed at St. Francis rose about 500 percent in the 1920s. While at least one German sodality (religious brotherhood) remained active, the newcomers formed distinctly Mexican lay organizations: women joined the *guadalupanas*; men joined the Santo Nombre. Membership in these lay societies offered one way to affirm *mexicanidad* while also becoming part of American parish life.[66]

The cultivation of Mexican piety attracted newcomers to St. Francis. Throughout the year the faithful avidly took part in worship. On Good Friday "the Roman soldiers, Pontius Pilate and his court, and biblical figures were the center of all eyes" in the overflowing church. Families decorated altars

TABLE 1. Membership, baptisms, and revenue at St. Francis of Assisi Church, 1917–1938

	Registered families	Baptisms	Revenue (in dollars)
1917		46	
1921	120	40	16,965
1922	108	58	18,040
1923	103	45	16,920
1924	70	90	22,993
1925	60	67	19,561
1926[a]	n/a	239	20,026
1927[b]	n/a	378	9,256
1928	n/a	315	14,314
1929			
1930		353	9,544
1931		334	10,157
1932		295	8,866
1933			
1934		241	7,028
1937		199	n/a
1938		200	

[a] Claretian priests assist Father Epstein.
[b] Claretian priests assume control.

for Corpus Christi. The novena and feast day for Our Lady of Guadalupe, which featured a tableau of her apparition to Juan Diego, were well attended. Mexican women added to that December celebration as they made tamales and fried *buñuelos*, then drizzled with sweet syrup.[67] Following Las Posadas and Nochebuena, many parishioners arrived for *la acostada*, the act of laying Niño Dios in the manger at 3:00 a.m. Later that day children enjoyed a party with a piñata at St. Francis.[68] The pronounced use of votive candles at St. Francis made it a uniquely Mexican space among the Catholic parishes of Chicago. Sales of votive candles doubled in the years that Mexicans took over St. Francis from German parishioners.[69]

Immigrant families also availed themselves of the Cordi-Marians, a Mexican female order that arrived in Chicago to further the Claretians' mission. Initially, the nuns staffed catechetical centers in the city's Mexican districts. By 1936 the Cordi-Marian Settlement had opened its doors four blocks from St. Francis; there and at St. Francis, the sisters prepared children for their first Communion. The "Mexican Sisters," as they were known in the community, also sponsored a preschool, after-school clubs and sports, and a summer day camp. Working parents found these services invaluable. While Hull House and other neighborhood settlements offered similar services, the Cordi-Marians became the most popular social service center for area Mexicans. Certainly, immigrant parents felt at ease with the Spanish-speaking nuns who helped them care for their children. In interviews, older Mexican Americans often refer to these nuns as "family friends." The Claretians' ministry at St. Francis explains much of what drew mexicanos to concentrate in the Near West Side, but the Cordi-Marians played a vital role for families who settled nearby as well.

■ ■ ■

Elidia Barroso wrote intimately about her youth in Mexico, the circumstances that caused her emigration, her first seven years coping as a mexicana in the United States, and the winding road that brought her to make a life in Chicago. Elidia and her siblings formed part of the first wave of Mexican immigrants in the early twentieth century; nearly one-tenth of Mexicans left their homeland between 1910 and 1930. Her diary offers a tantalizing personal glimpse into the indirect paths that carried the pioneering generation of Mexicans to Chicago. Like most mexicanos, neither Elidia Barroso nor Ignacio Valle entered the United States with a plan to move to Chicago. Yet in 1920 Chicago had the fourth largest concentration of Mexicans in the country. Why did immigrants move so far from home? Why did they choose to suffer Chicago's heat and cold? The simple answer is jobs. Work in the Chicago-area steel mills, train yards, and stockyards drew Mexicans until the Great Depression. Illinois trailed only California and Texas in the number of money orders sent to Mexico in 1926–27.[70] Without a doubt, jobs were essential. Yet Elidia's personal reflections remind us that so much more mattered when it came to setting down roots.

What did Mexicans undergo as they set about creating homes in Chicago, so far from Mexico or the borderlands? Recent published works on Mexican Chicago before 1940 stress a difficult entry and negative racialization of Mexicans there. Gabriela Arredondo posits Chicago as a hostile place for Mexican immigrants, who "increasingly found themselves isolated from whites." Michael Innis-Jiménez similarly puts forth that Mexicans in South Chicago were "confined to clearly demarcated community and workplace niches."[71] These historians emphasize oppression and Mexican resistance to it. Yet much evidence indicates that mexicanos encountered more varied and fluid situations. Many details in Innis-Jiménez's book, *Steel Barrio*, for example, indicate inclusion, respect, and some integration in South Chicago. Mexicans boarded with other ethnic groups. Management promoted some Mexican mill hands to foremen at the steel mills. Banks enthusiastically reached out to Mexican savers. Former steel workers opened small businesses, some of which catered to Chicagoans of any ethnicity. Irish American Catholics avidly supported the establishment of Our Lady of Guadalupe parish. When compared with the simultaneous migration of African Americans, the Mexican newcomers in Chicago unquestionably met with more respect and openness.[72] Skin color and dress clearly influenced how individual Mexicans were treated.

Catholicism proved decisive in the relative success of Mexicans' entry and integration in Chicago for decades to come. The archdiocese and many members of the Catholic laity actively included Mexican Catholics. The Spanish-speaking parishes enabled Elidia, her family members, and thousands of others to gain a toehold in Chicago, create new homes, and raise families in a place that became less diasporic and felt more like home.[73]

These new parishes would reflect roots in an evolving (and increasingly embattled) Catholic Church in Mexico. Even prior to the revolution, institutions and devotions were in flux and varied regionally. Edward Wright-Rios's work on Oaxaca shows multiple forces at work in Catholic Mexico. Late nineteenth-century Mexico saw much reinvigoration at the diocesan level, giving rise to a vigorous, controlling church in urban centers, where the faithful regularly took part in the sacraments. Rural parishes continued to be "Catholic in their own way": more festival oriented and less attached to the sacraments. Efforts to standardize Catholic devotion proved uneven beyond diocesan centers, creating "wedges of modernized Catholicism" amid the generally rural population of the period. Even in the towns and cities, the Catholic Church's intended hierarchical control gave way in the enduring, more local devotions to the Virgin Mary, with their pilgrimages and "mass, unmediated supplication."[74] Elidia Barroso, given her various residences within Mexico, had experienced these multiple, evolving paths to the sacred in Mexico.

Beginning in 1914, the Mexican Revolution unleashed anticlerical actions and generally challenged the Catholic hierarchy. Militant Catholics (known as Cristeros) responded by creating protective leagues and political parties, as well as promoting public devotions in the face of anticlericalism, which came to a head under President Plutarco Elías Calles (1924–28).[75] While the Barroso family emigrated years before the Calles regime, they joined Mexican parishes in the United States that formed precisely as thousands of Mexicans created a "Cristero diaspora."[76] Laypeople joined with hundreds of exiled nuns and priests. Cristero-era Catholics identified with the church in an almost militant fashion and by doing so expressed an identity rooted in Catholic Mexico. They would long keep alive the memories of martyred priests. Simultaneously, a liberal anticlerical immigrant stream settled in Chicago, voicing their politics in the local paper *México*, forming the Blue Cross benevolent society, and often aligning with Protestants. But as historian John Flores concludes, the liberals' efforts in Chicago waned during the Great Depression. Meanwhile, the more Catholic "traditionalist" Mexicans could count on the archdiocese's institutional support.[77]

Like tens of thousands of this immigrant generation in Los Angeles, Texas, Chicago, and elsewhere, Elidia Barroso maintained her faith and actively sought connection to Catholic congregations.[78] The panethnic Archdiocese of Chicago providentially inaugurated two Mexican parishes in the 1920s. This action influenced many people and institutions in Chicago to welcome the "strangers in our midst." Our Lady of Guadalupe in South Chicago and St. Francis of Assisi in the Near West Side became lasting centers of Mexican religious, ethnic, and community identities for the pioneering Mexican immigrants and the generations that followed. Making these Mexican parishes in the 1920s provided a ready home for new arrivals and subsequent generations. Of these two pioneering churches, St. Francis would become more than a neighborhood parish, in time emerging as Chicago's "Mexican cathedral."

2. *La catedral mexicana*

St. Francis of Assisi and the Mexican Near West Side, 1940–1962

A wooden house that looks like an elephant sat on the roof. An apartment so close to the ground people knock on the window instead of the door. Just off Taylor Street. Not far from Saint Francis church of the Mexicans. A stone's throw from Maxwell Street's flea market. The old Italian section of Chicago in the shadow of the downtown Loop.
—Sandra Cisneros, *Caramelo*

On Sundays Evelina went to Mass with her sons. She loved Father Tortas' voice, the way it threatened, reminded, scolded, urged. Loved his Spanish, so different from hers, his lisp. She never tired of hearing his voice, even when she didn't understand what he was saying. He was so educated. Sometimes she couldn't tell if he was speaking Spanish or Latin.
—Hugo Martínez-Serros, "Victor and David"

ON JANUARY 13, 1946, St. Francis of Assisi parish inaugurated a Catholic Youth Organization (CYO) gym on the school's top floor, featuring $15,000 of athletic equipment for use by all the Mexican youth, girls and boys. The gym accommodated basketball, boxing, volleyball, ping-pong, and billiards. The Sunday afternoon program featured master of ceremonies Eddie Cavanaugh, WGN radio personality, who introduced the Mexican consul, the 20th Ward alderman, the local police precinct captain, Irving Klein of a local businessmen's association, and several priests. Tito Guízar, star of screen, radio, and stage, headlined the event. The elegant Guadalajara native was a true crossover artist: he had sung and acted in many Mexican movies and six Hollywood movies.[1] That winter he played a run at the Blackstone

Hotel's swanky Mayfair Room. In the modest St. Francis CYO gym, Guízar presented the 1945 All-Around Mexican Athlete trophy to Jerry Mendoza, who excelled at baseball and football and lettered in basketball at Washburne High School. After the ceremonies, fans watched cross-town basketball rivals take the court: the Near West Side's Hidalgos played the Rancheros from South Chicago.[2] The afternoon's events showed St. Francis's strong pull among Chicago Mexicans, as well as its recognition by power-holders in wider circles.

On a Thursday not two weeks later, the Sisters of St. Francis of Mary Immaculate who staffed the parochial school finished up their classroom chores. When darkness fell the nuns returned to their convent next door, eager for supper, followed by a quiet evening of marking homework and prayer. But a fire soon broke out in the school. As the nuns fled their convent, Sister Juliana turned around and went to the convent chapel to remove the Blessed Sacrament. She rushed across the street with the monstrance to the rectory, where Father Victor, busy fielding phone calls, gave her permission to place it in the church's tabernacle. While firefighters battled the blaze, the sisters sought refuge down the block with the Reindls and the Rothbauers, two of the remaining German families. The winds blew hard that night and fanned the flames. Neighbors and parishioners watched in horror as water from the hoses rushed down "like Niagara Falls"; some cried as the brand-new gym and parts of the school were destroyed. None of the Newberry Avenue residents slept much that night, from the few older Jewish families (the Klaskins, the Bluesteins) to the newer arrivals from Mexico and Texas (the Acevedos, the Torreses, and fifteen others). After six hours, the firefighters managed to extinguish the blaze.

Given the fire's ferocity, amazingly, no one was harmed. The sisters noted that "somehow St. Agatha preserved us." With danger over, the sisters returned to "the shack," as they derisively referred to the convent. They found eighty years of accumulated furniture, personal items, clothing, and teaching supplies lost to water and smoke damage. The sisters and the new head pastor, Fr. Thomas Matin, CMF, were at a loss. Where would the sisters live? How could they continue the school year? The ruin of the gym and the school, both essential to the parish and work with the youth, stunned the Claretians. The fire seemed an act of sabotage. The sisters heard Father Thomas declare, "Never was a better plan laid."[3] After a week's break, classes resumed in temporary facilities. Pupils and teachers made do without desks and blackboards for months until the school's lower floors were deemed safe and had been cleaned and refurbished.[4]

Father Thomas wasted no time in publicizing the tragedy and campaigning for donations to rebuild. The Sunday following the fire, Tito Guízar again performed, this time in another Catholic church hall with the aim to help rebuild St. Francis's facilities. To encourage giving, the musician started a collection box, which circulated as he sang *canciones rancheras*, tangos, and medleys of famous Mexican songs, each number gaining thunderous applause. Father Thomas aggressively and successfully sought donations from beyond the Mexican community. He soon had pledges of support from neighborhood department stores, a nearby bank, and a window shade factory. He printed brochures and postcards with a photo showing the school engulfed in flames and with a fire truck in the dark Chicago night, and he invited donations by mail. Parish youth raised funds with dances and raffles. Laywomen began cooking meals every Sunday from 9:00 a.m. to 7:00 p.m. in the rectory. Those sales benefited the school. The energetic response to the tragedy showed how much Mexicans of different generations identified with this church.

Members of the parish gathered funds so quickly that they were able to rebuild the school that same year and even added a kindergarten and a cafeteria. Samuel Cardinal Stritch blessed the remodeled St. Francis School in August 1946. Parish children "attired in Mexican costumes, made the procession from school to church very colorful." The sight so pleased the cardinal that he had his picture taken with them.[5] That fall the school grew by one hundred additional pupils. A bus now transported children from outlying neighborhoods, a sign of the ongoing growth and dispersal of Mexicans in the city. In postwar Chicago's fast-growing Mexican population, St. Francis's reach was on the rise.

This chapter explores how St. Francis evolved at midcentury, taking in a new and sizeable wave of Mexicans who were drawn to Chicago's vigorous wartime economy. After the war and throughout the 1950s more and more Mexicans and *tejanos* continued to converge on Chicago. St. Francis became "el refugio de los mexicanos," a place that felt like home in a city that often did not. Many a newcomer found a familiar place to pray and sing hymns in Spanish. Much more than *misa en español*, this church offered newcomers a place to consult a Spanish-speaking doctor or a chance to meet a Mexican movie star. As the Mexican population dispersed, the faithful came from well beyond the Near West Side, enduring long streetcar rides, not to mention the cold on many Sundays. Word of this church extended beyond the shores of Lake Michigan. Its reputation spread throughout the Midwest and into Mexico.[6] It remained a true parish for Near West Side Mexicans, but it also achieved a citywide status as *la catedral mexicana*. Even today many call St. Francis of Assisi the "Mexican cathedral" of Chicago.

■ ■ ■

The Near West Side *colonia* survived the Depression. Repatriation had mostly been voluntary, with *solos* and families choosing to leave Chicago as they lost jobs in the early 1930s.[7] But most *mexicanos* who settled in the 1920s persevered through the trying years of the Depression and raised their children, born in midwestern boxcar camps or in Chicago itself. Kids scavenged for coal in the alleys, and boys took on after-school jobs with local storekeepers. Teens walked miles to high school to save the nickel for the streetcar. When the Italian merchants at the nearby South Water Market gave away lettuce at day's end to their Mexican employees, families learned to eat salads. St. Francis (and Our Lady of Guadalupe in South Chicago) offered food and clothing from Catholic Charities and the government.[8] According to historian Michael McCoyer, the rapid drop in Chicago's Mexican population (37 percent from 1930 to 1934) was crucial in reducing "the threat that Mexicans posed to white neighborhoods and white jobs."[9] Without fresh arrivals from Mexico in the 1930s, many Mexicans in the Near West Side rubbed shoulders with neighbors who spoke English and Italian and further adapted to life in the United States.

Public institutions furthered Mexicans' integration into American society. Some men, including Elidia Barroso's brother-in-law, found work on WPA projects. When the model Jane Addams public housing project opened in 1938, Mexican families moved in alongside Irish, Jewish, Italian, and other European Americans. (The Chicago Housing Authority barred African Americans from the new housing at that point.) The weekly newspaper written by Jane Addams Homes' residents indicates Mexicans' social inclusion.

> Mr. and Mrs. Melendez, 1212 W. Roosevelt Rd., were presented with a baby boy on Dec. 17. No doubt Tonio will be delighted with his new brother. This will make the 1212 W. Roosevelt Road building score as follows: 1 girl versus 9 boys.
>
> Mrs. Mary Valles, her daughter Delores and her mother, Mrs. Matilda Ramirez, have visited their old home in Durango, Mexico for the past two months. It has been 16 years since Mary left her childhood home to live in the United States. She was entertained by her brother and sister and many friends. Her husband Jose Valles of 1245 Cabrini, has been very lonesome but now he looks cheerful again.[10]

The nicknames and other signs of neighborly intimacy demonstrate Mexicans' inclusion in this multiethnic housing complex.

Mexicans similarly formed part of the twenty-five different nationalities enrolled at the Dante School's night program for adult immigrants. Mexicans made up 9 percent of the June 1940 graduates. Aurora Castillo arrived in Chicago in 1938 with six years of schooling; within two years she became her class secretary.[11] Isabel Horcasitas, then fifty years old, also completed the Dante School program. She shared the story of her daughter's high school graduation in an essay. The high school instructed families to send flowers to the principal's office prior to the graduation exercises. But on the evening of her daughter's graduation, as Isabel and her husband prepared to leave the house, "just then I remembered that I had forgotten . . . all about the traditional bouquet I expected to give my only child on that occasion." She sat through the ceremony, scarcely listening, "thinking only of the moment when my beloved daughter would receive her diploma without the expected flowers. I almost fainted, but when I heard my girl's name and saw the Principal giving her the diploma and a beautiful bouquet reading aloud 'from your mother' I could not believe my eyes and ears." Isabel wrote her story in clear English, expressing her gratitude for educators who taught her child. Soon after graduation, eighteen-year-old Dolores Horcasitas (born in Iowa) worked as a typist in a law office.[12] The adult immigrants who stayed in Chicago through the 1930s, a period of demographic decline for Mexicans, had to interact with people of other ethnicities and US institutions. Isabel Horcasitas was one of many who acculturated in the process.

As the US economy revived after 1940, young cousins and nephews in Mexico or Texas joined (or rejoined) family in Chicago. Some found jobs in the South Chicago steel mills or the packinghouses in Back of the Yards. Yet most newly arrived mexicanos gravitated to the Near West Side, with its steady access to jobs in the train yards, factories, and Loop establishments. In 1946 Union Station advertised in the Spanish-language paper *ABC* for men to fill year-round jobs at $7.93 for a nine-hour day, with paid vacation, overtime pay, and a pension.[13] By 1948 an estimated twelve thousand Mexican-origin people lived in the Near West Side, making it Chicago's largest, most central, and most visible Mexican neighborhood. Newcomers found that living in the Near West Side offered an array of Mexican shops and *iglesias* and increased the likelihood of running into *paisanos. Braceros* (Mexican male contract laborers) joined the throngs doing errands, shopping, or simply taking a walk on Halsted Street.[14]

At least ten specifically Mexican groceries operated in the Near West Side in 1946. At El Fénix, grocer Francisco Murillo offered "el más mexicano de los chorizos" (the most Mexican of chorizos), as well as imported bottled salsas and canned chiles from Mexican manufacturer Clemente Jacques. Mercado Vilchis, at the prime Halsted and Roosevelt corner, sold meat, offering discounts for boardinghouses. On Saturdays, hungry shoppers smelled hot *chicharrón* and *barbacoa* wafting onto the street, and they stopped at El Paisano Alfonso's shop. The Sunday specials of chicken in *mole poblano* and *puerco en adobo* drew diners to the Rio Rita restaurant.[15] La Gloria Panadería stayed open daily from 7:00 a.m. to 10:00 p.m., selling baked goods but also corn husks and *masa* for tamales. In 1950 railway worker and part-time tortilla vendor Raúl López quit his day job and opened his *tortillería*, El Milagro, just blocks from St. Francis.[16]

After a few paychecks, new arrivals headed to Villarreal Bros. Radio Shop to choose a radio; they could compare prices a block away at Casa Pan-Americana. Many American stores displayed "Se habla español" signs, relying on the Chicago-reared Mexican Americans as sales clerks. For Mexican records, Artes de México—formerly Ignacio Valle's El Arte de México—remained on Halsted. Music lovers could also shop for "the latest songs from Mexico" at Mundial, a gift shop a block away. Mexican newspapers and magazines, as well as Chicago's own Spanish weekly, *ABC*, sold swiftly at El Carrito de la Prensa, as it advertised, "always stationed in front of St. Francis Church, corner of Roosevelt and Newberry."[17] Entrepreneurial immigrant vendors roamed neighborhood streets, calling out their wares, such as *pantalones de mezclia* (denim pants) and *camisas de lana* (wool shirts).[18]

Translator Francisco López helped clients with English and Spanish documents seven days a week at his third-floor office near Hull House. He reminded potential clients who might need help with work papers or visas for family reunification that "only a Mexican understands the affairs of Mexicans." Men stopped in for a haircut and then might play a couple rounds of pool at Mike's Peluquería y Billares, run by Miguel Parra. Farmacia Atlas dispensed not only prescriptions but also medicinal oils and herbs. More serious medical problems brought mexicanos to Dr. Olimpo Galindo, who even had an on-site *rayos-x* machine, in the Mexican Welfare Council in St. Francis's former rectory. Mexicanos, their Chicago-reared children in tow, went to see Cantinflas, Jorge Negrete, and Tito Guízar movies at the Globe Theater.[19] Distinguished literary scholar Luis Leal (who studied at Northwestern University and the University of Chicago) summed up the Near West Side's importance in mid-twentieth-century Chicago: "You could find Mexican restaurants, barber shops, bookstores, grocery stores, and, of course, the Church."[20] At the *barrio*'s near-center loomed St. Francis of Assisi.

Mexicans and their children attended at least six Protestant congregations in the Near West Side, but none had the influence of St. Francis. In 1941 Eunice Felter, a University of Chicago master's student, surveyed the city's Mexican churches. She aptly gave primacy to the Catholic parish: "St. Francis has prestige among the Mexicans on the Near West Side. It has a large church

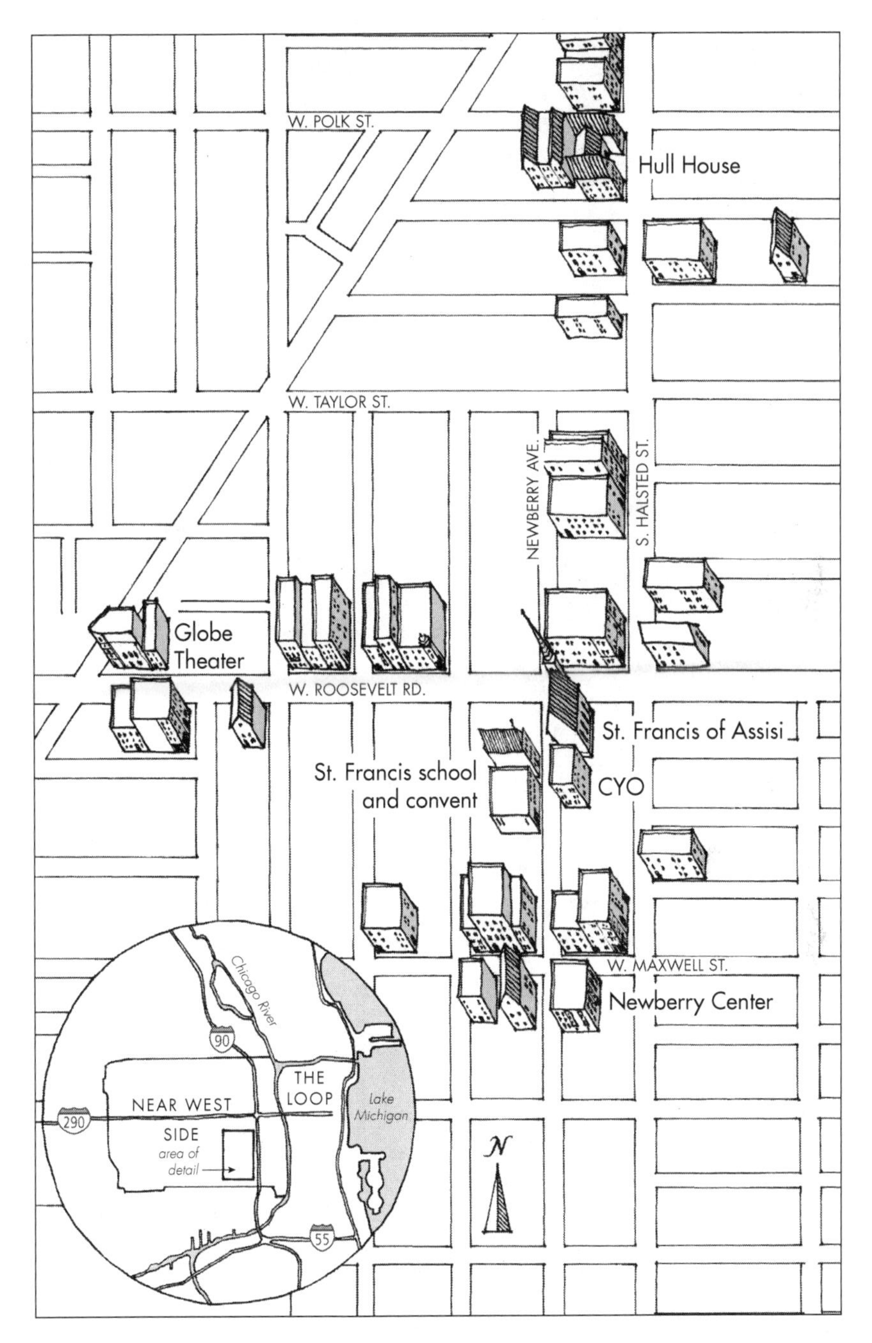

MAP 2. The Mexican Near West Side, 1948–61. Map by Molly O'Halloran.

and its program keeps its name before the public." Yet Felter underlined that "the Protestant churches in the area have become stronger." The Seventh Day Adventists had twenty-six members. The Methodist church El Buen Pastor had 125 Mexican members. Across the street from Hull House, one hundred Mexican Pentecostals worshiped regularly at Gethsemane Christian Church. Only a block from St. Francis, the Mennonite Misión Evangélica had twenty-eight members. In total, area Protestant churches had fewer than three hundred Mexican members. Ten thousand souls constituted St. Francis parish, of whom six hundred reportedly attended church on a regular basis; over three hundred children attended the parochial school. Felter, a novice researcher, just skimmed the surface of what it meant to belong to any of these Christian congregations.[21]

Immigration, often directly from rural Mexico and, after 1945, from Puerto Rico, continued unabated in the postwar era.[22] Young adults formed the bulk of new arrivals. As they started families, many lacked the support and social network of home. Dr. Jorge Prieto, himself a Mexican immigrant, saw many patients "suffering from distress caused by their living conditions, their poverty, and their alienation at finding themselves separated from their normal environment . . . from the whole support system they had enjoyed in Mexico." Some women endured alcoholic husbands and endless pregnancies, all "caught in a vicious cycle of poverty, isolation from friends and relatives, and marriages that were little short of permanent nightmares." One anguished husband called Dr. Prieto about his wife; she had suffered for months from "bronchitis" but was now coughing up blood. Visiting the family's "miserable four-room flat on Cermak Road," the doctor found a gaunt, pale young mother in bed as five children ran about. She needed treatment in a sanitarium, but the husband worried how he would hold on to his job and care for the children.[23]

Naive immigrants overpaid "shady employment agencies" for work leads and were at the mercy of undependable notary publics. They paid for sham documents and frequented the Gypsy fortune tellers on Maxwell Street with their personal and health problems. Social workers wrote about "Mexican problems," detailing cases of parents who struggled to maintain employment and properly supervise their children.[24] In the early 1950s roundups of ethnic Mexicans became common in Chicago, and the very real possibility of deportation created a climate of fear.[25] Certainly, many newcomers fought to gain a secure place in the city.

Some midcentury observers argued that Chicago's Mexican-origin population was "disorganized." Researchers and social workers decried what they perceived as the challenge of Mexicans' mobility, the breakdown of family forms, and the loosening of community identity. The ongoing arrival of braceros and others from Mexico meant that many in the Near West Side lacked the resources to find decent jobs, learn English, and care for their families' health. Mexican American organizations came and went and did little to meet community needs.[26] The clergy at St. Francis, many of whom had been born in Spain, came under fire for failing to cooperate with Protestant entities in tackling neighborhood problems. Outsiders recognized St. Francis's stature in the Near West Side Mexican community but doubted whether the Catholic church could meet the laity's many and diverse needs.[27]

To whom could the new immigrant turn for help in this "disorganized" community? Mexican American civic organizations relied upon volunteer staff and often busied themselves with social events.[28] Felter had cautioned that none of the area churches, Protestant or Catholic, was capable of helping immigrants adapt to city life. In 1948 Hull House–based Frank Paz similarly asserted that "the Catholic and Protestant Churches have not served the Mexican American community in a true sense." He faulted the Catholics for employing "missionaries from Spain," as he narrowly labeled the Claretians.[29]

On a day-to-day basis many immigrants did find succor at St. Francis. Immigrants in other US dioceses sought spiritual aid from clergy in Mexico: women and men wrote directly to the archbishop of Guadalajara for help with illness, marital problems, and devotional needs. By contrast, few Mexicans in Chicago requested this help.[30] The Claretian fathers, it seems, managed to meet immigrants' needs in Chicago. The Claretian clergy maintained good working relations with the Chancery, as well as with clergy in Mexico, which helped facilitate the faithful's transnational lives.[31] With its sizeable staff, its centrally located and large physical plant, and a highly committed core group of laypeople, St. Francis Church performed outreach to the arrivals from Mexico and, if less so, to those from Puerto Rico in ways large and small.

■ ■ ■

Fr. Thomas Matin, CMF, was remarkably adaptable. Within days of arriving in Chicago in the fall of 1945 as St. Francis's new pastor, the forty-five-year-old met with the sisters who taught at the parish school. The bespectacled priest spoke to them in English with a marked German accent about his plans to improve the school building. After his short talk, some of the sisters raised in German immigrant homes found that Father Thomas was from Bavaria. What a nice change from the Spanish pastors who preceded the new one! Many Mexican parishioners first encountered *el nuevo padre* that Sunday. They awaited the sermon and were pleased to hear his fluent Spanish. If not native, padre Tomás at least sounded much more Mexican than the Spaniards

FIGURE 4. Fr. Thomas Matin, CMF, and children, Near West Side, Chicago, Illinois. Photo by Sánchez-Itta. Courtesy of the Claretian Missionaries Archives USA-Canada.

who had served at St. Francis. He greeted parishioners after Mass and asked about their hometowns in Mexico and if their children attended St. Francis School. The other Claretian fathers who shared the rectory found that Father Thomas was both scholarly (he had recently completed his doctorate) and quite mystical in his faith.[32] As Father Thomas explained his ambitious plans for the parish, it became apparent that he was also very familiar with the mexicanos whom the team of priests served. He would spearhead many efforts at St. Francis to meet the needs of the newly arrived.

Memorialized as the "Advocate of Immigrants," Father Thomas had a unique life story. Born Thomas Matischok, he entered the Claretian seminary in Spain and was ordained in 1925. In 1933 the German Claretians sent him to the United States to learn English and to raise funds for their province. He preached missions and attempted to establish regular services for the Spanish-speaking in St. Louis in 1934–35.[33] In the late 1930s Matin served as pastor at Claretian-run parishes in Los Angeles. He became fluent in Spanish and helped establish a mission church, San Conrado, in the impoverished, heavily Mexican Palo Verde / Chavez Ravine neighborhood in 1939. With the war's outbreak, Matin found himself cut off from his German province. Padre Tomasito, as many still remember him in Los Angeles and Chicago, dedicated himself to the needs of his Mexican flock, even if it meant contradicting his superiors' orders. The ensuing conflicts led to his removal from Los Angeles and semibanishment to a Claretian parish in El Paso in 1943–44.[34] In 1945 Matin was transferred to St. Francis in Chicago, where he vigorously devoted himself to the religious and material needs of Mexican people for a decade. He took seriously his mission to immigrants, reaching out to them in any way possible.[35]

Six months after arriving in Chicago, Father Thomas began broadcasting his *Hora Católica Mejicana*. The priest soon sought Cardinal Stritch's blessing of the "half hour radio program in Spanish for the Latin American Colony of this city" on Saturdays at 2:30 p.m.[36] Listeners across the city heard the priest's orations, songs by local singer Chiquita Rangel, and commentary by doctor and civic leader Dr. Olimpo Galindo. Father Thomas claimed that "St. Francis Assisi on the Air" had led to 426 conversions and revalidation of 311 marriages in just over two years. The broadcasts also raised revenue for the parish.[37] Using radio to proselytize and build a citywide community of the Spanish-speaking faithful represented an assertive and modern form of pastoral work.

The very idea of pastoral work by radio seems odd given the usual confluence between (ethnic) neighborhood and parish in most of Catholic Chicago.[38] But the initiative in some ways fits the distinctive reach of St. Francis, which, since 1926, never corresponded strictly to the geographic boundaries of the Near West Side. Rather, St. Francis served "the Mexicans" or "the Spanish-speaking Nationalities," regardless of their location in the city. After World War II, Mexicans and Mexican Americans began to reside beyond their three traditional enclaves in Chicago, with some settling far from St. Francis. The Spanish-language Catholic radio show may have appealed especially to these distant listeners. One mexicana, who had lived in Chicago for thirty years, attended Mass at St. Ambrose (in the Hyde Park / Kenwood neighborhood) and then tuned into the *Hora Católica* "so that she can have a sermon which she completely understands." The thousands of Puerto Ricans who moved into areas other than the Near West Side may have tuned in as well.[39]

World War II—and the start of the Bracero Program—sparked a period of sustained demographic and economic growth at St. Francis parish extending into the 1950s. New families arrived from Mexico and Texas seeking the ample work opportunities of wartime Chicago. The number of baptisms nearly quadrupled between 1941 and 1951. During the war, the Claretian fathers simply gave up attempting a count of the parish as a whole. In 1946 the priests claimed to serve nineteen hundred families and eighteen thousand souls. In 1947 they recorded three thousand families and twenty thousand souls.[40] Parish reports after that year simply avoided either statistic. The mushrooming numbers at St. Francis stand in marked contrast to many non-Mexican parishes in that era.[41] This tremendous growth of people and income reflects Chicago's expanding Mexican-origin population in the World War II era and beyond.

Surging revenues at St. Francis enabled major improvements to the parish's physical plant. Annual parish revenue at St. Francis increased from $10,743 in 1941 to $38,475 in 1951. While Mexican people in Chicago had struggled in the 1930s, now they had spare cash as they found full-time employment and extra shifts during the war. They filled collection baskets in the 1940s with their contributions, and visiting braceros added coins and bills. Parish members and priests used the money to renovate aging structures and to expand the parish's appeal. In 1943 the priests had the pews and church exterior cleaned, in addition to installing a new boiler. On a May Sunday in 1944 parishioners toured St. Francis School to see the new library and the "new, modern toilets"—blessed that afternoon. Later that day a procession composed of first communicants, altar boys, and the St. Francis Girls Club marched to the church. They entered a sanctuary scented by thousands of peonies, filled beyond capacity, for the blessing of a new painting and altar of Our Lady of Guadalupe.[42] In 1948 the addition of a spanking new, state-of-the-art CYO gymnasium made St. Francis one of the largest recreational facilities in the entire Near West Side, Mexican or otherwise. The investment in the gym showed the diversification of goals and programs at the Mexican parish. Renovations and building formed just one aspect of the growing parish's outreach and optimism about its future.

▪ ▪ ▪

Researcher Eunice Felter doubted that Mexican Catholicism could thrive in Chicago: "The Catholic churches try to appeal to memories of the church in Mexico. The use of the name 'Our Lady of Guadalupe' and of the slogan *Viva Cristo Rey* are examples of this. They try to carry over the fiesta at the time of baptisms and weddings, thus keeping the same place in the social life of the people." Attempts at continuity, she felt, proved insufficient: "But the communities in Chicago are so different from the Mexican communities that this is not enough."[43] Mexican Catholicism, she argued, could not withstand the realities of the urban-industrial North. Felter, a young Protestant

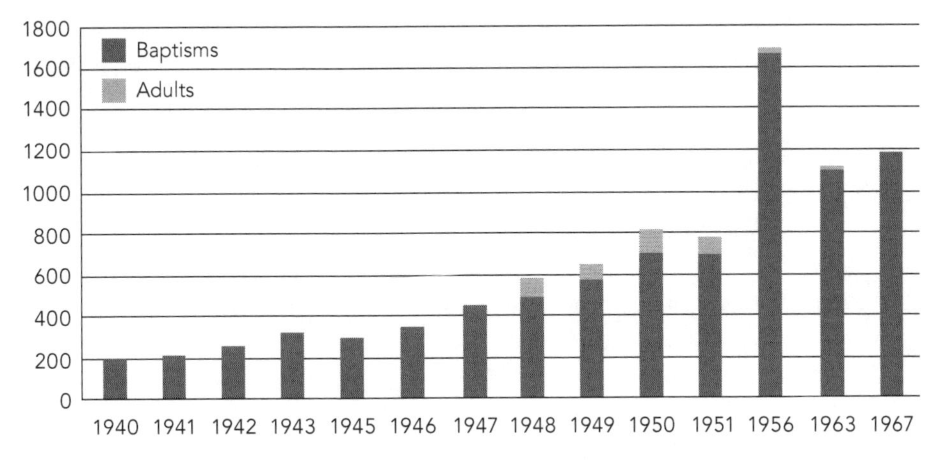

CHART 1. Baptisms at St.Francis Church, 1940–1967

graduate student, had a limited understanding of the complex, multiple, and overlapping levels of worship that took place in any Catholic church, let alone the diasporic and communal meanings in a national (or ethnic) parish. St. Francis of Assisi, in fact, exerted a palpable Mexican and devotional pull for thousands who walked into its sanctuary. Some came daily for Mass, and many more came weekly. Others found St. Francis's doors open when needed.

By the time Mexicans arrived in Chicago, regular Mass attendance had taken root in the city's parishes. Leslie Woodcock Tentler describes how Pope Pius X (1903–14) and, eventually, many American clergy promoted daily Communion and urged laypeople to "take advantage of this great means of grace." It became a hallmark of early twentieth-century US Catholicism, if slower to develop in many ethnic parishes.[44] In cities like Chicago, densely populated by Catholics, churches offered multiple Masses on Sunday and on weekdays as well. At St. Francis in the 1940s, the devout could attend Mass at 7:00 or 8:00 a.m. on weekdays. On Sundays mexicanos attended Mass with a Spanish homily at 6:00, 8:00, and 10:30 a.m. Masses with an English homily at 9:00 a.m. and 12:10 p.m. appealed more to US-reared children, some of whom whispered prayers for the White Sox.[45] St. Francis offered yet more opportunities for worship in the church each week. After the Sunday midday Mass, the tabernacle stayed open, exposing Su Magestad, the Host. Laypeople returned to church for the final hour of silent devotion and found comfort in chanting the rosary at 8:00 p.m.[46]

During World War II, parishioners gathered on Thursday evenings for Hora Santa (Holy Hour) for their loved ones serving in the military. The pastor invited each St. Francis family with a member in the armed forces to choose a date for that person: "All who come to the Holy Hour may pray especially for him or her." The special worship drew so much attention that the priests added a second Holy Hour on Sunday evenings through 1945. Señora María de Jesús Galván sponsored a Thursday Holy Hour twice that year, seeking the parish's prayers for her sons Fidel and José. Even people who lived well beyond the Near West Side sponsored these events. For example, señor and señora Julián García, who resided in Bensenville, dedicated a Thursday evening Holy Hour for their son Arturo. Although the Garcías lived over twenty miles away, Saint Francis was their parish. People came to these Holy Hours from the northwest side, Douglas Park, and Chinatown; one family came from Freemont, Indiana. The parish monthly newspaper, the *St. Francis Crier,* publicized these wartime Holy Hours in Spanish, indicating that Mexican immigrants sought and followed this schedule of worship. Fr. Severino López, CMF, recalled the well-attended wartime Holy Hours: "One of the side altars of the church was completely filled with pictures of these soldiers brought in by mothers and sweethearts." Not incidentally, the announcements—compiled by rectory staff—spelled names correctly, including accent marks.[47] When Mexican people joined other parishes, staff frequently bungled this basic recognition of self and devotion.

Novenas proved as frequent and popular at St. Francis as they were throughout US Catholic parishes in the mid-twentieth century.[48] Novenas there promoted devotions unique to mexicanos, as well as devotions familiar to all Catholics. Each December people made their way to church for nine evenings of worship, leading up to the yet more popular events of December 12, the feast day of Nuestra Señora de Guadalupe. In addition, the parish sponsored periodic novenas throughout the year to both la Guadalupana and the Immaculate Heart of Mary. Like many Chicago parishes, St. Francis sponsored a novena to la Madre Dolorosa (the Sorrowful Mother) three times each Friday: at noon and at 7:00 and 8:00 p.m.[49] The Claretians, devoted to the Immaculate Heart of Mary, encouraged participants at a weekly novena to the Sagrado Corazón de María on Sunday afternoons in 1947, in addition to the annual nine-day novena in October.[50] These devotional events attracted people who faced special challenges and sought divine intercession. While a person could pray a novena at home, many found comfort in the communality of the church novena. At church, in the words of one Catholic layperson, "You would pray with other people aloud and loudly." The experience was emotional and left some people feeling less alone with their troubles.[51] Women may have enjoyed these events as a chance to leave the apartment. The clergy found that novenas proved a way to increase devotionalism, to further ties to the parish, and to raise revenue. For immigrants from Mexico, the majority from small towns and *ranchos*, attendance at a church novena had been a rare event.[52] The Chicago parishes offered them the chance to practice their faith more regularly and publicly.

Days of obligation and feast days filled the calendar and expanded the daily and weekly opportunities to visit St. Francis throughout the year. The parish ushered in the New Year with a sanctuary filled at midnight: fervent hymns and prayers of thanksgiving rang out. Some faithful remained through the night for adoration of the Host. A 4:00 a.m. Mass brought in the New Year, followed by a celebratory breakfast, with live Mexican music courtesy of parishioner and neighborhood butcher Alfonso Zúñiga. On January 6, Día de los Reyes (Epiphany) featured celebratory Masses. In the afternoon the sisters walked their four hundred pupils to the church to visit the crib. The kindergartners knelt there and sang "Silent Night." All the grades sang more seasonal hymns, and Father Thomas gave the Benediction with the Blessed Sacrament. "Following a Mexican custom, Father then presented the Baby Jesus at the Communion rail for veneration. As each child kissed the Baby Jesus and made an offering, the server gave him a medal or a holy picture." The European American sisters found the custom noteworthy, adding that all the boys and girls took a "very special interest" in the visit. On February 3, St. Blaise Day, even on a weekday, adults and children made time to visit the church: after each Mass, the priest blessed each worshipper's throat, warding off respiratory illnesses so common in winter. The blessings continued into the evening. Lent began soon after. St. Francis clergy kept busy on Miércoles de Ceniza (Ash Wednesday): "Every hour during the day ashes were distributed to those who came for that purpose."[53] With ashy crosses on their foreheads, the faithful hurried to work at train yards, hotel kitchens, and candy factories. Others returned home to cold-water flats.

As the long Chicago winter finally seemed to end, Semana Santa (Holy Week) arrived. The sisters again marveled at the Mexicans' elaborate observances at St. Francis. Good Friday began with the Unveiling of the Cross and the Mass of the Presanctified at 8:00 a.m. At noon people came for Tre Ore Devotions; they witnessed the Washing of the Feet, where the priest knelt before the twelve servers who acted as the apostles. At 8:00 p.m., with darkness settled in, crowds lined Newberry Avenue and witnessed the procession that began at St. Francis School and made its way to their church. The parishioners watched intently as the Drummer Boy and two men dressed as Roman soldiers led the Via Crucis, which featured twenty more costumed reenactors. Ten more soldiers marched, followed by five girls dressed in blue, each of whom bore an instrument of torture on a cushion. Four men dressed in long purple robes carried the glass-enclosed Christ known as Jesús Nazareno. After the final figure, the Weeping Woman entered the sanctuary, the faithful followed. Young children wondered if the "soldiers" weren't in fact seventh- and eighth-grade boys from St. Francis School. The packed church began to chant the rosary in Spanish. After Father Thomas's sermon, the laity approached the ritual objects. They slowly filed by and kissed the instruments of torture and the Corpus. Parents took their sleepy children home as the devotion ended about 10:00 p.m. Those children, impacted by the evening, would long remember Viernes Santo at St. Francis. Families returned for the 7:00 a.m. Mass the next day, especially if their children sang in the choir.[54]

In 1950, a month later, the Claretian fathers urged the parish to attend the 10:00 a.m. solemn High Mass that celebrated the canonization of Blessed Antonio María Claret, the founder of their order. Later that Sunday, many returned at 3:00 p.m. to witness the procession that welcomed Cardinal Stritch to St. Francis. The cardinal presided over the event, which included the unveiling of a painting of the new saint and concluded with his Benediction of the Blessed Sacrament. The Mexican choir from South Chicago's Our Lady of Guadalupe Church sang.[55]

Family and friends gathered on the final Sunday of May to witness the First Communion of St. Francis School at the 8:00 a.m. Mass. The small girls attired in pink silk gowns carried lilies; others wore white with blue capes. Older girls dressed in white with wings "flitted through the crowd to escort the little ones back to their pews."[56] Many people returned to the church for an afternoon novena, the May Crowning, and the consecration of the First Communion girls and boys. At this final ceremony a priest enrolled the children in the scapular, sprinkling them with holy water, then placing the thin cords over each child's head so that the postage-stamp-sized brown cloth *estampita* hung below their collarbones. Parents looked on proudly as the priest explained to the children, "The Scapular is a mirror of the humility and purity of Mary: through her simplicity she invites us to live modestly and in purity. By wearing the Scapular day and night, it becomes a sign of our constant prayer and of our special dedication to the love and service of the Virgin Mary. By wearing the Scapular, you renew your baptismal vow to put on our Lord Jesus Christ. In Mary, your hope of salvation will be safeguarded, because in her the God of Life has made his abode."[57] First communicants in many US parishes received the scapular, publicly marking their body with this token of Marian devotion. Meant for continuous wear, according to Paula Kane, "as an object of popular Marianism, the scapular flourished before Vatican II."[58] Notably, wearing *el escapulario* persists as a popular practice among Mexican Catholics. Many immigrants crossing the

Arizona desert wear one. Even today, street vendors in Chicago's Pilsen and La Villita neighborhoods sell a variety of scapulars to the mexicanos who dominate these neighborhoods.

The year came to a busy close each December at St. Francis. The well-attended novena to Nuestra Señora de Guadalupe began on December 3 and culminated in a boisterous Misa de Gallo (Rooster's Mass) in the predawn hours of December 12. No matter the ice or snow, the *guadalupanas* insisted on a procession from the gym to the church. Upon entering St. Francis, women, men, and children—including costumed Juan Diegos—received roses, which they then placed at the altar, crowded with bouquets and candles. Especially large crowds appeared in 1943, whether due to wartime anxieties or the fine preaching of a visiting Claretian priest from Los Angeles. The increased attendance included the recent influx of newcomers from Mexico as well. Las Posadas, another nine-day observance and celebration, began soon after and ended on Christmas Eve. Yet that year, due to a cold snap, attendance was limited.[59]

St. Francis followed the same liturgical calendar as the rest of the archdiocese, with the addition of the feast of Our Lady of Guadalupe. While this church did nurture certain devotional traditions from Mexico, at the same time it carried out the habits of devotionalism shared by Catholics of many nationalities in mid-twentieth-century Chicago. Eileen McMahon writes evocatively of the pre–Vatican II world, in which "it was not uncommon to find St. Sabina parishioners wearing a scapular, carrying a rosary in their pocket, or tipping their hat when they passed a church."[60] The same could be said for St. Francis.

Like all parishes, St. Francis drew in family, neighbors, and a community of faith for the sacraments that marked life events. Baptisms, always celebratory, had a special resonance in a parish so heavily comprised of immigrants as families laid down new roots. Mexicanos gathered too at their church to mark deaths and to remember the departed. In 1924 Elidia Barroso had requested a Mass for her late parents' souls. She had left them behind, buried in Guanajuato; however, at the store-front precursor to St. Francis, others joined Elidia in Chicago to pray for her parents. The church brought together kin, friends, and neighbors a few weekday mornings each month for a funeral Mass of someone who had passed away at home or in a West Side hospital. Family, friends, and customers attended the November 3, 1945, funeral High Mass for Miguel Parra, a local musician and proprietor of Mike's Peluquería y Billares, a block north of the church. On April 11, 1945, the parish held a High Requiem Mass for Pvt. Mike Hernández Jr., killed in action on Corregidor weeks before. Miguel Hernández and his wife raised Mike just a block away from St. Francis—certainly many members of both generations came that day to pray for his soul's repose.[61]

The funeral Masses held at St. Francis on Saturday, March 4, 1944, demand special remembrance for the four Mexican men buried that day. José Aguirre (age fifty-seven, native of León), Juan Casino, Juan López, and Socorro Santoyo (age fifty) all died in a train accident two days prior. These men, who apparently had no family in Chicago ("nuestros paisanos," as memorialized in the parish newspaper), were likely braceros working on area railroads. The *St. Francis Crier* featured a front-page Spanish-language article in February 1944 that welcomed the first braceros to Chicago, praising their sacrifices for the war effort, and it reminded Mexican residents to help these sojourners in all ways. The anonymous author finished: "The good will, I won't say of neighbors, rather of brothers, is what the Chicago colonia knows to provide the Mexican railways braceros. Welcome to Chicago!" But railway work was dangerous. These four men had their lives end tragically far from home and the loved ones whom they wanted to support in Mexico. Three priests sang the funeral Masses, for two men at noon and two later that afternoon, before burial in Chicago cemeteries.[62] Many St. Francis parishioners worked in the city's rail yards and roundhouses; most of the settled families had, at one time, worked on the tracks. Many children had been born in boxcars somewhere between Texas and Illinois. Attending the funerals of these men, unknown, perhaps, but whose lives so paralleled their own, was an essential act of accompaniment to these men who would be interred so far from home.[63] For those who did not attend the Mass and read about it in the parish paper, it stirred up memories of personal journeys and sacrifices in migrating to Chicago. Certainly, the four paisanos' tragic demise led some to say a prayer and light a candle at St. Francis in their memory.

The possibility of traditional Mexican devotion at St. Francis proved crucial in the parish's recruitment and retention of Catholics from Mexico. From 1940 to 1960 votive candle sales generated 9 to 29 percent of the parish's annual revenue. By contrast, Our Lady of Guadalupe, the South Chicago Mexican parish, netted 2 to 9 percent of its annual revenue from votive candle sales. (A sample of revenue sources in several nearby non-Mexican parishes shows only 1.7 to 5 percent of income from candle sales.)[64] Obviously, St. Francis welcomed these devotional offerings. Other traditional practices of seeking intercession via the saints and the Virgin Mary took place at St. Francis. Some faithful left *milagros*, tin *retablos*, and crutches at altars as they prayed to specific religious images.[65] Today at St. Francis, the faithful kindle the vast majority of their candles before a large Jesús Nazareno, already scourged and bloodied. Mexican parents in the 1930s and 1940s taught their children to

FIGURE 5. Altar of the Immaculate Heart of Mary, St. Francis of Assisi Church. Note the retablo and milagros to the left. Courtesy of the Claretian Missionaries Archives USA-Canada.

revere the image as Christ the King, or Cristo Rey, suggesting an important link to the Cristero rebellion, which reverberated in Chicago's parishes.[66]

This kind of popular piety, stressing the cult of the saints, flourished in the 1940s and 1950s at St. Francis, as well as in immigrants' homes. Whenever I asked elderly Mexican Americans about their childhood homes in Chicago, with a smile they named their immigrant parents' beloved images: el Santo Niño de Atocha, la Virgen de San Juan de Lagos, la Virgen de Guadalupe, or a picture of the Sacred Heart. The celebrations of the novena and fiesta of the Virgin of Guadalupe throughout this era exemplify a vibrant and unifying Mexican devotion at St. Francis. The parish established its own store featuring religious items. One could choose from a variety of rosaries and crèches and a wide range of images, "above all the Sacred Heart of Jesus and the Santo Niño de Atocha" (as advertised in 1946).[67] The store's inauguration built upon the strong sales of votive candles, which distinguished St. Francis from other parishes. Its presence in the church facilitated ongoing individual acts of supplication and devotion, often unconnected from the scheduled communal liturgy at St. Francis.

The church added to its display of images. In 1954 Father Thomas wrote to the archbishop of Guadalajara requesting an image of the Virgin of San Juan de los Lagos. "We are going to make an altar in this church," for which a meter-high statue of the devotion was urgently needed.[68] In this case, I imagine that "we" meant that the Claretian priests were acting on the growing devotion to the Virgin of San Juan among newly arrived men and women in Chicago. As Christina Heisser documents, this once-regional devotion was spreading in the mid-twentieth century. The Virgin of San Juan was becoming "the virgin of the migrants," her devotion expanding within Mexico and among immigrants and braceros.[69] Father Thomas, with previous pastoral work in Los Angeles and El Paso, was attuned to Mexicans' piety and devotional styles.

Beyond the opportunities for individual devotion, some parishioners wanted even more opportunities to express their devotion as part of a community. In 1946 Father Thomas backed parishioners' desire to initiate Perpetual Adoration of the Blessed Sacrament in their church. As their priest explained to the cardinal, "I have been asked time and time again by my people to have Perpetual Adoration. The Mexican people do have a deep devotion to the Blessed Sacrament and there is hardly a Mexican town in which you do not find Perpetual Adoration in some one of the churches." While he wrote as though he had witnessed such devotion in Mexico, the German priest was more likely familiar with the Mexican laity's participation in Perpetual Adoration from La Placita Church in Los Angeles. In his personal devotional practices, Father Thomas shared much with many devout mexicanos.[70]

The Mexican laypeople's desire for this round-the-clock devotion in their Chicago church is notable on many levels. Their request indicated a strong devotion to Jesus, as represented in the sacrament.[71] In late nineteenth-century Mexico, Vela Perpetua became a very popular practice in parishes that was backed by priests and laity alike.[72] When the laymen and laywomen of St. Francis carried out this rigorous practice of accompanying the Blessed Sacrament with silent meditation, they demonstrated a deep commitment to their faith and their parish community on a daily basis. The cardinal, however, denied the mexicanos' request for Perpetual Adoration. Yet parish records from years before and after this request show that dozens took part in the Vela Perpetua at St. Francis, reaching 150 members in 1952.[73] The persistence of the unauthorized devotion suggests both the strength of lay piety and Father Thomas's tendency to break rules to support immigrants' needs.

In the 1940s and 1950s parishioners asserted their Mexican religious preferences time and time again, even though their priests, the Claretians, campaigned to foment the cult of the Immaculate Heart of Mary. Glorification of this mystical cult fills the order's internal publications. The Claretians built chapels, established archconfraternities, and sponsored novenas to promote this particular devotion. St. Francis's sanctuary featured large murals portraying the Immaculate Heart of Mary. Despite persistent promotion of this Claretian cult, Chicago's Mexican Catholics stood unmoved in their devotion to the patroness of Mexico.[74] The Claretians established a vicariate in Chicago's Back of the Yards neighborhood in 1945: they named it Immaculate Heart of Mary. But the Mexican faithful never took to that name, which referred to the Claretians' special devotion. "The people didn't like it," recalled Fr. George Ruffalo, CMF, who served there in the late 1950s.[75] Instead, parishioners called their converted storefront church "la Capilla" (the Chapel), short for la Capilla de Nuestra Señora de Guadalupe, in honor of the Guadalupe image, which attracted Back of the Yard Mexicans. The Claretian fathers likewise tried to encourage devotion to their order's founder, St. Anthony Mary Claret, without apparent success.[76]

■ ■ ■

For the braceros and other mexicanos who arrived in Chicago in the 1950s, St. Francis was often a touchstone in their first days. The priests sent parish teens to the nearby rail yards to escort lone travelers to St. Francis. When Vicente Zúñiga finally managed to "arreglar papeles" (to get a visa) and bring his wife, Amelia, north to settle with him, she nervously flew to Chicago. That very day, her first in the United States, the reunited couple went to St. Francis for Mass and to offer prayers of thanksgiving.[77] Mexican immigrants found a familiar place at St. Francis: the Virgin of Guadalupe was prominently displayed, her gilded altar aglow with candlelight and the Cristo Rey within reach. The people in the pews and the rectory staff all spoke Spanish. "I felt comfortable [at St. Francis], seeing so many people of *la Raza*," recalled

FIGURE 6. Sanctuary, St. Francis of Assisi Church, 1948. Photo: Chicago Architectural Photographing Company. Courtesy of the Claretian Missionaries Archives USA-Canada.

Rubén Castillo, who arrived as a young man from Oaxaca in 1950.[78] For the immigrant in need, prayers to the Virgin or el Nazareno provided some solace to the hungry, jobless, or those fearful of deportation.

A trip to the St. Francis rectory often brought immediate, tangible help. The Claretians, a religious order committed to the poor, provided food and other charity to the needy. The priests permitted newly arrived braceros to sleep in parish buildings and actively helped them find employment. Father Thomas explained that "there are hundreds of Mexicans that come to Chicago from different parts," and he did "his best to take care of them. Many of them are without funds and hungry and they know that they can obtain aid in St. Francis Rectory and so they flock there." Father Thomas hosted groups of migrant men for meals in the rectory.[79]

Father Thomas took assistance to another level. In 1949 Immigration Department officers charged that he had helped obtain work for some Mexicans who sought to overstay their temporary work contracts. In one instance he himself employed a man at the parish. Officials further charged that "Fr. Thomas baptized a man who turns out to be here on a temporary visit permit and puts on the baptismal certificate that he was born at Chicago." The Immigration Department asked the Chancery to see that Father Thomas avoid the legal problems that similar acts might invite in the future.[80]

To serve the Mexican population more systematically, St. Francis established the Mexican Welfare Council (MWC) in 1945 with Mrs. Emma Saravia, a Catholic Charities case worker, at the helm. The agency took over a building within the parish complex and developed a strong support and membership network within the parish itself. Its programs ranged from health and legal services to the prevention of juvenile delinquency. MWC letterhead notably used all Spanish, while rival Mexican Civic Committee letterhead (and correspondence) was in English. Possibly, the MWC more consistently conducted its programs in Spanish, thus increasing its appeal to the newly arrived. For whatever reason, the St. Francis–based MWC was deemed "strongest of all" and "most active" of the colonia organizations in 1947.[81]

Laypeople used their affiliation with the parish to aid other mexicanos in less formal ways. Consider the president of the guadalupanas, who took "the comadre role seriously, choosing devout friends for the godparents of her children. She is godmother to many children herself. She mentions that she has helped many friends fill out job applications and other forms."[82] Within a few years of his own arrival in Chicago, Rubén Castillo delivered food from St. Francis to needy Mexican families in the neighborhood. The young medical doctor Jorge Prieto recalled eagerly establishing his first practice in 1952 in the parish compound: "Together Father Thomas and I painted three rooms in the old wooden convent building across the street from his church." Prieto hung a bronze plaque at the street entrance: "Dr. Jorge Prieto, Universidad Nacional de Mexico." For the next twenty years he attended to mexicanos at that location.[83] The actions of priests and lay leaders alike secured St. Francis's reputation as an institution that cared about Mexican immigrants in tangible ways.

Yet "the Mexican cathedral" had its critics. P. J. Miranda, who grew up in the Near West Side, readily noted St. Francis's central role for neighborhood Mexicans in the mid-1950s. This Hull House–based social worker declared that "many families center their lives around this Church and depend solely on it for all their needs." He noted the breadlines for new immigrants at the church, which earned priests the reputation as "saints." Miranda acknowledged St. Francis's centrality for Mexican people yet heaped criticism on its priests for their failure to cooperate with other neighborhood churches (Protestant and Catholic) and agencies.[84]

The postwar arrival of Puerto Ricans also led to criticisms of the Claretians' control of St. Francis. Some diocesan clergy took note of the Puerto Ricans' spiritual needs in the 1950s. At their urging, the Cardinal's Committee for the Spanish-Speaking (CCSS) formed with a focus on this newest population. Fr. Leo Mahon felt that Puerto Ricans needed special attention. Mexicans, he believed, had fewer needs, as they carried "in their culture a sound piety, a sound religiosity." The Archdiocese of Chicago no longer permitted the establishment of national parishes, so Puerto Ricans never had their own Catholic churches. As Puerto Ricans dispersed into the city's west and north sides, no parish was made "Puerto Rican."[85] Moreover, many parishes shunned Puerto Ricans. Many Puerto Ricans settled near Our Lady of Pompeii, yet in 1954 the priest there brushed off any possibility of adding a Spanish Mass. Sermons were offered in Italian and English; "if he added Puerto Rican it would greatly lengthen the time of masses."[86] The fact that many European Americans ascribed a negative racialization to Puerto Ricans did not help their situation.[87] The CCSS tried to implement new plans to incorporate *puertoriqueños*, but Father Mahon recalled that St. Francis did not support these initiatives. Some of the Claretians "thought that all Hispanics were their province and we were stealing them away." Father Mahon argued, "There was no way you could handle all these people, and they ought to be getting into their [neighborhood] parishes."[88]

Many Puerto Ricans did find St. Francis welcoming. While Italian churches on the Near West Side proved hesitant (and possibly hostile) to their new neighbors from Puerto Rico, St. Francis's doors were open. In the late 1950s the parish held a novena to Our Lady of Divine Providence, the island's patroness.[89] Many Puerto Rican couples opted to marry there in the 1950s. While they undoubtedly heard that St. Francis "belongs to the Mexicans," Puerto Ricans still went there because the parish "was the one there was. . . . [I]t was the most known."[90] In the early 1960s twenty-three Chicago parishes reported that Puerto Ricans attended Mass. Leading all, St. Francis reported that an average of fifteen hundred Puerto Ricans attended on Sundays.[91]

■ ■ ■

St. Francis of Assisi, a place that many immigrants experienced as "el refugio de los mexicanos," reached its apogee in the 1940s and 1950s. With a fully staffed rectory and convent, vigorous religious participation, solid school enrollment, and a great many clubs, services, and events for new immigrants, long-time residents, and Mexican American youth, Roosevelt and Newberry truly was a vital center for Mexican Chicago. When Tito Guízar packed the house in 1946, St. Francis's star was ascending; the incredible fund-raising push that rebuilt the school and gym within seven months made this clear. Two years later the parish expanded again with a free-standing youth center / gymnasium, a concrete stake in the Mexican church's future.

Yet as a parish—providing religious and secular services, succor, and community for adults and children every day and at any hour—St. Francis's influence declined along with the Near West Side neighborhood, which underwent a speedy demise after 1961. Chapter 3 details how Mexicans lost their homes to make way for the University of Illinois's new Chicago campus. Without parishioners nearby, St. Francis essentially became a "weekend parish," with tremendous, enthusiastic attendance on Sundays, during Semana Santa, on December 12, and on similar occasions throughout the year. In 1966 the CCSS opined that the Claretians' St. Francis "treated itself as the Spanish-speaking Cathedral."[92]

The appeal of this church, *la catedral mexicana* (or sometimes called *la catedral hispana*), continues today. Despite (or perhaps because of) its near demolition in 1996, St. Francis stands tall. Prior to 1960 Latino Catholics could only attend Mass with a Spanish-language homily at three churches: St. Francis, Our Lady of Guadalupe, and Immaculate Heart of Mary (a vicariate in Back of the Yards). Now they can do so at over one hundred Chicago-area churches. While choices abound for Latino Catholics, St. Francis's pews spill over seven times each weekend, although its mainly immigrant attendees do not live nearby. Each Saturday, dozens of families choose to baptize their children at St. Francis. The Virgin of Guadalupe, held aloft by Juan Diego on his *tilma*, now holds pride of place over the main altar. As such, the image of Guadalupe is not an accessible offering site at present-day St. Francis. The faithful worship at multiple side altars. They bring milagros, notes, photos, and other offerings to el Santo Niño de Atocha, San Judas Tadeo, and el Nazareno. Before these images, women and men light dozens of votive candles. The side altar for the Virgen de San Juan, sought by Father Thomas decades ago, has become the preferred spot for people with family members who served in Iraq or Afghanistan.

In the past decade the sanctuary became home to the Virgen de la Nube, inviting Chicago's growing Ecuadorean population. Hundreds gather here each May to celebrate the image of la Madre del Ecuatoriano Ausente.[93] At the 8:00 a.m. Mass on a rainy June Sunday in 2015, six votive candles glowed at her altar. I watched as a gray-haired man, after taking Communion, approached; he touched and kissed the Virgen de la Nube. He then gathered his lunch sack and plastic Dunkin' Donuts cup and left the church, off to work. After Mass, a middle-aged woman lit a candle before the Virgen de la Nube, knelt in silent prayer for several minutes, then crossed herself. The priests meanwhile offered a post-Mass exposition of the Santo Sacramento. Most of the congregation (still overwhelmingly ethnic Mexican) stayed, kneeling, in silence for ten minutes. At the sanctuary's rear, four men approached el Nazareno for prayer. They added their offerings to the four dozen votive candles aglow at this ever-frequented corner of St. Francis.[94]

The physical and social landscape of the Near West Side—once home to "the Mexican boulevard"—changed forever in the 1960s, but St. Francis perseveres. Whether with saints and candles, free bread, Mexican movie stars, or the familiar sound of Spanish, the parish always drew people in and earned St. Francis a special status in Mexican Chicago. Puerto Ricans too found a welcoming Spanish-speaking religious home, if not especially attentive to their piety. Dr. Prieto highlighted the crucial pastoral work of the mid-twentieth century: "In this otherwise cold northern metropolis . . . the Claretian Fathers and the Cordi-Marian Sisters" provided "a source of solace, unity, and strength."[95] St. Francis's standing as la catedral hispana changed as Catholic churches elsewhere in Chicago slowly added Spanish-language services and integrated Latino devotions. Its aura persists, however, for the multitudes of Chicagoans whose families consider St. Francis of Assisi their mother parish, now for multiple generations.

3. Red, White, and Blue and Mexican

Mexican Americans in Midcentury Chicago

¡Nada le intimida y con brio avanza! ¿Cómo se ha de temer si en sus venas corre sangre mexicana?

Nothing intimidates him, and with spirit he advances! How could he fear if in his veins runs Mexican blood?
—María Serrano, "Vuelve a nuestra casa" (Return to our home)

After I was enlisted in the Air Force and I was sent overseas on a squadron detail, I had the plane named after the parish team "The Wildcat."
—Vincent Barba

TEÓFILO ARÉVALO, a corporal in the Army Corps of Engineers, had survived two harrowing years in England during which Nazi bombers had turned London into "Buzz Bomb Alley." By early 1945 his unit had made its way to France, where he saw liberated Paris. The ballyhooed road to Berlin seemed a cruel joke during the hard winter at the Bulge, but now the Americans were certainly on their way to Germany. As Teó ate his chow one afternoon, a truck rode into camp, pulled up to the commanding officer's tent, and dumped the familiar gray sacks there. The guys perked up. Mail call stirred every enlisted man, waiting anxiously to hear his name and to receive letters from parents, a younger sibling, or maybe a sweetheart. With "A" at the top of the list, Teófilo never had to wait long to see if he had a letter. "Abbott!" the sergeant called out. "Anderson!" Hearing "Ar-EE-vAAlo!"

Teófilo trotted up to get his mail. The large envelope caught him off guard, but the return address—1206 S. Newberry Avenue, Chicago, Illinois—was as familiar as his own home. He stepped away from the tent, pulled out his knife, and carefully slit open the envelope. He smiled broadly as he unfolded the January issue of the *St. Francis Crier*.[1]

With twelve pages of news from his Chicago parish, much of it written by childhood friends, Teó found himself transported from the war-ravaged French countryside and back to the familiar Mexican faces and worn blocks of the Near West Side. Just to glimpse the ads took him home. Alfonso's Grocery on Peoria Street, where his *mamá* bought the family fresh meat and chiles from Mexico. Casa Mexicana bookshop, where his *apá* stopped in to see newspapers from his homeland. Leavitt Brothers, on the corner of Halsted and Maxwell, open day and night—Teó's stomach growled at the mere suggestion of the joint's hot kosher corned beef sandwiches.

Then Teó lost himself in the features. He pored over news from the other boys in the service: Pfc. Manuel Martinez, "stationed somewhere in the Philippines"; Cpl. Sixto Zaragoza, "somewhere in New Guinea." Pvt. Joseph Reyes was "somewhere in Holland." Teó remembered seeing Joe, a South Chicago boy, play basketball with the Yaquis when they took on his own team, the Hidalgos. Chuck Aragón, lucky guy, was home on furlough from Camp Blanding in Florida. The girls would be glad to see Chuck again, with his "million dollar smile" featured in a small photo in the paper. Only the call back to work with his unit shook Teó from his Chicago reverie.

In the next days, the young corporal would read the *Crier* cover to cover: from Armando Galvan's sports section, devoted to Chicago's Mexican basketball teams, to Lupe López's review of a new Charles Boyer movie. The Musical Parade began with news of Glenn Miller's tragic disappearance over the Channel. He nervously studied the Gossip column, envious to read about the guys on furlough, recent engagements, and the pretty girls of his high school days, like Betty Cruz and Stella Lopez, at the St. Francis socials. Teó was relieved to find nothing about Lupe Murillo, the girl he was sweet on.[2] Given his long absence, he worried that she might take up with a neighborhood boy or even one of the Mexican *braceros*.

Teó proudly shared his paper with the other Mexican boys in the unit—Hernández, Ramírez, Guerrero, and others. He reflected that in France, "we sorta have a Mexican community in our company." Although the boys were from California, New Mexico, and Texas, they enjoyed reading the *Crier*'s few Spanish articles and learning about Chicago's good-looking young Mexican women presented in the Girl of the Month. Even an Irish guy from a northside parish enjoyed reading the paper for its taste of Chicago.[3] Feeling gratitude for his parish paper's monthly arrival, Teó Arévalo wrote to the editors, "It does my heart good to read about all my friends who are at home and in the Service." He continued humbly, "I guess a fellow like me needs something like the CRIER to sorta bring home near."[4] The little paper did just that.

On the other side of the globe that spring, another St. Francis boy landed at Iwo Jima, digging into the black volcanic sand under constant Japanese artillery and mortar fire. Artie Arriaga, a marine, had been overseas since the fall and wrote home about his landing at Iwo Jima. Within minutes of landing, Artie watched two of his buddies take Japanese fire. In return, he boasted, "I fired three thousand rounds of ammunition at the 'Hot Rock' known as Mt. Suribachi. We are about a hundred yards away from it and 'Old Glory' is on top, which is a good sight to see." From Chicago, Artie's brother had written encouragingly, "Maybe those nips will give themselves up," but no such luck. Closing his letter, Artie sent regards to all the folks in the neighborhood. Before enlisting, his gang of friends had pompously worn their draped suits on Chicago's West Side.[5] The *Crier* proudly printed Arriaga's letter in May 1945. That same month the Iwo Jima flag-raisers toured the home front, Chicago included, to drum up continued public support for the war effort, especially the Mighty Seventh War Loan. ("Don't forget. It's not over yet.") With the American flag-raising at Iwo Jima an omnipresent symbol of American fortitude, St. Francis's youth emphasized their parish's sacrifice there.

Teenagers published the *St. Francis Crier*'s first issue on November 11, 1943. They directed the monthly paper at parish sons (and a few daughters) in the military to keep them connected to home.[6] Professionally typeset, illustrated with photos and cartoons, the *Crier* averaged twelve pages. English-language sports, music, fashion, and gossip columns and cartoons ran alongside Spanish-language features that mostly spotlighted the church itself or announcements directed at the older immigrant generation. The paper carried numerous advertisements from neighborhood businesses. While most of these ads came from Mexican establishments, Jewish- and Italian-owned businesses also bought ad space. Local merchants recognized the *Crier*'s sizable readership and sought the growing Mexican clientele for their businesses. Ferrara, an Italian bakery on Taylor Street, advertised in the *Crier*. Their cannoli-filled cake became a favorite at many Mexican American weddings.

The *St. Francis Crier* spotlights the talents and desires of the Mexican American generation that came of age in the 1940s.[7] Like other Chicagoans of that era, the teens at St. Francis were sports crazy and joiners.[8] Before the war they formed teams and social clubs at local settlement houses and at church. The paper grew out of the St. Francis Social Athletic Club, formed in

1940, for parish boys to play baseball and football and sponsor dances. After Pearl Harbor, the club lost its members, one by one, to the armed forces. With club members scattered around the globe, the idea arose to create a paper "of interest to all the boys and girls in the service." The editors also proclaimed that the paper was "dirigida en su totalidad por Jovénes [*sic*] Mexicanos, ha nacido con el sano propósito de servir a la misma . . . para formar Ciudadanos dignos" (directed completely by Mexican youth, born with the healthy aim to serve the same . . . to develop worthy Citizens).[9] The paper soon had a regular volunteer staff of eight (of whom half were women), plus a string of reporters. Upon printing three thousand copies each month, the staff—all of whom had siblings, neighbors, or old schoolmates in the service—gathered in their office in the rectory and devoted hours to addressing hundreds of copies to the intended readers. The staff also organized fund-raisers for the paper, including bimonthly dances at Hull House. At first, they mailed the paper mainly to training centers scattered throughout the country, but it soon went to places the Chicagoans had never imagined. The *Crier* made its way to "Saipan, Iwo Jima, and Okinawa in the pocket of some Marine." It "was stained with blood at the Anzio Beachhead" and lay by "some lifeless body of a Yank in the shores of Normandy." Prisoners of war read the paper over and over in the prisons of Manila and Germany.[10] The paper proved a comfort to men stricken with malaria in Asian jungles or recuperating in a Battle Creek, Michigan, hospital. Pfc. Anthony López had himself photographed on Iwo Jima: helmeted and grinning, he held up the *Crier* he received there in February 1945. For López, reading each issue was "a piece of heaven, consolation and joy."[11]

On the paper's second anniversary in November 1945, the staff looked back in amazement at how their hard work had enabled "the American youth of Mexican descent in Chicago to have a periodical they can call a newspaper." With peacetime finally upon them, they vowed to continue publication "in the shadow of the red, white, and blue."[12]

This chapter examines the rise of Chicago's second generation. Published works on Mexican Chicago largely ignore the emerging Mexican American generation in the 1940s. Their parents may have arrived as sojourners and faced obstacles to full inclusion and recognition, but the second generation grew up as Chicagoans. They spoke Spanish at home, but outside they played cowboys and Indians, learned to shoot hoops, and danced the jitterbug like their peers all over the country. They flocked to Hull House for appearances by Benny Goodman and Fiorello LaGuardia.[13] Discussing the emerging second generation in Los Angeles, George Sánchez contends that Mexican American youth faced "considerable internal conflict" as they balanced "the desires of their immigrant parents and the reality of their American existence."[14] I find a very different story. As revealed in oral histories, the *Crier*'s rich material, and St. Francis School records, these young women and men lived easily with their hybrid identity. They did not call themselves "Spanish" but instead proudly called themselves Mexican, American, and Catholic.

Growing up at St. Francis fostered a positive Mexican identity that Chicagoans could share with their immigrant parents. Beyond the integrated spheres of school and work, these young people lived in a social world almost entirely of Mexican origin. As members of Club Juárez, they held dances. As Wildcats and Cobras, they played baseball. A weekend retreat for the Young Ladies' Sodality (a lay Catholic devotional group) meant prayer and socializing with Lupes, Marías, and Teresas. Mexican American GIs from Texas and California on furlough easily mingled on the Near West Side, including at the *Crier*'s monthly Victory Socials.[15] After the war, Mexican Americans formed their own American Legion Post, honoring parish son Manuel Pérez, posthumously awarded the Congressional Medal of Honor.[16] The veterans met in the St. Francis parish complex. When they married in the 1950s, often moving into other neighborhoods, they returned to baptize their children at St. Francis. They also celebrated relatives' and friends' weddings and baptisms at the "Mexican cathedral." The second generation, in sum, generally elected to live in a Mexican American social scene, much of which was rooted in their evolving Catholic parish. As parishioners they also belonged to the American Catholic world—in Chicago this meant respect. All of this began when they were children.

▪ ▪ ▪

Kids called Johnny Hernandez "Slugger." This recent St. Francis School graduate was quite the baseball player. As a regular at the Chicago Boys' Club down the street, he joined other Near West Side boys on a club-sponsored camping trip to an Indiana lake. There Johnny set out in a canoe and paddled toward some swans. Not "as handy with a paddle as with a baseball," the thirteen-year-old lost control, the canoe capsized, and he drowned. Thirty-five youngsters from the Boys' Club marched in the procession that brought his casket from the Salerno funeral home, with six boys as pall bearers, to St. Francis, where a High Mass was sung for his soul. The Sisters of St. Francis, touched by their former student's untimely passing, noted that the casket also contained his beloved pitcher's glove and a "new league ball, signed by all thirty-five boys." The *Crier* lauded Johnny's pals who sought donations from Mexican groups to defray the funeral costs. They gave this money to his widowed mother, Mrs. Lupe Hernandez, who lived one block from the church.[17] With his love of sports, Catholic education, and connections to St. Francis, John Hernandez's life sounds like that of hundreds of young people who grew up in Mexican Chicago.

In the 1940s a new Mexican American generation emerged. Raised in the United States by immigrant parents, they had limited personal contact with Mexico. Of a sample of one hundred St. Francis School pupils in the 1940s, just two were born in Mexico; 76 percent had been born in or near Chicago.[18] Elidia Barroso's sister Sofía, for example, raised seven kids in a Peoria Street flat two blocks from St. Francis. She and her husband, Guadalupe Cabrera, increasingly spoke English with their children, who grew up with Italian neighbors, ascended through local public schools, and made friends at church with newcomers from Texas. The many Mexican children enrolled at nearby public schools formed a minority in their classes and learned alongside children from Italian and Greek households; over time, their Jewish classmates moved elsewhere, and more African American children moved in.[19] Informants who grew up in the Near West Side recall speaking Spanish at home but English in public settings, even with Mexican American friends. Alfred Galvan, the son of Mexican immigrants and a graduate of St. Francis School, claimed he knew Yiddish before he knew Spanish (as a boy he worked for a Jewish businessman on Maxwell Street). Galvan further reflected that when he first visited Mexico as a young adult, "I was embarrassed there because I didn't know how to order a hamburger in Spanish."[20] Laura Vasquez, daughter of New Mexicans, arrived in Chicago at age five. As a teen she sold tickets at the Globe, a local Mexican movie theater; because she did not speak Spanish, she had to ask other employees to handle phone calls from Spanish speakers. Vasquez appreciated that she had free admission to the theater—for its American movies.[21] Although the generation that came of age in the 1940s grew up in a tightly knit Mexican social world, most of their interests, education, and aspirations overlapped with those of other young Chicagoans.[22]

Even in the heavily Mexican St. Francis School, this generation had a solidly American education. Their teachers, the Sisters of St. Francis of Mary Immaculate (a predominantly German American order based in Joliet) had taught at St. Francis School since 1867, when most pupils were also German. As school enrollment became more Mexican, the nuns did not change much. They neither spoke Spanish nor fostered Mexican culture in their school. "The nuns hollered," one *tejana* remembered of her enrollment at the school, and "I learned English quick."[23] The sisters had minimal interactions with the Mexican families on the nearby blocks.[24] The teaching sisters seldom acknowledged the Mexican culture of their students' homes (as evinced in their convent annals from 1939 to 1964). Instead, they taught in English and used the Catholic American curriculum offered at parochial schools across the archdiocese. Only in the postwar era, challenged by the increasing numbers of non-English-speaking children, did the nuns set up separate classrooms for the newcomers.[25]

Attending St. Francis School meant belonging to Chicago's powerful, multifaceted Catholic network. Each December, children enjoyed Christmas parties and gifts courtesy of the Knights of Columbus or the American Legion. The new school library received funds for books from Catholic Charities. Donning diminutive habits, select school boys and girls—dressed as Claretians and Joliet Franciscans, respectively—ventured off to the north side, where they marched in the Mission Day procession at Holy Name Cathedral. Mixed in with hundreds of other parochial school children, they represented their school and their church at the epicenter of Chicago Catholicism.[26] When the St. Francis Boy Scout troop was organized in 1950, they took communion together; later that day, Bishop Bernard Sheil himself received their oaths. Sheil, the founder of the CYO, was a nationally known figure.[27]

No kid could doubt their parish's importance when twelve hundred Chicago policemen took over St. Francis Church for a St. Jude League Mass. The same for the youngsters who stood on a slushy corner and watched as row after row of police, in full dress, filled block after block of Roosevelt Road as the league solemnly processed to the church, accompanied by the police band.[28] Decades later they recalled Fr. Patrick McPolin's gleaming, black, new police vehicle, parked on Roosevelt Road. "Father Pat," a Claretian, headed the St. Jude League beginning in 1943; later he became a force-wide chaplain. Riding along in his chaplain's car made a St. Francis kid feel "like royalty because every police officer on duty on the streets of Chicago waved when they saw him."[29]

Even the St. Francis School patrol boys received a special nod. Ensuring the safety of young schoolmates crossing four lanes of traffic on Roosevelt Road was a significant responsibility. On a March evening in 1950, boys from the St. Francis safety patrol met at the rectory. From there Father Pat chaperoned them west to Riis School, where the 22nd Police District honored the neighborhood's patrol boys. The St. Francis kids, however, felt a special pride when Father Pat, their priest, delivered the program's invocation. They returned home carrying new raincoats, bestowed upon them by the police.[30]

St. Francis School children were firmly educated in the era's Catholic American traditions. They took part in May Crownings and novenas. They heard vocation talks and visited convents. Their first Holy Communion day ended with receiving the chocolate-brown scapular of Our Lady of Mount Carmel. Despite the run-down conditions of the Near West Side, in 1946 the sisters directed their charges to collect pennies for "the starving children in Europe." When the "Pilgrim Virgin," Our Lady of Fatima, toured Chicago parishes, she stopped at St. Francis. Schoolchildren and other parishioners joined the throngs who came face to face with this image of Mary, which was gaining popularity throughout the United States in the 1940s.[31] Likewise, St. Francis pupils participated in a "Catholic action" to pray for the conversion of Russia in 1951.[32] Historian Colleen McDannell underscores the role of parochial education: "American Catholics were learning how to be Catholic at school even more than at home."[33]

School could challenge the piety that many children learned at home. Mexican-born Esperanza Godínez recalls St. Francis School in the 1940s:

> One day, as several of us (second graders) were making the sign of the cross as our parents had taught us at home, one of the European nuns called out to us, "Stop that you dirty little Mexicans, How can you kiss those filthy fingers of yours?" We had no answer for her. We had been taught that as we would say "Por la señal de la santa Cruz . . ." by the sign of the holy cross . . . we made a cross putting our thumb over our forefinger, and as we said "Amen" we would kiss our "filthy" thumb.

Godínez reflects that "in order to belong I had to learn a new way of making the sign of the cross, a new way of being part of the Catholic Church."[34]

Yet belonging to a Mexican parish directed by the Claretians did prompt a degree of *mexicanidad* at St. Francis School. On December 12 (following a solemn High Mass at 8:00 a.m.) pupils had a free day. At some parish novenas, the schoolchildren sang in Spanish.[35] Bishop José María Preciado, CMF, from Panama confirmed many young people in the 1940s and 1950s. On the final day of classes in June 1944, the entire school went to see *San Francisco de Asís*, a Spanish-language movie released just months earlier in Mexico.[36] The sisters led the pupils down Roosevelt Road to the Globe Theater, the Mexican movie house that many children knew well as the place to see *charro* movies and Cantinflas comedies. The Mexican consulate regularly selected the school for special projects, inviting St. Francis pupils to attend its Christmas party or to decorate the Mexican tree at the Museum of Science and Industry's annual *Christmas around the World* exhibit. All in all, St. Francis provided multiple spaces in which its younger parishioners could experience and meld American and Mexican worlds.

■ ■ ■

As the second generation grew into teens and young adults, to what extent did a generation gap develop? In the 1940s few signs emerge of Chicago Mexican

Americans struggling, as Sánchez suggested, to balance their immigrant parents' desires and life in the United States. Certainly, many immigrant parents may have worried how well their kids who went to "jaiscul" (high school) spoke Spanish. A few may have anguished over the sons who chose to "vestir como pachucos" (dress like zoot-suiters), but there was little sign of a pachuco panic. Francisco López, an immigrant and a professional translator in the neighborhood, voiced some of these concerns in his periodic *Crier* columns on language, "Conviene Hablar Bien" (To speak well is best). Even López had to admit that, over the years in Chicago, immigrant parents' own Spanish had declined.[37] His musings demonstrate the fact that American influences entered immigrants' homes. López's own Chicago-reared daughter illustrates how the second generation deftly navigated the American world of school, work, and leisure time and the more Mexican world of home and family.

Lupe López, a steadfast *Crier* contributor, was born in Chicago in 1928. She attended public schools until transferring to St. Procopius Catholic High School for her final years; her favorite subject was shorthand. Her brown eyes sparkled at the "mention of any classic, swing, or rhumba number," but she loathed the jitterbug. Like so many Americans in 1944, she declared her favorite song as "I'll Be Seeing You"; Bing Crosby's version topped the charts that summer. Yet in the same year, Lupe sang "Virgen ranchera" at the musical night St. Francis Youth on Parade.[38] Lupe loved going to the pictures, and as the *Crier*'s movie reviewer, she described dozens in its pages. She mostly wrote about Hollywood movies, for example, *Meet Me in St. Louis* and *State Fair*, as well as many of Hollywood's Catholic-themed pictures, including *Going My Way*, *Song of Bernadette*, and *Keys of the Kingdom*.[39] Lupe also saw Mexican movies, including *Distinto amanecer*, starring the dashing Pedro Armendáriz. She wrote several reviews in Spanish.

Lupe López spent many of her leisure hours at St. Francis. She stopped by the rectory where Rufina, Jesse, Eddie, and the gang assembled the *Crier*. She looked forward to chatting with handsome Chuck Aragón, typing up his parish history for the paper. But in 1944 Chuck was inducted and went off to train in Florida. Lupe took part in the St. Francis Girls' Club: on the first and third Sundays she joined other Mexican American girls after the 10:30 Spanish Mass. The club chose Lupe to crown the Virgin with roses in May 1945. The Girls' Club sponsored an eighth-grade graduation banquet to honor "the Mexican students of Chicago." Lupe, who was the club's vice president, and the girls went skating at the Roller Bowl.[40]

Lupe's popularity extended beyond the St. Francis set when the sixteen-year-old's photo went out to thousands as the *Crier*'s Girl of the Month in November 1944. Following readers' nominations, the paper highlighted

Page 6 May, 1945 ST. FRAN

VOTE FOR THE G

EMMA PEDROZA
May, 1944

Delia Santisteven
June, 1944

"NO GIRL"
July, 1944

MARY VARGAS
August, 1944

"ST. FRANCIS CRIER"

To Hold

MAY DANCE

AT WEST - END

—o—

On May 28th, The St. Francis CRIER will hold a May Dance at the West End Women's Club, on Ashland and Monroe street. Manolo and his orchestra will furnish the music. Time of entree is 7:00 p. m. Admission price is $1.00.

"A LAS MADRES"

Vamos todos a cantar
Con tod el corazón
El himno más grandioso
Más lleno de emoción.

Y todos a una voz
Gritemos con placer
Que viva nuestra "Madre"
La MARTIR del deber.

Con el alma radiante de gozo,
Yo anhelaba llegar a este dia
Y estas flores, oh Madre querida,
Te dan prueba de amor, Madre Mía.

For the last twelve months w
lovely young lady whom we call "T
these girls automatically beco a
Year." Now, in order to choos e "
in the service should be the ones to pi
For this, THE CRIER is send
receiving the paper, with the name of
it in. Any blank sent in not directly t
for the contest.
After all the ballots have been
votes will be crowned "Girl of the Yea
The date for the dance will be annou
will be awarded a special prize.

ESPERANZA BARBA
December, 1944

JOSEPHINE MANCILLAS
January, 1945

THERESA BELMARES
February, 1945

FIGURE 7. Nominees for Girl of the Year, with Lupe Lopez (following page *top right*), *St. Francis Crier*, May 1945. Courtesy of the Claretian Missionaries Archives USA-Canada.

IRL OF THE YEAR

VIOLET CASTILLO
September, 1944

MARY TORRES
October, 1944

LUPE LOPEZ
November, 1944

› have been presenting each month a he Girl of the Month." Each one of cand' 'e for the title of "Girl of the Girl ıe Year", we feel that the boys k her.
ing a blank to every boy who is now each candidate and asking him to mail THE CRIER, will be held ineligible

abulated, the candidate with the most s" at a dance to be held in September, nced later. The girl winning the title

The Girl of the Month
May 1945

Lovely Angelina Caballero was born in Ollwein, Iowa, on October 31. She attended and was graduated from the Ollwein High School in 1935. Mr. and Mrs. Braulio Caballero are proud of their daughter who has won many friends with her pleasant personality and radiant smile in the short time she has been in Chicago. Angelina lived with her parents who still reside in Ollwein, Iowa, until a few years ago, when she came to Chicago to seek employment, with success for she is now employed at Mackevich's Grocery Store, 1146 S. Halsted St.

She is 5 ft. 2½ inches tall, has brown eyes and black hair. Red is her favorite color and she is fond of slacks, dancing, flowers and perfume.

Her hobby is collecting records and taking snapshots of her brother Michael.

She dislikes people who criticize, gossip, cheat, and who are destructive.

She likes Chicago boys best and she writes to many of them who are in the Service.

Her favorite song is, "If I Knew Then."

ELSIE GAMEZ
March, 1945

Miss Lupe Canchola
April, 1945

Angelina Caballero
May, 1945

Mexican American young women with a photo and a short profile.[41] These headshots, likely yearbook photos, were strikingly wholesome and modest compared to the pin-up girls featured in publications such as *Yank*, the US Army's weekly.[42] In May 1945 the paper devoted two pages to all of the year's featured girls. Editors asked servicemen to vote for their favorite and enclosed paper ballots with the eligible girls' names: the winner would become "G.I. Queen of 1944–45." Ballots returned that summer from Okinawa, Italy, the Philippines, and elsewhere. Frank Rodriguez, a neighborhood boy stationed in Austria, enclosed a letter with his ballot. "Thanks a lot for letting me vote for the Girl of the Year. The way I picked her I let all my buddies look at the contestants' pictures and we had our own little contest." Sgt. Manuel Barrientos, a Laredo native stationed in Germany, came across the paper, which greatly impressed him, as he had "always been interested in the achievements of the Mexican youth in the United States." He found the girls "the most attractive and charming looking young ladies. . . . European girls can't hold a candle to any one of those twelve." The *Crier* staff welcomed his letter, added him to their subscription list, and promised to introduce Barrientos to these young women should he visit Chicago.[43] For *tejano* vets, returning to Texas meant a return to persistent discrimination and segregation in public facilities.[44] Chicago offered a much more open landscape for people of Mexican descent.

By the time of the GI queen crowning, the war had ended at last. When the V-J news reached Chicago, cars honked everywhere, and celebratory crowds descended upon the Loop. In the Near West Side, people danced in the streets. Italians set up tables in the middle of May Street, ate spaghetti, drank red wine, and played tambourines. Others set bonfires, drawing fire trucks. As they did at churches nationwide, parents and young people came to St. Francis for thanksgiving prayer. The Claretian clergy dedicated a Holy Hour to the Immaculate Heart of Mary, and the faithful thanked "her for deliverance from this horrible war."[45]

Spirits ran high as the Mexican patriotic celebrations began in September 1945. On September 8 Lupe López was crowned GI queen at the St. Francis School Auditorium as part of a larger celebration that inaugurated the parish's Mexican Welfare Center (an agency that would primarily serve immigrants, as discussed in chapter 2). That event featured the singing duo Tarasco and *baile folklórico* presentations. The next week, Lupe left the Near West Side's familiar confines as she led the September 16 parade to Grant Park, where Mexicans from all parts of Chicago and beyond celebrated Mexican Independence Day. Lupe cheered on the St. Francis girls' softball team, which included many of her friends. Bigger crowds gathered for the day's featured game between the St. Francis Wildcats and the Rebels, the well-known Mexican team from Moline. Lupe, as queen, presented trophies to the winning teams.[46]

One wonders what Lupe's Mexican parents thought of their daughter's display. Long before the *Crier* shared her photo with strangers, the gossip column teased: "Charles Aragon and ? ? ? have a crush on Lupe Lopez. May the best man win!"[47] Many Mexican parents had modified their stance on appropriate female behavior. Their daughters went to high school and joined sports teams, and some girls even went roller skating with strangers. As much as modest incomes allowed, daughters tried to follow Hollywood fashion trends.[48] But for hundreds of Mexican American young women on the Near West Side, all this happened at or under the shadow of St. Francis. Families there knew each other, and immigrant parents may have felt less need for traditional chaperonage. The youth formed Mexican clubs that were, as Elizabeth Escobedo puts it, "socially sanctioned, but not fully controlled."[49] Lupe's parents, Frank and Margaret (who had lived in Chicago for two decades), could not have been much bothered when Chuck Aragón, discharged from the army as a well-decorated sergeant who served in Belgium and Germany, began to date their now eighteen-year-old daughter. Gone for two years, Chuck quickly rejoined the *Crier* and returned to writing serious articles, for example, on the Republican victories in recent elections. To mark the paper's third anniversary, the staff grouped for a photo: Chuck, neatly dressed in civvies, stood behind a demurely smiling Lupe.[50] Not long after, these two *Crier* staffers married.

Being Mexican, American, and Catholic fit together easily for that generation. As one Chicagoan recalls, "It was a Sunday tradition for Mexican families to go to church at five in the morning so that they could spend the whole day at the park playing and watching ball games."[51]

Johnny "Slugger" Hernandez and Lupe López both embodied the second generation. These teens had very American likes and habits and at the same time immersed themselves in a Mexican-origin social world. For Johnny and Lupe and so many of their generation, St. Francis parish anchored their hybrid identity.

▪ ▪ ▪

Many Mexican American young adults experienced a growing interest in Mexico and Mexicans on their own terms, often distinct from the México of their immigrant parents' memories. Chicago Mexican Americans made connections with a modernizing, urbanizing Mexico—not the Mexico of *haciendas* and *serenatas* that Elidia Barroso and others had left behind decades earlier. During the war and after, Mexican Americans engaged in wide-ranging transnational connections.

The economic opportunity of wartime work opened up an array of personal contacts with Mexico. During the war, many Near West Siders traveled to Mexico for the first time. The *St. Francis Crier* regularly reported on vacations to Mexico. In 1944 the paper congratulated "Miss Lupe Abarca who finally made that long desired trip to Mexico."[52] The goals of such trips varied. Some visits seemed more explicitly like tourism (Connie Soto "left for Mexico where she will spend two weeks sightseeing"). Others centered more upon time with family ("Silvia Martinez is spending most of the winter in Mexico visiting her relatives"). Charles Galvan graduated from high school, visited Mexico, and upon his return enlisted in the army.[53] Meanwhile, Mexico came north in the shape of braceros. The *Crier* often needled local girls for their interest in the newly arrived. Mary Vera reportedly could not "make up her mind between the fellows of the neighborhood or the fellows from Mexico." A bracero named Tony ("six foot tall, another Clark Gable only this one is from Mexico") regularly attended dinners at St. Francis's mission in Back of the Yards. Antonia Martinez apparently enjoyed "the Mexican movies in the company of a fellow from south of the Border."[54] Priests at St. Francis sent young neighborhood men to the nearby train yards to invite arriving braceros to the parish. The braceros found free food, lodging at the parish school, and even job leads. They also encountered young women of Mexican descent. One-time parish secretary Ruth Galvan met her husband, Javier López, a bracero from Guanajuato, this way. When they first met, she remembered with a laugh, Javier wore *huaraches*.[55] The older generation would sometimes offer lodging to *paisanos* from their home state; young Chicago women met young men from Mexico this way too. Many contacts were more ephemeral. Neighborhood kids, for example, went to Douglas Park to watch Club Necaxa's soccer games.[56]

Mexican Americans in 1940s Chicago had remarkable access to the latest cultural production from Mexico and incorporated it into their passions, chatter, and social relations. Many of the second generation had gone with their parents to the Mexican movies at the Globe Theater. (As Sandra Cisneros, a Chicago native, writes, "We like Mexican movies. Even if it's one with too much talking.")[57] As young adults, with friends or on a date, many persisted in seeing these movies. The *Crier*'s Tips for Teens advised that a good date consisted of sitting together, sipping a chocolate soda, or "taking her to see the latest Jorge Negrete picture co-starring Maria Elena Marquez, with all the trimmings of technicolor."[58] Young people enjoyed the latest from Cantinflas and awaited the comedy king's appearance in Chicago. *Crier* columnists interjected, "Ay, Jalisco no te rajes!" referring to the 1941 ranchera song and movie of the same name.[59] On the screen, Mexican Americans saw a Mexico of singing charros and *rebozo*-clad women: a folkloric and highly romanticized version of the rural life that their parents had left behind. The movies also showed them the metropolis of Mexico City, with its boulevards and neon signs for Goodyear Tires and Carta Blanca, its street-wise women in heels and mustachioed men driving sedans. The Chicago visits of Mexican basketball teams also intrigued Mexican Americans. On a 1945 goodwill tour, the national university's men's team played the Lin Dahl Foundry. Cheering on the Mexican visitors, Mexicans and Mexican Americans alike packed the De LaSalle Gym. Two months later Chicago fans came out to see Mexico's women's basketball champs, the Politas. These athletic women in shorts and high-tops, with the team's "flashy, hustling forward" and "rangy, aggressive guard," certainly showed a new, modernizing Mexico.[60]

Mexican Americans kept up with Mexican popular music. Travelers to Mexico "brought back records of the top Mexican tunes" and played them for friends in Chicago. The song "Traigo mi cuarenta y cinco" (I carry my .45) was a big hit with "the Halsted Street Boys." Immigrant parents loved Tito Guízar, but so did their kids. A foursome of neighborhood youths went to the Opera House to hear the Mexican singer and movie star (who would raise funds for St. Francis in 1946).[61] Some Mexican Americans tracked the Mexican hit parade, available on a weekly radio program on Chicago airwaves.[62]

In the Pan-American era, with Latin music tremendously popular in the United States and US influences strong in Mexico, national boundaries blurred along musical lines. As the *Crier* music editor, Paul Gasca, commented in 1945, "South of the Border has become a jitterbug world. They are crazy for swing . . . for instance, 'Sin Pantalones,' 'Dulce y Agua,' . . . 'Avena con Leche,'" with music by Chicago-raised Gene Krupa. Gasca noted the flow south: "Most of our favorite songs are being translated into Spanish and becoming hits in Mexico. For instance, 'As Time Goes By' is known as 'A Través de los Años' . . . 'At Last' as 'Por Fin.'" The bolero "Bésame Mucho," penned by Mexican songwriter Consuelo Velásquez, became a big wartime hit in the United States.[63]

During the war this Pan-American swirl played out on Chicago radio stations, on the dance floor, and at the pictures. In a single column, Gasca covered the death of Lucha Reyes (interpreter of "Ay Jalisco, no te rajes"), an upcoming Chicago appearance by Frank Sinatra, singer Miguelito Valdés's movie debut in *Mi reino por un torero* (My kingdom for a bullfighter), and a Count Basie performance. He urged readers to attend regular shows at Hull House by Manolo and his Royal Latins in which their versions of

"Bésame Mucho" and the "St. Louis Blues" "really get the crowd in a dancing mood."[64] In the realm of music and movies, the contacts with Mexico were many and positive. As scholar Anthony Macías argues for midcentury Los Angeles, "People used popular music, dance, and style to articulate a point of view—an identity—both Mexican and American."[65] Chicago Mexican Americans readily consumed the culture of their ancestral home alongside US popular culture.

■ ■ ■

World War II sent St. Francis's second generation far beyond Chicago as soldiers served all over the world. In the barracks and on the front lines, Mexican Americans served in regular units—in contrast to African Americans and (some) Puerto Ricans, who served in segregated units.[66] Mexican American soldiers underscored their American patriotism time and time again in letters to the *St. Francis Crier*. They wrote of their antipathy to Hitler but displayed true virulence against the Japanese. Tony Martínez, stationed in the Pacific, closed a letter in typical fashion: "Let's hope those Nips and Heines wash up, so that we can be together again. So long!" When Tony came home on a furlough (after thirty-eight months), the *Crier* noted that "in the Southwest Pacific[he had been] tossing trouble to the apemen of Nippon." From Iwo Jima, Artie Arriaga bragged of the "Jap souvenirs" he collected, including a canteen and field manuals, "but best of all a belt of a thousand stitches, that the Japs use before committing 'Hari Kari,' but we sort of help them in the process."[67] Mexican Americans, like other Americans, readily demonized the Japanese enemy.

Mexican American soldiers from Chicago voiced their US patriotism, albeit laced with a bicultural tinge. When John Flores returned home on furlough, a *Crier* writer asked what he felt upon single-handedly capturing fifteen German soldiers. Flores responded, "It seemed as if I heard our cry, the cry of the Mexican revolutionists, 'Mexico, No Se Raja.'"[68] Many from St. Francis carried a card (*estampita*) of the Virgin of Guadalupe. The *Crier* declared (in a Spanish-language article) that no better talisman existed for the Mexican soldier than that of the Virgin of Tepeyac. The article included a small image of Guadalupe that some soldier-readers might have cut out and saved for worship.[69]

Meanwhile, their old friends on the Near West Side made the war their own, stamping it with a Mexican and Catholic flavor. The *Crier* published María Serrano's poem, dedicated to her little brother in the service, entitled "Vuelve a nuestra casa" (Return to our home).

¡Nada le intimida
Y con brio avanza!
¿Cómo se ha de temer
Si en sus venas corre
Sangre mexicana?

¡O Virgen Morena
Y gran Generala!
Cuídalos a todos
Los de piel tostada,
Y haz que mi hermanito
Vuelva a nuestra casa.[70]

Nothing intimidates him
And with spirit he advances!
How could he fear
If in his veins runs
Mexican blood?

O Dark Virgin
And powerful General!
Care for all those
With toasted skin,
And insure that my little brother
Returns to our home.

Serrano's wartime appeal to the Virgin of Guadalupe to protect all those of "piel tostada" (browned skin) exhibited a strong sense of Mexican distinctiveness and pride.

The *Crier* habitually highlighted the many ways that local soldiers had profound connections to their Catholic parish. The paper wrote admiringly of the furloughed GIs who attended Mass at St. Francis, stopped by the socials, or dropped in at the rectory. Ramon Barba, after tours of duty in North Africa and India, received a week's furlough. During his short Chicago stay, "his friends and family were honored to have him serve the 4 a.m. New Year's Mass at St. Francis." His brother Vincent Barba served in the air force. While overseas on a squadron detail, Barba boasted, "I had the plane named after the parish team 'The Wildcat.'"[71]

Twice weekly the church sponsored Holy Hours, when parents and friends dedicated special prayers for their loved ones overseas. St. Francis held special novenas to the Virgin of Guadalupe for the soldiers' protection. More often, however, the church sponsored novenas to the Immaculate Heart of Mary, "praying for peace and the safe return of our boys in the service of our country." During the novenas many mothers brought framed photos to the altar dedicated to the Immaculate Heart of Mary at the front of the sanctuary; in doing so, they "placed their sons under the protecting mantle of the Mother of God." Dozens of photos, small and large, crowded the lace-covered altar. By 1945 the parish had erected a more permanent and orderly devotional site: a wood and plastic plaque stood ten feet high and six feet wide, again at the Immaculate Heart of Mary altar. This Honor Roll bore the names of 258 soldiers in February 1945. Three flags topped the plaque: the American, Mexican, and papal.[72]

That spring the *Crier*'s office filled with sadness, hope, and drama. In early April the staff learned that Charles Galvan had been wounded again in Luzón—his brothers Jesse and Armando played key roles for the paper. Their mother, Carolina, cook at the rectory, sponsored a Holy Hour for Carlos in April and again in May. Then on April 12 news of President Roosevelt's death stunned the young writers and editors, who asked each other, "Is it true?" In Chicago, State Street stores shuttered and Catholic schools closed on the day of Roosevelt's funeral. The *Chicago Tribune* ran a headline, "Army Believes Nazi Collapse Is Few Days Off."[73] Soon V-E Day came, but celebration was muted, as so many from St. Francis remained in the Pacific in harm's way.

Just weeks after President Roosevelt's funeral the Treasury Department unrolled its Seventh War Loan bond campaign. Posters emblazoned with the stirring image of the Iwo Jima flag-raising urged support for the war and proclaimed, "Now—All Together." The painted image drew heavily from the iconic photo, which appeared in papers nationwide on February 25. Joe Rosenthal's photo "spoke of group effort, the common man. . . . The very facelessness of the heroes sanctified a common cause. . . . [T]hey were just American boys, and they made war on behalf of all Americans." The official posters went up in movie theaters, banks, and factories and at train stations. Every time *Crier* staffers boarded a bus or trolley that May, they saw the striking campaign placards: again with the flag-raising, but also with a monumental number seven.[74]

The bond campaign's national tour of the Iwo Jima heroes filled the news. On May 19 the tour drew one hundred thousand people to State Street. The next day a patriotic crowd filled Soldier Field, just a mile east of St. Francis, to witness the heroes reenact the flag-raising upon a replica of Mount Suribachi.[75] In May the *Crier* included a small version of the iconic Rosenthal photo with labels of the supposed flag-raisers, including John Bradley, Rene Gagnon, and Ira Hayes. The paper asked readers, "Are you helping them by buying war bonds?"

Inspired by the ever-present bond campaign, the *Crier* created its own take on the Mighty Seven. For the May 1945 issue, the editors selected seven individuals with connections to St. Francis and inserted their photos into a large number seven nearly a page tall. Together it formed an eye-catching tribute to the parish's contributions to the war. Some of St. Francis's Mighty Seven remained on the front lines. David Martinez, a St. Francis School graduate, was in the Philippines. Ramón Villadonga, the Argentina-born, Florida-raised nephew of St. Francis parish priest Fr. Joaquín de Prada, CMF, landed with the marines at Iwo Jima. Frank Macías, a local father of two, had sustained head wounds in Germany that February; he was under treatment in a Michigan hospital. Two of this Mighty Seven, Fr. A. Pinto, CMF, and Ramon Barba, seem an odd choice. Barba, a navy coxswain with strong connections to the parish, was stationed in Panama. Father Pinto, previously assistant pastor at St. Francis, currently served in a Claretian mission in Panama. There the two met up and talked about the St. Francis community. Barba wrote to the *Crier* that Father Pinto "goes out into the jungle to try and make Christians out of these savages. They still aren't civilized to this day." Barba attended Mass at the missionary's cathedral. He knew that St. Francis GIs would appreciate this update, since many once served as altar boys with Father Pinto.[76] As the paper's staff fashioned their own, parish-level version of the Mighty Seven, apparently doing battle as a missionary fit with this paean to service and sacrifice.

On May 18, the day before the Seventh War Loan tour hit Chicago, the War Department informed Carolina Galván of her son Charles's death in Luzón. Friends recalled twenty-year-old Charles as "a happy-go-lucky boy" who played with the St. Francis baseball team. This loss cast a heavy shadow over the paper's staff.[77]

St. Francis's links to the war, military service, and its icons continued in peacetime. In the fall the parish learned that Charles Galvan and Edward "Lalo" Velasquez, both of whom attended St. Francis School, had been awarded the Silver Star. Carolina Galván received her son's military decoration at a public ceremony in the St. Francis School hall, followed by the screening of a Mexican movie. In the heady days following the war's end, the paper dramatically pictured how "Somewhere on Iwo Jima, Pfc. Manuel Valtierra (U.S.M.C.) certainly must feel proud because . . . his son Manuel Abraham, was baptized at St. Francis Church."[78] The *St. Francis Crier* savored every opportunity to mention parish connections to the war's emblematic people and places.

FIGURE 8. US Treasury poster, 1945. Library of Congress, http://www.loc.gov/pictures/item/95501013/.

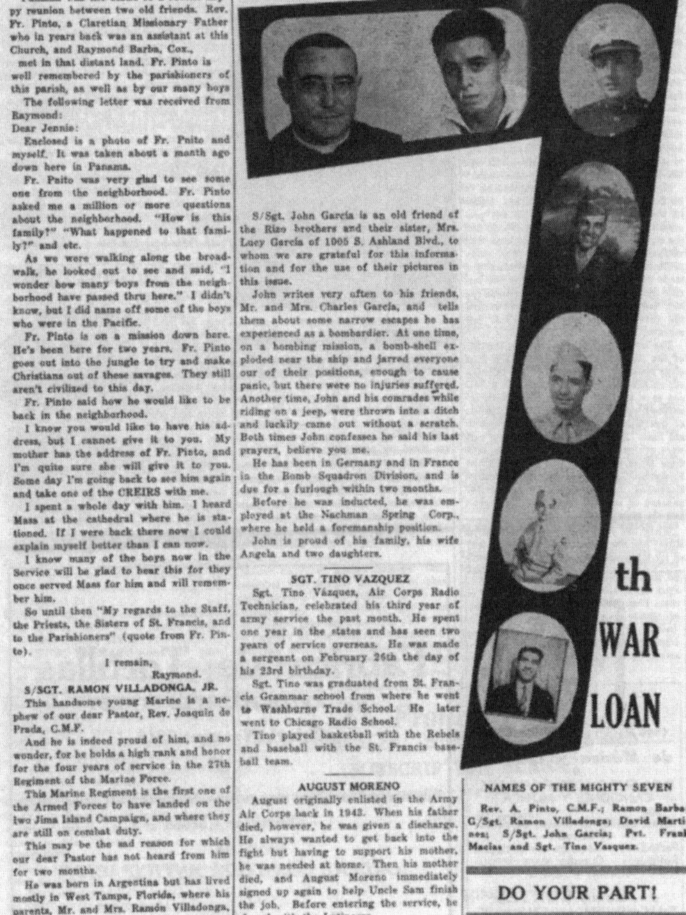

Page 4 ST. FRANCIS CRIER May, 1945

They were glad to meet

Panama was the scene of a recent happy reunion between two old friends. Rev. Fr. Pinto, a Claretian Missionary Father who in years back was an assistant at this Church, and Raymond Barba, Cox., met in that distant land. Fr. Pinto is well remembered by the parishioners of this parish, as well as by our many boys

The following letter was received from Raymond:

Dear Jennie:

Enclosed is a photo of Fr. Pnito and myself. It was taken about a month ago down here in Panama.

Fr. Pnito was very glad to see some one from the neighborhood. Fr. Pinto asked me a million or more questions about the neighborhood. "How is this family?" "What happened to that family?" and etc.

As we were walking along the broadwalk, he looked out to see and said, "I wonder how many boys from the neighborhood have passed thru here." I didn't know, but I did name off some of the boys who were in the Pacific.

Fr. Pinto is on a mission down here. He's been here for two years. Fr. Pinto goes out into the jungle to try and make Christians out of these savages. They still aren't civilized to this day.

Fr. Pinto said how he would like to be back in the neighborhood.

I know you would like to have his address, but I cannot give it to you. My mother has the address of Fr. Pinto, and I'm quite sure she will give it to you. Some day I'm going back to see him again and take one of the CREIRS with me.

I spent a whole day with him. I heard Mass at the cathedral where he is stationed. If I were back there now I could explain myself better than I can now.

I know many of the boys now in the Service will be glad to hear this for they once served Mass for him and will remember him.

So until then "My regards to the Staff, the Priests, the Sisters of St. Francis, and to the Parishioners" (quote from Fr. Pinto).

I remain,
Raymond.

S/SGT. RAMON VILLADONGA, JR.

This handsome young Marine is a nephew of our dear Pastor, Rev. Joaquin de Prada, C.M.F.

And he is indeed proud of him, and no wonder, for he holds a high rank and honor for the four years of service in the 27th Regiment of the Marine Force.

This Marine Regiment is the first one of the Armed Forces to have landed on the Iwo Jima Island Campaign, and where they are still on combat duty.

This may be the sad reason for which our dear Pastor has not heard from him for two months.

He was born in Argentina but has lived mostly in West Tampa, Florida, where his parents, Mr. and Mrs. Ramón Villadonga, Sr., reside at 1506½ N. Albany Avenue.

THE MIGHTY 7th WAR LOAN

S/Sgt. John Garcia is an old friend of the Rizo brothers and their sister, Mrs. Lucy Garcia of 1005 S. Ashland Blvd., to whom we are grateful for this information and for the use of their pictures in this issue.

John writes very often to his friends, Mr. and Mrs. Charles Garcia, and tells them about some narrow escapes he has experienced as a bombardier. At one time, on a bombing mission, a bomb-shell exploded near the ship and jarred everyone our of their positions, enough to cause panic, but there were no injuries suffered. Another time, John and his comrades while riding on a jeep, were thrown into a ditch and luckily came out without a scratch. Both times John confesses he said his last prayers, believe you me.

He has been in Germany and in France in the Bomb Squadron Division, and is due for a furlough within two months.

Before he was inducted, he was employed at the Nachman Spring Corp., where he held a foremanship position.

John is proud of his family, his wife Angela and two daughters.

SGT. TINO VAZQUEZ

Sgt. Tino Vázquez, Air Corps Radio Technician, celebrated his third year of army service the past month. He spent one year in the states and has seen two years of service overseas. He was made a sergeant on February 26th the day of his 23rd birthday.

Sgt. Tino was graduated from St. Francis Grammar school from where he went to Washburne Trade School. He later went to Chicago Radio School.

Tino played basketball with the Rebels and baseball with the St. Francis baseball team.

AUGUST MORENO

August originally enlisted in the Army Air Corps back in 1942. When his father died, however, he was given a discharge. He always wanted to get back into the fight but having to support his mother, he was needed at home. Then his mother died, and August Moreno immediately signed up again to help Uncle Sam finish the job. Before entering the service, he played with the Latineers.

NAMES OF THE MIGHTY SEVEN

Rev. A. Pinto, C.M.F.; Ramon Barba; G/Sgt. Ramon Villadonga; David Martines; S/Sgt. John Garcia; Pvt. Frank Macias and Sgt. Tino Vasquez.

DO YOUR PART!

FIGURE 9. St. Francis's "Mighty Seven," *St. Francis Crier*, May 1945. Courtesy of the Claretian Missionaries Archives USA-Canada.

■ ■ ■

After the war, Mexican Americans continued to anchor their social world around St. Francis. New spaces and activities emerged to engage them and to maintain allegiances to the Mexican parish. But across the 1950s, things gradually shifted in the surrounding neighborhood and challenged the St. Francis community. The Near West Side population reached 19 percent native-born Mexican.[79] Puerto Ricans arrived in the thousands. The African American population rose there and in the city of Chicago. Plans for neighborhood rehabilitation and for land clearance created an air of uncertainty, rising to crisis levels by 1960. In the immediate postwar period, however, St. Francis seemed unstoppable.

One late Sunday afternoon in August 1948, Samuel Cardinal Stritch led a singular procession through the Near West Side. The pageant featured several floats; one depicted the apparition of the Virgin of Guadalupe. The Knights of Columbus marched, as did the parish youth in "all the clubs dressed up with their brand new jackets." With Mexican, American, and papal flags, the procession made its way up Halsted, "north to Taylor Street, west to Blue Island, south to Roosevelt, east to Newberry," before arriving at its destination: the St. Francis CYO gymnasium.[80] This route took St. Francis well beyond its parish complex, where most neighbors were Mexican or parishioners. The procession boldly announced the parish's growth to the larger neighborhood. At the packed, open-air dedication, Cardinal Stritch commended St. Francis parishioners as "grandes y buenos Católicos" of a nation consecrated to the Virgin of Guadalupe. "Vosotros," the cardinal urged, "deberaís dar buen ejemplo, de pueblo Católico para el resto de nosotros en Chicago" (You should offer a good example of the Catholic people for the rest of us in Chicago).[81] The reason for that day's grand procession—the gym's inauguration—seems a mild, almost secular show of Catholic and Mexican American identity. Yet establishing the gym in a brand-new two-story building in the decaying Near West Side signaled St. Francis's certitude in its future, as well as the archdiocese's recognition of the Mexican parish.

The CYO gym (also known as the St. Francis Youth Center) opened up a new space for Mexican American teens and adults.[82] A Hull House–based social worker described St. Francis's CYO in the 1950s as "one of the largest and newest in the city": it boasted "shower facilities, library, a movie room, club rooms, two game rooms, two kitchens, and facilities for other gymnastic activities." The gym held "sports tournaments in which about thirty clubs participated."[83] Established local teams, including the Hidalgos, moved to the gym and began a formal affiliation with St. Francis. Young athletes initiated

FIGURE 10. Dedication of the St. Francis Youth Center, August 1, 1948. Fr. Thomas Matin, CMF, and Cardinal Stritch in the doorway. Courtesy of the Claretian Missionaries Archives USA-Canada.

more sports teams for the parish. The gym offered the chance to enjoy the camaraderie of a volleyball team or to train as a Golden Gloves contender, and it was simply a warm place to play marbles. The gym hosted dances almost every week. Young people crowded the gym to hear live (usually Latin) music and to dance and mingle, despite the basketball court's horrible acoustics. Daughters found that their strict immigrant parents were more likely to let them attend dances at St. Francis than elsewhere.

Until the gym opened, few options existed for young women to involve themselves at St. Francis. Some, including Lupe López, had joined the St. Francis Girls' Club, a sodality in which they attended Mass together once a month and displayed their banner by the front altar. Occasional retreats at the rectory featured spiritual talks by one of the Claretian priests. Members of the St. Francis Girls' Club wore their two-tone, college-style sweaters as they marched in the procession that preceded the gym's inauguration.

This sodality quickly changed its meeting place from the rectory to the gym. Soon after, the girls' sodality transformed itself into an athletic club, the Cobras. At the gym these young Mexican American women learned to play volleyball. Former Cobras members recall how male coaches helped them break down their hesitance on the court to become stronger, more aggressive players. "We were terrible," remembered one player. "We'd see the ball coming between two girls, and we'd look at it." Soon the Cobras took up softball and ventured beyond the Near West Side, representing St. Francis at city parks. The Cobras' founder, Loretta Jaimes—niece of Elidia Barroso (see chapter 1)—gladly retired the more sedate club sweater and proudly put on an attention-getting blue-and-white jacket emblazoned with a cobra.[84]

When the daughters of Mexican immigrants began to organize and play sports, especially in public parks, it spelled a variety of changes. For one, they had gained their parents' approval for greater mobility beyond the accepted spheres of home, school, and church. Lupe (née Parra) Almendarez had an especially protective mother: "I couldn't even have girlfriends, let alone boyfriends. I wasn't allowed to go here and there." Her mother limited her socializing with girlfriends as a teen, fearing that "me esten trayendo mensajes de los muchachos" (they were bringing me boys' messages).[85] Former Cobras coach Aggie Santos observed, "At the time you didn't see very many girls playing sports." When the Cobras' parents left Mexico (or Texas) in the 1910s and 1920s, girls' sports were a rare thing, even in the large cities. Santos had to go to the girls' homes to ask parents' permission to let their daughters go to practice ("they trusted me and let them go"). Then the parents began to go watch their daughters' games. The parents, Santos explains, came "to accept the girls being tomboys for certain things; parents saw the girls having a good time, and there was nothing wrong, girls against girls."[86] For the players, the Cobras provided an acceptable social group in which to play sports that many had enjoyed as girls with their brothers.

The emergence of female teams, all teams in fact, also signified the economic stability and increased leisure time among Mexican Americans in the 1940s. For softball games, the Cobras purchased blue-and-white uniform blouses. The players wore these with jeans and gym shoes, items that, just years before, these Depression-era children might not have owned. (Friends filmed the Cobras at some of their games—with cameras that used color film, no less.) Whereas taking part in the St. Francis Girls' Club as a sodality meant a monthly commitment, with a religious component that took place at the church, being a Cobra meant at least a weekly practice or game for purely social and physical reasons that was often well beyond the shadow of St. Francis's spire.[87]

The emergence of these female teams marked a fairly self-conscious transformation. The *Crier* declared in 1946, "The stay-at-home gal is a creature of the past. The Mexican girl of today is not only an interested spectator at sports meets, but also a participant in athletic activities."[88] This growing female confidence may have manifested itself as the war created fundamental shifts.[89]

For young people, the gym became one of St. Francis's greatest assets and fostered allegiance to the parish and its social world. This space, however, primarily belonged to the Mexican American parishioners. Logistically, newly arriving *mexicanos* and *mexicanas* would have little time for the gym as they looked for work, took night classes, and accustomed themselves to Chicago. If they (and here I specify the men) did dedicate leisure time to sports, they sought out soccer games, a sport gaining popularity in the Mexican provinces at the time.[90] Notably, St. Francis never sponsored a soccer team, favoring instead sports deemed "American," just as the CYO did. In any case, "English, English, English" dominated the locker rooms and the basketball court.[91] Young women who called themselves "Cobras" seemed a strange thing to their peers from Mexico. The gym, as well as the *Crier*, represented an invisible divide that crossed St. Francis in the postwar era: an opaque delineation of activities directed at the growing proportion of Mexican-raised Mexicans versus American-raised Mexicans. Notably, when I spoke with long-time parishioners who arrived in Chicago as adults, they mentioned the gym only if I specifically asked. "The gym," recalled one parishioner from Mexico, "they had it. It was more Mexican American."[92]

Time and again, Mexican American informants insistently told me about the gym: "When the gym opened up, that was a real positive thing for us."[93] Dozens of clubs, teams, and other secular parish activities brought a constant stream of youth to St. Francis. Mexican American girls joined Chicago's first Mexican Girl Scout troop there. Male teens formed an American football team. Others planned (but cancelled) a minstrel show. Dozens eagerly joined a male glee club that performed in white button-downs and black bow-ties, perhaps inspired by the 1944 movie *Going My Way*. These clubs and activities generated a great deal of confidence, cooperation, and experience among the participants.[94]

By the late 1950s, the gym was in decline. The pastor refused to open the youth center to non-Catholics.[95] Some male teenagers retreated to private clubs. The Vikings and the Saints, for example, often gathered at Hull House or at the St. Francis gym. The Near West Side had become a "gang crossroads" as Mexican, Puerto Rican, African American, and Italian groups engaged in more violent confrontations.[96] This turn toward delinquency worried local police, business people, and social workers. In 1958, as part of the Chicago Area Project's (CAP) Hard to Reach Youth Program, Frank Delgado met with the Royal Kings, a group of fifteen-year-old boys whom he termed "good kids" from poor families. Members purchased jackets and sewed on their club emblem. The Royal Kings told Delgado that they broke into parking meters, drank, played dice; possibly they stole cars. The Royal Kings liked to play pool at the St. Francis gym, but Fr. Robert Billet, CMF, told Delgado he was not "too happy about our club coming round." St. Francis Youth Center now required membership (twenty-five cents per week); Hull House was free.[97]

As Mexican-descent people moved to outlying neighborhoods, they returned to St. Francis for Mass and many came back for the dances and athletic activities at the gym. Aggie Santos, for example, occasionally went to St. Francis for liturgical events. But once the gym opened, the twenty-nine-year-old father of two, who lived several miles away, began to coach the Cobras and to shoot hoops there with the Hidalgos. "I was there every day" for years, Santos remembered.[98]

Much of what took place at St. Francis—team sports, putting out a paper, club sweaters, singing in a glee club—would have occurred for European Americans of a certain class at preparatory high schools or college. But even with the GI Bill, few Mexican Americans of that generation would have the experience of attending college. Instead, Mexican Americans created intersecting social networks among themselves that, for most of them, were tied to the Catholic world of the parish.

■ ■ ■

At midcentury, the Near West Side was home to Chicago's largest Mexican-origin population. Still, it never became a majority Mexican neighborhood. Mexicans and Mexican Americans shared blocks with Italians, ever smaller numbers of German Americans and Jewish Americans, and ever growing African American neighbors. The 1940 census and qualitative evidence suggest a significant African American presence in the blocks that surrounded St. Francis. Mexicans and African Americans coexisted on Newberry Avenue, 14th Place, and their environs. By 1950 African Americans made up 40.9 percent of Near West Side residents.[99] But significant interaction between Mexicans and African Americans was limited. A Mexican American housewife commented: "We don't dislike Negroes, but we can't let our children be identified with them. They suffer enough from prejudice."[100] Mexicans aligned themselves with the Catholic world of St. Francis, which was more closely associated with white Chicago. A block in the old neighborhood, as commonly recollected by elderly Mexican Americans, was "mostly Mexicans and Italians. We all grew up like one big family."[101] Young black males, meanwhile, avoided walking on Mexican-dominated Newberry Avenue, where "they would beat you."[102]

The *St. Francis Crier* offered few direct references to Chicago's race relations and how Mexican Americans fit in the city's black/white divide.[103] The paper mentioned popular African American musicians and Frank Sinatra's 1945 push for school integration in Gary, Indiana. But the young staffers wrote nothing about their African American neighbors who lived on the same blocks, frequented the same parks and settlement houses, and attended the same public schools.

Meanwhile, the Sisters of St. Francis, from their convent's perch on Newberry Avenue, mentioned and, further, problematized the neighborhood's African Americans. The sisters found it noteworthy that "negresses" won several prizes in a 1945 parish raffle. Of a spring 1946 parish carnival, the nuns remarked that "the colored flocked and spent much money. . . . [T]he Mexicans feared the negroes, so they stayed home."[104] The sisters offered catechism classes for neighborhood children who attended public school. When "some colored children applied" in September 1952, the sisters faced a dilemma. Following tradition, the sisters barely paused, as these children "had to be referred to St. Joseph's School for colored children, because St. Francis School does not as yet admit colored children."[105] In this case, it seems that the European American nuns acted as gatekeepers in preserving the school as Mexican or white. I have no record of what Mexicans thought of this practice.[106]

Mexican Americans had substantial connections to the European Americans who grew up in the neighborhood and played on the same teams. The St. Francis football team all enjoyed a spaghetti dinner to celebrate the 1944 season's end at the home of an Italian American player. Mexican and Italian youth together watched warily as blacks entered Hull House for a dance in 1943.[107] The *Crier* shared the news when a St. Francis GI ran into a German American boy from the old neighborhood while stationed overseas.[108] St. Francis was a Mexican parish. But above all, it was a parish that served all (white) Catholics in the area. A few German American families remained very involved at St. Francis in the 1940s, including the Reindl family. Everyone walking on Newberry in 1945 admired the three-star flag in the family's window. With his three brothers deployed overseas, young Eddie Reindl took part in everything St. Francis had to offer: he played on its sports teams, oversaw the *Crier*'s distribution for three years, and sang and acted in the parish's musical revues. When the gym opened, he was a regular. The gym's hot showers, he confessed, were a real draw, given that his family only had cold water.[109] The white non-Mexican minority simply formed part of the parish mix. African Americans may have been neighbors, but due to either religious affiliation or race, they stood outside the parish's Mexican and Catholic orbit.[110]

■ ■ ■

St. Francis of Assisi parish entered the postwar era with many institutional strengths. Its varied Claretian staff met the needs of the growing Mexican American and Mexican immigrant populations. The Claretians' European priests generally tended to the adult immigrants. Meanwhile, the American Claretians, with more basic Spanish-language skills, applied themselves to the Mexican American youth, often coaching parish teams. After school and work, children and young adults spent many hours at the gym. The head pastor, Fr. Thomas Matin, CMF, had overseen the gym's erection and steadfastly advocated for immigrants' religious and secular needs. He sought a statue of the Virgin of San Juan de los Lagos and encouraged Dr. Prieto to open his Spanish-speaking practice in the parish. The American Legion Manuel Pérez Post literally arose in the parish complex. Mexican American grass-roots leadership there took on the advocacy of veterans and Mexican Americans and remained tied to St. Francis.[111]

Changes, at first subtle, would challenge the parish's postwar growth and vitality. The Mexican-origin population, so centered on the Near West Side, if never exclusively, fanned out farther. Mexicans mostly moved west into newer and better housing, for example, to Pilsen and Lawndale. The suburbs must have intrigued families with good salaries. Many people from the Near West Side's aging, cold-water flats bought church raffle tickets in 1946 with an eye to the grand prize: a six-room colonial house in suburban Park Ridge. The raffle benefited St. Francis; even parish priests sold tickets. For fifty cents, anyone had a chance to move to Park Ridge, where "the spirit of America, of neighborliness, of mutual interest and generous tolerance . . . makes it a good place to live."[112] Few Mexicans moved to the suburbs in those years, but families did relocate at greater distances from St. Francis. They enrolled their children in the closest parochial school but often returned to St. Francis on Sundays for Mass, for a hot dog on Maxwell Street, and to shop at the *tiendas*.

Tougher immigration enforcement also impacted St. Francis. Federal immigration authorities launched the quasi-military Operation Wetback in the summer of 1954 to apprehend and deport undocumented Mexicans. St. Francis School faced a sharp enrollment drop that September. The sisters explained that the decline partially reflected that "the Immigration Board tightened its laws. This required 'wet backs' to return to Mexico" and thus resulted in the loss of pupils.[113] But enrollment rose significantly over the fall, indicating the ongoing migration from Mexico in the face of immigration policies and the continuing pull of St. Francis. Still, Operation Wetback impacted all Mexican-origin people in Chicago. The media and law enforcement increasingly viewed Mexicans in a negative light, as untrustworthy and prone to breaking laws.[114]

Like parishes elsewhere in the forward-looking Archdiocese of Chicago in the 1950s, St. Francis experienced a certain aggiornamento well before Vatican II. Even the parish school underwent some opening up to the changes in the world. The school began to be involved with the Back of the Yards Neighborhood Council. In 1953 the teaching sisters received a television for their convent. In 1956 the archdiocese asked parents to donate to a fund for WTTW, Chicago's public television channel. In 1958 two lay teachers joined the staff. The sisters faced the challenges of teaching "modern math" and incorporating the Stanford Achievement Tests into their calendar. In 1961 St. Francis pupils took part in the Race to the Moon fund-raiser, complete with space ships on the bulletin board. Change was in the air, and the children looked toward a modern age. At the same time, the first communicants continued the centuries-old tradition of donning the brown scapular and took part in May Crownings of the Virgin Mary. Catholic traditions—Mexican and American—persisted and saturated St. Francis through the early 1960s.

As the Spanish-speaking population, fueled by arrivals from Mexico and Puerto Rico, continued to rise in the 1950s, people packed the pews at St. Francis's weekend Masses.[115] In fact, the only other Catholic churches that offered *misa en español* were also Claretian administered: Our Lady of Guadalupe in South Chicago and Immaculate Heart of Mary in Back of the Yards. With an increasing proportion of Latinos well beyond these enclaves, the Claretians could not provide the kind of local, 24-7 Catholic community that had flourished in earlier decades at St. Francis. By 1960 Latino demographic growth and dispersal had overwhelmed Claretian resources. The Mexican Americans, English-dominant and Chicago-raised like the *St. Francis Crier*'s former staff, joined new parishes as they dispersed across Chicagoland. Meanwhile, recent arrivals from Mexico, Puerto Rico, and Cuba needed parishes that could understand and minister to their needs. The CCSS pushed the archdiocese to encourage more Spanish-speaking priests and to end the Claretians' virtual monopoly of Latino Catholics.

The most effective challenge to the Claretians' dominance and St. Francis's centrifugal status did not originate with the archdiocese. That challenge was land clearance. The process of Mexican dispersal had begun in the 1940s, and it quickened as Near West Side residents heard talk of land clearance for their "blighted" neighborhood. Construction of the Congress Street Expressway (later renamed the Eisenhower) began in 1949 and removed the neighborhood's northern edge.[116] With various urban renewal plans and land clearance projects in the news, uncertainty loomed over the neighborhood in the 1950s. Social scientists cautioned against wholesale removal of blight and instead recommended conservation. The area "enjoys a distinctive wealth in its schools and churches. These institutions took long years to acquire and build. It is very probable that clearance followed by new construction would cause mass relocation, the destruction of a well-integrated neighborhood, and consequently, the breaking up of existing congregations and parishes. Existing institutions may never again be used to the fullest possible extent."[117] This warning proved thoroughly appropriate.

It seemed possible that a new University of Illinois campus would replace the Mexican Americans' neighborhood. As Lilia Fernandez puts it, "The Near West Side was being dismantled bit by bit, disfigured by expressways, abandoned by those who had means, and increasingly relinquished to poor, predominantly African American, public housing residents."[118] While the decision to place the campus on the Near West Side was not finalized until February 1961, anyone seeking new housing in the late 1950s looked elsewhere. With the announcement of their neighborhood as the site for the future campus, young Mexicans protested in torch-lit marches in 1961. Their elders, the newspapers reported, filled St. Francis to pray for their homes.

Amid the bulldozers and tumbling bricks, the Mexican church somehow stood fast. On Sunday, September 17, 1961, when the parish marked Mexican Independence Day, Alfred Cardinal Meyer visited the church and delivered the homily in Spanish. The school installed a new sprinkler system to the tune of $20,000. On December 12 the sky lit up around Halsted and Roosevelt as parishioners set off "brilliant fireworks in Our Lady's colors," announcing that evening's Mass for Nuestra Señora de Guadalupe to the emptying neighborhood.[119] Prayer and protest did not stop the demolition of homes, businesses, and neighborhood institutions, including the predominantly Italian Holy Guardian Angel Church and the Hull House complex. Groundbreaking for the campus's construction took place in October 1963. Streetscapes changed forever: entire residential blocks were erased. Halsted Street, north of St. Francis, lost its *supermercados*, *taquerias*, Italian shops, and Greek diners and gave way to expansive parking lots.

As the city forced remaining families to leave their homes, enrollment plummeted at St. Francis School. In September 1961 303 pupils enrolled, but in 1963 there were just 130 pupils. That year, only five teachers staffed the school. While the Sisters of St. Francis attended archdiocesan meetings on the Second Vatican Council, at the Newberry Avenue convent talk centered more on their school's future. By spring, the archdiocese decided the school would close "on a suspension basis for a period of about four years." Graduation that June was bittersweet; younger children sadly realized they would not have the

FIGURE 11. Land clearance looking southwest from Halsted Street. St. Francis of Assisi rectory, church, school, and convent, 1965. Courtesy of the Claretian Missionaries Archives USA-Canada.

chance to graduate from their school. During a scorching summer several sisters undertook the great task of closing the school, packing up the convent, and securing nearly a century of school records. On an August morning in 1964, Sister Agreda "locked the doors of St. Francis of Assisi convent and school." As she handed the set of keys to the pastor, Fr. Raymond Bianchi, CMF, they both understood that an era had ended. The Sisters of St. Francis not only had administered and taught at the school since 1867 but also had run the choir, played the organ for all the services, trained the servers, and kept up the church.[120] The parish's future was in doubt. Long-time parishioner Rubén Castillo, like many at the time, thought the neighborhood's demise spelled "el fin de San Francisco" (the end of St. Francis).[121]

But a surprising number of people returned each Sunday from faraway neighborhoods and suburbs. Increasingly after that point and through today, St. Francis serves immigrants. New arrivals from Mexico would take over *las guadalupanas*, pushing aside the parish-raised Mexican American mothers. The gym, the parish's great pride in 1947, closed for sports in the 1960s, and the building was converted into a temporary shelter for new arrivals.[122]

St. Francis of Assisi's heyday as a center of Mexican American life was rather short if indelible in thousands of memories. Annually, at a memorial

Mass held in a Catholic school gym marking October 4, the day of St. Francis, and at fund-raising dinners in the southwest suburbs, silver-haired members of the St. Francis Wildcats still reminisce about their childhood parish, Father Pat, and the "old neighborhood." The Cobras, the female volleyball team formed in the late 1940s, gathered for a reunion lunch in 2014. Their founder, Loretta Jaimes, now in her nineties, proudly displays the team's trophies in her living room. A photo hangs nearby: a twenty-something Loretta in an embroidered *blusa mexicana*, smiles alongside the Mexican movie star Pedro Infante and Father Thomas.[123]

With the exception of St. Francis Church and the Youth Center, the Roosevelt Road / Halsted Street environs of today would be unrecognizable to the *St. Francis Crier* staff who spent so much of their formative years there. Now the area is a place of well-kept university athletic fields and residence halls. A dozen historic facades front the businesses that comprise "University Village Maxwell Street," which offers "an eclectic mix of cuisines to please a variety of tastes."[124] While the gym stands, its doors are usually locked. It has not hosted dances or basketball games for many years.[125] For a few decades, however, from the 1930s through the early 1960s, St. Francis—the church, rectory, school, and gym—provided a lively, nurturing home for Mexican American young people. They may have grown up in poverty, but with a parish to call their own, they did not feel marginalized. The Mexican church anchored the community, and its children grew up with a positive grounding in Mexican and US Catholic traditions. This experience would manifest itself as thousands of Mexican-origin people entered new neighborhoods, including Pilsen, in the 1960s. In new parishes dominated by European Americans, many former St. Francis members would assume a vanguard position.

4. Making Parishes Mexican

Pilsen, 1947–1970

[Pilsen] wasn't a ghetto, it was a good neighborhood, nice and strong.
—Grace González

St. Ann's was an old Slavic neighborhood that had become Spanish. . . . Father Wojek, the pastor, could say the service in five languages—Latin, Polish, Ukrainian, English, and Spanish. The altar boys now were Mexican kids, their poor-looking gym shoes sticking out from black cassocks.
—Stuart Dybek, "The Wake"

AFTER WORLD WAR II, St. Pius V Church buzzed with activity each day at the corner of Ashland Avenue and 19th Street in Chicago's Pilsen neighborhood. Over four hundred children attended the parish school. The CYO sponsored sporting activities and dances. The shrine to St. Jude attracted parishioners and outsiders alike. Wives belonged to the Rosary Altar Society, husbands to the Holy Name Society. Each March the once-Irish parish held its St. Patrick's Homecoming Party. In August they hosted an eleven-day carnival that brought in funds from neighborhood fun seekers. Every October this Dominican-run parish sponsored a Rosary Sunday procession in which as many as fifteen thousand faithful paraded their devotion through area streets. Mass was celebrated five times each weekday, with Mass intentions printed in the weekly bulletin. One week in 1947 the Masses were said in the memory of deceased women and men with Slavic surnames such as Nawrocki, Koterba, Mizejewski. This prosaic list embodied the ethnicity and religious devotion of St. Pius parish, but one notice sticks out. The Friday 7:00 a.m. Mass was dedicated to thank "San Juan de los Lagos," the Virgin

Mary from the Mexican city of that name.[1] Apparently, St. Pius had at least one Mexican parishioner in 1947.

At that time, Pilsen encompassed thirteen principally Slavic parishes. By 1970 it would become the city's first majority Mexican neighborhood. This chapter explores Pilsen's transformation through the prism of its many parishes. Mexican entry into local churches was gradual, almost tentative in the 1950s. When the unnamed parishioner at St. Pius declared his or her gratitude to the Virgin of San Juan de los Lagos, that lone act of Mexican devotion marked a first step to making that church home. It surely went unnoticed by the larger, mostly Slavic parish. Yet in the 1960s, as one priest recalls, "it just kind of changed dramatically. That presented a lot of problems obviously, both for the ones coming in and for the ones who were left here."[2] These stories and others from Pilsen illustrate the fraught transition from the parish as European American ethnic enclave to a shared congregation. In time, most churches became de facto national parishes serving the needs of Mexicans and Mexican Americans.[3] Mexicans asserted distinctive devotions and remade parish after parish, with increasing effect throughout Pilsen. The neighborhood became ever more Mexican *and* Catholic in the 1960s.[4]

■ ■ ■

It only takes thirty minutes to walk from one end of Pilsen to another. Stand on some corners, and you can see three or four church spires. Pilsen, also known as the Lower West Side, is a two-mile swath that centers on 18th Street (from the Dan Ryan Expressway to Western Avenue), narrowly framed on the north by the railroad tracks and on the south by 22nd Street (Cermak Road). Within this compact geography, Pilsen became home to thirteen parishes between 1874 and 1915. The territorial parish of St. Pius V was established in 1874. Early parishes included the Poles' St. Adalbert and the Czechs' St. Procopius; parishes dedicated to serving Slovenians, Germans, Slovaks, and Lithuanians followed.[5] Each parish maintained a church, rectory, school, and convent. Some parish complexes occupied an entire city block (St. Pius, St. Adalbert), while others took over existing buildings in a more jumbled way. At Providence of God, for example, the Sisters of St. Casimir's convent was on a different street (although its backyard offered easy access to the school's back door). In addition to regular Mass attendance, each parish had its weekly and annual gatherings. Distinct peer groups met at the Holy Name Society and the Mothers' Club or on bunko nights. The parish as a whole came together for periodic novenas, carnivals, and processions. Designed to shelter and separate ethnic groups, the Pilsen parishes embodied the vital, disciplined, and cohesive world of 1950s Catholic America.[6]

Saturday is the feast of St.Albert the Great, O.P., Doctor of the Church, Patron of our Dominican Province. There will be a Solemn Mass in honor of this great 13th century scholar at 10 A.M..

C.Y.O DANCE!
The C.Y.O. is sponsoring a Sadie Hawkins Dance on next Sunday night beginning at 8:30. At this dance the girls of the parish will have a chance to ask the boys to dance with them instead of following the customary procedure. Eddie Gray and his Orchestra will supply the music.

CHILDREN'S RAFFLE!
Here are the winners of the highly successful raffle held by the school children last week. Mr. Melvin Gordon, 2152 W. 18th Street won the bicycle, Michael Famartino, 3136 W.16th Str. won the Electric Clock and Jay Bauml won the wagon for selling 18 cards.

HIGH MASS INTENTIONS FOR THE WEEK

Monday-----8:00 Honor of Blessed Martin
7:30 Deceased Members of Legion of Mary
7:00 Michalina Rosako,deceased
6:30 Gertrude Schive,deceased
Tuesday----9:00 Andrew J.Cuslak,deceased
8:00 W.C.O.F-Deceased Members-St.Pius Court
7:30 William Nawrocki,deceased
7:00 Gertrude Schive,deceased
6:30 Anton Koterba,deceased
Wednesday--9:00 Sarah Stephan,deceased
8:00 William Nawrocki,deceased
7:30 Annie Gilfillan,deceased
7:00 Jimmie Espitto
6:30 Mr.& Mrs. Jos. Placzek,deceased
Thursday---9:00 Sarah Stephen,deceased
8:00 Mary Kupferschmidt,deceased
7:30 Sixta Marron,deceased
7:00 William Nawrocki,deceased
6:30 Gertrude Schive,deceased
Friday-----8:00 Joseph P. Geary,deceased
7:30 Thanks- St.Jude
7:00 Thanks-San Juan delos Lagos
6:30 Mrs.Catherine Mizejewski,deceased
Saturday--10:00 Peter Gardan,deceased
9:00 Teresa Cousins,deceased
8:00 Morrison & Nicolls Families,deceased
7:30 Thanks-St.Jude
7:00 Mr. Albert J. Gruenke
6:30 Mrs. Bertha E.Gruenke

FIGURE 12. Mass schedule, St. Pius V Church, *Chicago Dominican*, November 9, 1947. Dominican Provincial Archives, Province of St. Albert the Great.

Despite the parishes' physical proximity to one another, postwar Pilsen well exemplifies John McGreevy's observation that "each parish was a small planet whirling through its orbit, oblivious to the rest of the ecclesiastical solar system."[7] Priests, concerned solely with their own flock, seldom cooperated with the parish standing just two blocks away. Parishioners likewise demonstrated strong devotional and social allegiances only to their particular parish. Even in the 1950s the national parishes embodied qualities of the "immigrant church" from decades past.[8] Unless a person was Polish or Lithuanian or Czech, these were not easy churches to enter.

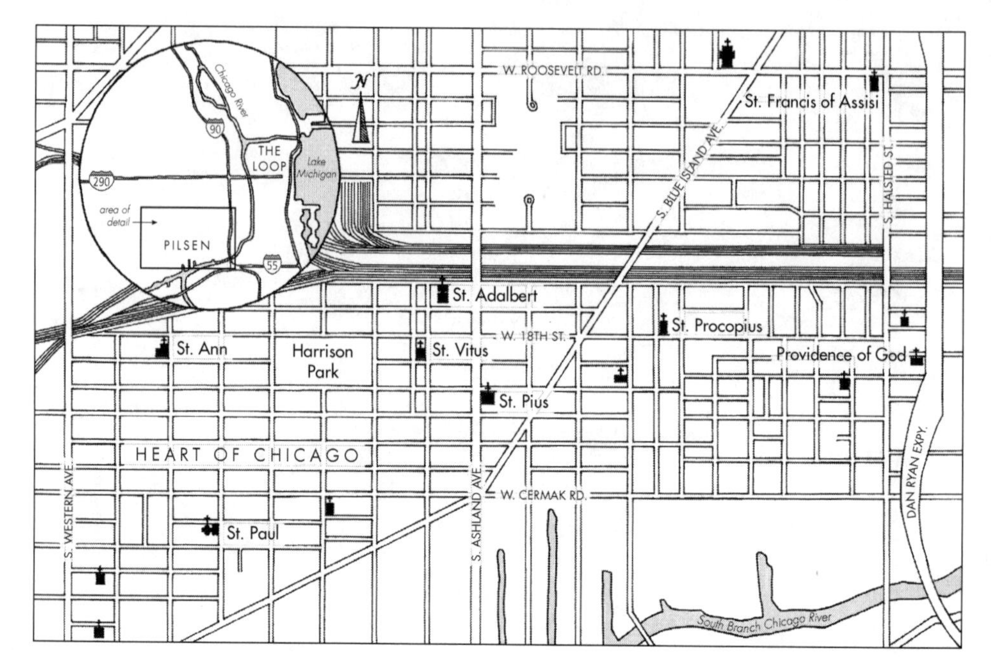

MAP 3. The Pilsen neighborhood and its Catholic churches, 1950s. Map by Molly O'Halloran.

A lively working-class neighborhood surrounded the many Catholic churches in the mid-twentieth century. Meat markets, bakeries, banks, bowling alleys, candy shops, newsstands, and hardware stores lined Pilsen's commercial streets. "In the little independent groceries the grocer knew most of his customers and he often carried on an animated discussion with them, inquiring about their families." Families could pick out something new at the Sadowski Furniture House or find sheet music and records at the Balkan Music Company, both on 18th Street. Bohemian women brought their treasured *perinas* (down comforters) to be re-covered at the Jewish Bohemian–owned Leader Store. Polish American girls shopped at the local cut-rate department store, the Lion Store, while dreaming of better things from Marshall Field's in the Loop. Their brothers, St. Adalbert boys, formed the Ashland Cardinals and played football at nearby Harrison Park. Workingmen could stop by the Polish-owned chili parlor on 18th Street or the dozens of corner taverns advertising "ZIMNE PIWO" (cold beer). The neighborhood had a dozen billiards halls and over three hundred liquor establishments.[9] In mid-twentieth-century Pilsen, few mothers worked outside the home. Instead, the Lithuanian and Polish housewives scrubbed their steps and stoops, regularly

TABLE 2. Establishment of Pilsen parishes and ethnic affiliation

1874	St. Pius V	"territorial"
	Sacred Heart	"territorial"
	St. Adalbert	Polish
1875	St. Procopius	Bohemian
1876	St. Paul	German
1888	St. Vitus	Bohemian
1898	St. Stephen	Slovenian
1903	St. Michael	Italian
1904	Providence of God	Lithuanian
1906	Our Lady of Vilna	Lithuanian
	St. Joseph	Slovak
	St. Ann	Polish
1915	Holy Trinity	Croatian

took part in their parish and PTA, and added to the prevalent sense of safety and familiarity for everyone in the neighborhood.[10]

The placement of the national parishes shaped residential choices. Most Czechs lived near St. Procopius or the smaller mission at St. Vitus. Of all the Slavic groups in Pilsen, the Czechs included many "freethinkers," who organized themselves beyond the Catholic church. Their *sokols* (athletic and social clubs), theaters, and music academies dotted nearby streets. The neighborhood park, long a recreational center for area Czechs, was officially named for the composer Antonín Dvořák in 1913.[11] Two blocks from St. Procopius, Presbyterians ran Howell Neighborhood House, a settlement house established in 1905 to serve the impoverished Czech immigrants with Americanization classes, clubs, and safe play areas. Francis Nemecek opened his photo studio in 1903; in the early 1950s this Czech studio competed with Steven Garwacki's and John Gora's studios just a short walk away.[12] While Chicago Czechs had long proved great organizers and patriots, the establishment of an independent Czechoslovakia in 1918 fueled yet greater nationalist expression. Pride in Czech origins received citywide approval with Anton Cermak's election as mayor of Chicago in 1931. In 1945 Howell House director Gertrude Ray would fondly reminisce that "to stand on the corner of Blue Island and 18th Street thirty-five years ago was to stand in the heart of a Czech city with a population second only to Prague. The signs on the windows, the language of the streets, proclaimed this to be a city of Czechs."[13] At midcentury the Czech influence in the neighborhood remained palpable, despite the drop in immigration coupled with an outmigration to the Lawndale neighborhood and suburban Berwyn and Cicero.[14]

Pilsen-raised poet Philip Kolin conjures deep Czech Catholic traditions in "The Pilsen Saints."

> Their saints sailed with them—
> Ludmila, Procopius, Vitus—
> to be enshrined in copper tower churches
> confirming that God was born in Bohemia.
> They witnessed every sacrament,
> signed and sealed in a Czech tongue,
> from baptizing a steam of *Vaclavs* and *Jiris*
> to marrying stocky brides with white aprons
> and braided veils to sending souls off
> to eternity via St. Adalbert Cemetery.[15]

Here, as in other poems, Kolin underlines the connections between Czech ethnicity and Catholicism during his childhood and prior generations of immigrants.[16]

St. Procopius, the Czech parish founded in 1875, still nurtured a strong ethnic identity in the 1950s. Czech-speaking Benedictine priests and brothers (from St. Procopius Abbey in Lisle, Illinois) staffed the parish, which also housed the Bohemian Benedictine Press, publisher of Czech Catholic magazines and *Národ*, a daily paper for the Chicago area. The laity remained almost exclusively Czech in 1950. Many sodalities and benevolent societies bore Czech names, including Marianska Druzina (Sodality of Our Lady) and the Zdruzeni Jednot (Consumers' Cooperative).[17] Parishioners showed special devotion to the Holy Infant of Prague, the sanctuary's most venerated image along with Our Lady of Fatima.[18]

In 1953 the parish gathered to celebrate the rededication of St. Procopius School with a Sunday afternoon reception and dinner. Many arrived on foot, walking from the modest two-flats with clean-swept stoops.[19] Others drove in from the suburbs back to the old neighborhood to spend the afternoon at their home parish, where they had been baptized and married. The reception formally commenced as aged immigrants, joined by their Czech American children and grandchildren, sang "The Star-Spangled Banner" and "Kde Domov Můj," the Czech anthem. Parishioners dined on turkey or roast pork, accompanied by dumplings, sauerkraut, and rye bread, and enjoyed a flaky kolachky with their coffee. Musical entertainment featured a Dvořák piece. After the meal, families toured the new school facilities.[20] Although the school had begun to enroll some of the first Mexican children in the neighborhood, their families had no recorded presence that day. The

MARIÁNSKÁ DRUŽINA
(Od leva) Josefa Domovich; Bessie Hodouš; dp. Augustin Studený, O.S.B.; Rosalie Hucek

IMMACULATE CONCEPTION SODALITY
Left to right: Helen Struhart, Josephine Blazic, Violet Hornik, Mildred Juric, Rev. Augustine Studeny, O.S.B., Rosemary Kopp

FIGURE 13. Lay sodalities, St. Procopius Church, 1950. From the souvenir book *Diamond Jubilee of St. Procopius Parish, Chicago, Ill. Diamantové Jubileum Osady Sv. Prokopa*. Archdiocese of Chicago's Joseph Cardinal Bernardin Archives & Records Center.

rededication program was an overtly Czech afternoon, as befit the seventy-eight-year-old Czech parish.

The resolutely Czech American banquet masked St. Procopius's questionable future as many members left the neighborhood. By the 1950s younger families had departed cramped two-flats and three-flats, among the city's oldest housing. As Kolin writes of the time, "We endured life in Chicago's Pilsen in a $53 month flat across from a tavern with no windows on a side street."[21] Czechs moved to newer neighborhoods and single-family homes in the suburbs. Overall, the neighborhood population declined, and it grew older. At St. Procopius, weddings and baptisms had been declining since the 1920s and bottomed out in the Depression years.[22] Plummeting membership concerned the priest, Fr. Peter Mizera, OSB, who realized that the parish, once home to 3,000 families, could claim only 350 families in 1952. With a new school to pay for, the departure of young families especially concerned the priest. He mused that "as long as the Czechs have children of school age, they generally remain in that place where their children begin going to school. The physically improved school building and the parish playgrounds will be further inducements for our parishioners to remain here." By 1956 Father Mizera bemoaned the difficulties of enrolling a kindergarten class; few of the children whom he had baptized in 1951 remained to register at St. Procopius School.[23] Priests across Pilsen (and many ethnic parishes in Chicago) experienced the same worries as parish membership declined.

Half a mile west, St. Adalbert Church had massive membership, which spoke to the Catholic Church's centrality for the majority of US Poles. In 1941 St. Adalbert counted 1,973 families, or some 9,000 souls, as members. Close residence to the Polish church was essential in order to send children to the parochial school. In Chicago, 70 percent of Polish children attended parochial schools.[24] St. Adalbert School enrolled 1,828 children in 1931 but only 614 children in 1941.[25] The decline reflected the impact of immigration restrictions, the Depression, and the aging of the parish. When St. Adalbert's Polish American men returned from the service, many looked at their childhood neighborhood with new lenses. They had grown up in a constricted working-class neighborhood, often in housing from the 1870s and 1880s. Any personal dreams of education or mobility were largely deferred during the 1930s.

Wartime and after, with its higher wages and the GI Bill, offered a way out. For women and men in Pilsen and throughout (white) urban America, the private home became an attainable cornerstone of American prosperity. As the children of Polonia married and started families, they too were intrigued by the much-touted promise of brand new housing. Newspaper ads led to weekend drives beyond the city to "see what the fuss was about." They stepped "into houses so new that the contractors hadn't bothered to sand the floors yet."[26] The GI Bill or maybe a job in a new suburban factory enabled younger Polish Americans and other European Americans to leave Pilsen. Cardinal Stritch saw this as a citywide concern. In 1952 he warned, "Chicago is emptying out into its suburbs. Thousands and thousands are going out into little homes in the suburban areas."[27] St. Adalbert's had 1,862 families on its parish rolls in 1945; within a decade that dropped to just 1,000 registered families.[28] Pilsen epitomized the postwar shift that Dominic Pacyga describes: "a place of ethnic stores and churches and old industries that might fondly be remembered as the place 'we grew up' but not as a place to raise the postwar generation."[29]

But not everyone left. In Pilsen's Polish-dominated sections, older parents and grandparents remained in their flats, walking to St. Adalbert for bunko and sodality meetings. The old-timers, standing in line at the bakery or coming to Mass, found new arrivals from the "old country." Cold War refugees gave the parish a new infusion of Polish language, culture, and nationalism in the late 1940s and the 1950s. St. Adalbert School enrolled Polish refugee children, whose scrubbed white faces blended in with those of their Chicago-born classmates.[30] At the same time, a few darker-complexioned kids with Spanish surnames also took seats in many classrooms. The new Europeans also arrived at Providence of God parish. In the 1950s many Lithuanian refugees made the Pilsen church their spiritual home in Chicago. At the same time that the Czech membership at St. Procopius had shrunk to a minority in the quickly Hispanicized church, Fr. Adalbert Vit arrived from Czechoslovakia. He revived Czech Masses, which drew in old-time parishioners along with recently arrived refugees (or displaced persons, commonly called DPs).[31]

In the immediate postwar era, younger members of Pilsen's ethnic parishes were generally Chicagoans, with no personal connections to the old country. But each church's celebration of ethnic distinctiveness persisted long after entries at Ellis Island had reduced to a trickle. Kolachky and sauerkraut had graced banquet tables at St. Procopius for as long as anyone could remember, and parishioners found no reason to change things. The Irish likewise had exited Pilsen even earlier, but St. Pius Church continued to anchor its social and fund-raising world on the annual St. Patrick's Homecoming Party.[32] Many historians underline the emergence of a panethnic (and white) Catholic culture in the postwar United States, noting the ascendance of "postethnic devotions" such as Our Lady of Lourdes and St. Jude.[33] In postwar Pilsen ethnic lines remained sharply etched. The arrival of Cold War refugees led to an unexpected reinvigoration of Old World customs and language.[34] The

FIGURE 14. Class photo, St. Adalbert School, 1960. Archdiocese of Chicago's Joseph Cardinal Bernardin Archives & Records Center.

many national parishes still emphasized what separated them. In sum, ethnic succession in Pilsen had complicated threads. Demographic change here was certainly not "white flight," a simple race-based reaction to the arrival of Mexican newcomers in the 1950s and 1960s. Lilia Fernandez similarly finds that "whites did not abruptly abandon Pilsen en masse."[35] She conjectures that European Americans saw Mexicans as less racially different than African Americans.

I argue further that Catholicism offered common ground. Ultimately, as this chapter shows, the desire to maintain parish structures explains European Americans' willingness to live with Mexican newcomers. In many ways, the outward flow of Lithuanians and Poles had little to do with race. Rather, Pilsen's transformation began as the younger people left for newer homes and parishes. The process was prolonged due to the new arrivals from Europe.

Parish priests warily watched the neighborhood's slow but sure ethnic diversification. Father Mizera complained to the Chancery in 1953 about St. Procopius's dwindling membership, adding that "the recent infiltration of the Mexicans and of Negroes makes things worse."[36] As he tried to make sense of the parish's rapid decline, the priest initially saw the two non-Czech groups similarly, but he treated each differently. When African American parents tried to enroll their children at St. Procopius School, Father Mizera sent them to St. Pius, Pilsen's territorial parish.[37] Yet he did allow Mexicans to enroll their children in the early 1950s, albeit grudgingly, thus beginning the ethnic integration of the heretofore solidly Czech parish.

The pressing issue for many white Chicagoans and Catholic parishes in the mid-twentieth century was the growing African American population, not the Mexican influx.[38] Sections of Pilsen, especially to the eastern and more decayed edge, did see the entry of some African American residents. Given the overall pattern of black movement into other white neighborhoods and white reactions, old-time Pilsen residents with apartments to rent and buildings to sell simply found Mexicans less objectionable. In 1955 Catholic Charities reported on the recent "immigration of Mexicans" into Pilsen. "Mexicans are still viewed as 'invaders' by the older residents [many] of whom still retain their own ethnic outlook and language. However, the Mexican is considered a much lesser evil than the surrounding Negroes."[39] Pilsen priests apparently viewed Mexicans, who were mostly Catholic, in the same way. In the end, black penetration of the neighborhood would be limited.[40] None of the Mexican individuals interviewed for this study recalled any trouble renting or buying in Pilsen in the 1950s.

■ ■ ■

Many of Pilsen's first Mexican-descent residents came from the adjoining Near West Side, where St. Francis of Assisi was their parish. By the late 1940s Mexican Catholics had overwhelmed resources at the city's extant Mexican parishes. Recognizing this growth, in 1947 the archdiocese approved a "mission" church—not a parish—for Mexicans: Immaculate Heart of Mary in Back of the Yards (also under Claretian administration). No parishes were designated to serve the thousands of Puerto Ricans who arrived in the 1950s.[41] By 1950 nearly 40 percent of the city's Mexican residents lived beyond the neighborhoods that housed the three Claretian churches.[42]

By the 1950s the new and old components of the Mexican population had essentially spilled out of the Near West Side. With good postwar paychecks coming in, who wanted to keep their family in the "ghetto" cold-water flats around Hull House? Mexicans and Mexican Americans sought housing throughout the city. The process of dispersal quickened as Near West Side residents exchanged news of land clearance plans and a new University of Illinois campus slated to tear down their supposedly blighted neighborhood. People who sought new housing in the late 1950s looked beyond the Near West Side.[43]

Loretta (née Cabrera) Jaimes, Elidia Barroso's niece, grew up on the Near West Side and had strong ties to St. Francis parish. A newlywed, she went apartment hunting in the mid-1950s: "Although we looked in Bridgeport, it was obvious they didn't exactly go for Mexican people." The Jaimes family had better luck in Pilsen. They signed a lease just blocks from St. Pius.[44]

Despite the Near West Side's proximity, Pilsen was terra incognita. Consider the trickle of Mexican American students who enrolled at St. Procopius High School. In 1947 Blaze Pérez wondered at the contrast between the Near West Side, her home neighborhood, and Pilsen. "It was Polish, and it had so many nice stores. Cookies, ice cream on the corner of Blue Island. The couple times I walked from St. Procopius down to Blue Island & 18th, it was so nice . . . a different world." Even her classmates seemed different. As Pérez remembered, "We had a lot of girls that were Polish and Bohemian. And they were tall and big. They were very fast-talking girls. I always looked at them. They didn't pay attention to me." Grace González, who graduated third in her class in 1950, similarly described her St. Procopius classmates: "Bohemian, Czech, Lithuanian. They dressed nice. They had nice clothes, nice shape." The Mexican girls from the Near West Side: "We were plain Janes." As Catholics, the Mexican Americans could enroll at the high school, but they never really fit in; small class differences bloomed into social slights at sock hops and proms.[45]

By 1955 Grace González and Blaze Pérez, now married and starting families, had joined a growing stream of people from the Near West Side who pioneered the Mexican entry into Pilsen. They found Pilsen a step up. Grace González's mother purchased a building. At that time, González observed, "everything was clean, there were flowers in the park, everything was clean. 18th Street was clean. People used to be very clean. The little old ladies would come out and scrub their stairs. They were super clean." Looking back, González considered: "People used to say to me it was a ghetto. I said, a ghetto? Those houses were made out of stone, and we had a bathroom. We used to have to share a bathroom [on the Near West Side], and it was down the hall. Or downstairs." Pilsen, compared to the Near West Side, was a good neighborhood.[46] The Mexican newcomers describe the neighborhood as safe in the mid-1950s. Families walked home from the local movie theater at midnight without worry.[47] My informants have positive memories of Pilsen's physical spaces, if marred by the scant number of *tiendas* in the majority Slavic neighborhood. Soon enough, Supermercado María Cardenas, Tortillería El Pescador, and El Nopal Bakery would open their doors.

Pilsen had no "deadlines" for Mexicans; redlining and restrictive covenants did not impact them. Mexican-descent people who moved to Pilsen in the 1950s easily bought property or rented an apartment. Yet many faced uneasy encounters on the streets and in the pews. Mexicans did not meet straightforward ethnic hostility in Pilsen, at least not the overt reaction and violence that unfolded in multiple neighborhoods as African Americans arrived.[48] But slights occurred on a new block and at a new parish. Only slowly did Mexicans make Pilsen and its parishes their own.

The individuals I interviewed have mixed memories of initial personal interactions in Pilsen. Each remembered being among the first Mexican residents on their predominantly white street. Landlords and close neighbors often acted kindly as neighborly relations formed. Grace González characterized her new street as "white, prejudiced," but regarding her neighbors, "some of them were nice, others were not." Stuck in González's mind was an incident that involved her brother Peter when he was in his twenties. He went "out for a walk, on 18th Street, just to explore. There were some children playing on the next block, and one of them said, 'Look at that dirty Mexican.' So that's the type of stuff we came into."[49] By contrast, Loretta Jaimes, who moved near St. Pius, reflected that "there weren't many prejudiced people around here." She readily mixed with (mostly Polish) housewives at the local settlement house, Gads Hill, or at the Mothers' Club at St. Adalbert School, where she enrolled her children. Nevertheless, she overheard complaints about other Mexican newcomers. As she told it, the Polish women took issue with Mexican housekeeping, especially windows. The old-timers would gripe, "Look at the way they got their shades." Jaimes explained that the Polish women "didn't like the idea of their curtains flying out the windows. . . . They didn't like the idea of the way they [Mexicans] used to have their windows open in the summer, with the curtains flying out the windows. It just didn't look right."[50]

Certainly, Mexicans and Mexican Americans faced some prejudice from the existing community, if little outright hostility. Mexican American and European American young people played sports together at Pilsen community centers, and friendships formed.[51] Tensions were mild compared to the often violent responses when African Americans moved into other white Chicago neighborhoods.

A marked generational difference distinguished Pilsen's long-time residents from the much younger Mexican families. While Spanish speakers comprised only one-quarter of area residents in 1960, three-quarters of Pilsen's children were Latino.[52] When Julia Rodríguez moved to Chicago in 1955 she missed the close-knit world she had left behind in Pharr, Texas (but not the migrant life of *la pizca*, or the cotton harvests, living in shacks as far away as Mississippi). "But with time," Rodríguez recalled, "we began to like being here. Getting to know more people and such." As for her white neighbors, "In fact, we got along well with them. Next door lived an older couple; were they Bohemian or Polish? The lady couldn't walk very well, and I used to go to the store for her. Or my oldest daughter would bring her things. We got along well with them and with those across the street. There weren't many of them [old-timers] left, because they had started to move out. And the Mexicans were coming in."[53] Her daughter mused that Bohemian neighbors had a good rapport with her mother, whom they often called Julie.[54] The generational differences often created an agreeable balance, with younger arrivals helping out older neighbors in need. Even so, some parents feared upsetting the older Polish and American residents on the block and warned their children to "stay on our side."[55]

Some of these children attended parochial schools and pioneered Mexican entry into the parishes. Father Mizera worried about the loss of Czech American children at St. Procopius School and the school's viability; at the same time, he bemoaned the increasing Mexican enrollment. In 1956 the priest feared that the kindergarten would be "stuffed with Mexicans who generally neglect to pay their bills." Father Mizera sounded an alarmist note as he sought the teaching sisters' support in pressuring Mexican parents to pay their tuition: "What do we do? Refuse to admit their children to our school?"[56] Mexican parents' relative poverty certainly challenged school budgets. Nevertheless, by 1960 Mexican American children had become the majority at St. Procopius Grade School.

Evangelina (née Campos) Skowronski attended St. Procopius School in the 1950s. Decades later she still vividly remembers the small ways that the nuns privileged European American pupils. If the teacher needed a child to take a note to the office or to take part in a May Crowning, "You knew you would never get picked. You would all be raising your hand, hoping, but you knew you would never get picked."[57] School could challenge the piety that many children learned at home.[58] Certainly, the religious orders that taught Chicago's Mexican children had little knowledge about or apparent interest in the newcomers' culture. In some instances, Mexican schoolchildren were forced to learn in an absurd manner. Some Mexican Americans at parochial school reported learning the catechism in Lithuanian: "Can you beat that? All these little Mexican kids reciting the catechism in Lithuanian."[59] Slights and awkward moments notwithstanding, by 1955 six parochial schools in Pilsen had enrolled Mexican children.[60] The children formed the vanguard of ethnic succession in the parishes. In addition to school days with the sisters and priests, parochial students had to attend Sunday Mass with their classmates.

Mexican parents, for their part, often chose not to attend Mass locally. Priests throughout Chicago alleged that Mexican parents failed to involve themselves in their local parish. Some schools enrolled dozens of Mexican American children; however, "none of the Mexican-Americans living in these parishes are in their church societies or attend Mass there."[61] Some priests at first attributed this odd pattern to Mexican indolence or impiety. In time, they recognized the persistent draw of the "Mexican cathedral," St. Francis back in the old neighborhood.

Consider the story of Julia Rodríguez, a newly arrived *tejana* in Chicago in the 1950s. Once settled in Pilsen and then a new mother, she started attending Mass at nearby St. Procopius. Her initial experience was uncomfortable: "¡Los polacos como que no!" (With the Poles, no way!).[62] While Rodríguez could not pinpoint an inhospitable act at her new parish, she did not feel welcome. She supposed that the older European American parishioners did not like the noise her baby made. Although Julia and her growing family did attend St. Procopius, more often they went to Sunday Mass at St. Francis. She did not know many people there, but she felt more comfortable because the priests and parishioners spoke Spanish. Sundays at St. Francis brought other advantages, most notably, Maxwell Street, the city's famous street market. Rodríguez lit up recalling Sunday Mass, followed by shopping at *la pulga*, and then a Mexican movie, all with her kids in tow. The Campos family, also parishioners at St. Procopius, went to St. Francis monthly, where the Mass was "more special" for the immigrant parents.[63] The Pilsen parishes did not mistreat these families, but St. Francis, not far away, offered a much more welcoming alternative.

St. Francis's power of attraction was undeniable. The faithful arrived from all over the city, enduring multiple bus transfers even on frigid Sundays. In 1960 Masses drew five thousand people to St. Francis each week. For two generations already this church had served as a welcoming oasis for *paisanos* and a home to their Mexican American children. Spanish-speaking priests and rectory staff helped people with job and housing leads. The sanctuary dedicated a large altarpiece to Our Lady of Guadalupe, who was properly venerated with a novena and a dawn Mass in December. Here the Latin American Catholic was a fit. An immigrant who arrived from Jalisco in the 1960s recollected feeling at St. Francis "como si estaba yo en mi pueblo" (as if I was in my village).[64] Only St. Francis celebrated a memorial Mass in 1966 for Pedro Infante, Mexican singer and movie idol, on the ninth anniversary

TABLE 3. Estimated Mass attendance by Spanish-speaking people at selected churches, 1960

Claretian-administered parishes	
St. Francis of Assisi	5,000
Our Lady of Guadalupe	2,000
Immaculate Heart of Mary	700
Pilsen parishes	
St. Procopius	700
St. Pius V	400
Providence of God	300

Source: Partial list from Cardinal's Committee on the Spanish Speaking, report for 1961, cited in Kelliher, "Hispanic Catholics," 168.

of his untimely death.[65] At that point, Pilsen parishes simply failed to provide what newcomers needed and wanted.

Mexican Americans and their immigrant neighbors had differing needs and aspirations. English-dominant Mexican Americans were raised in Chicago's parochial and public schools, served in the military, and liked baseball much more than *fútbol*. What did they look for in their new Pilsen parishes? Individuals such as Grace Gonzalez and Loretta Jaimes wanted to be acknowledged as US educated and churched. As English speakers they expected to be included in their new parishes, deserving of respect for their experience and skills honed at high school and at their home parish of St. Francis; in their youth, they had mattered there. The Mexican Americans I spoke with did not yearn for ethnic devotions such as Guadalupe, albeit familiar from St. Francis and from their parents.

The immigrants from Mexico and South Texas had a different set of hopes for their local parish. They wanted and needed priests who spoke Spanish. Ideally, the church would help them feel at ease in Chicago (as was the case at St. Francis and other Claretian parishes). *Mexicanos* responded well to clergy who greeted them warmly and showed some understanding of their plight as people uprooted, facing challenges as the working poor, often as parents of young children. These immigrants desired something akin to the national parishes established across the city half a century earlier. In this unfamiliar, often hostile city, mexicanos longed for a church that would feel like a refuge.

Julia Rodríguez did not like Chicago when she arrived in the 1950s. She yearned for the intimate world of the Rio Grande valley. She missed walking with friends and family from Pharr to nearby San Juan and its sanctuary, dedicated to the Virgin of San Juan, for Mass.[66] A decade would pass before Rodríguez regained a comparable feeling of a faith community in Chicago. Elidia Barroso's generation had experienced the same search in the 1920s. All in all, the Pilsen parishes proved inadequate for the Spanish-speaking laity for too long. These shortcomings explain the perpetual pilgrimage to St. Francis.

The clergy in Pilsen (and everywhere beyond the three Claretian-administered churches) stood challenged linguistically. As the 1960s commenced, despite the obvious ethnic shift, not a single Pilsen rectory included a Spanish-speaking priest. The CCSS noticed the archdiocese's deficiency as it sought to reach out to Chicago's emerging Puerto Rican population. Efforts to develop Spanish-speaking clergy within the diocese were piecemeal and often inadequate.[67] Fr. Alex Kaspar typified the clergy's limitations. Thinking back to his arrival at St. Pius parish in 1961, he stated, "I didn't know a Mexican in the world before I came here" and added, "I didn't know that much about them." His formal Spanish training amounted to a two-week Berlitz course.[68]

At St. Procopius, Father Mizera openly acknowledged the need for Spanish-speaking staff by 1960. He directed his assistant pastor, Fr. Matthew Herda, OSB, to take a ten-week Spanish class at Berlitz and encouraged his work with Mexican parishioners. As Father Mizera saw it, Father Herda was "very sympathetic with the helpless and illiterate Mexicans. He visits their homes. They took an unusual liking to him." Based on this promising start, Mizera sent Herda to Mexico for six months to improve his Spanish and, most importantly, "to learn all he can about their character, their disposition, their likes and dislikes and their attitudes towards religion, marriage, etc."[69] Parishes in Pilsen struggled to develop and maintain an adequate Spanish-speaking pastorate. St. Francis never had this trouble. The Claretians, originally a missionary order from Spain, required Spanish-language training of their US seminarians. At St. Francis, the homily and popular evening novenas were in Spanish. In Pilsen, hymns might be sung in Polish or Lithuanian, novenas held in English. Over at St. Francis, meanwhile, the Spanish-speaking faithful could participate more fully. In this unique atmosphere, a Mexican American daughter recalled, "It felt like they were all singing with their heart."[70]

St. Francis also bested other parishes when it came to meeting immigrants' devotional leanings. The lack of an altar to Our Lady of Guadalupe in Pilsen's sanctuaries may not have bothered Mexican American Catholics, but immigrants noticed the absence.[71] In 1960 not a single Pilsen church had a Guadalupe image. To make good on a *promesa* to Guadalupe required a trip to St. Francis (or distant South Chicago); there one could leave *milagros* or other devotional offerings. The parish store at St. Francis did a brisk business in candles and devotional cards of saints well known in Mexico. Who knows what Mexicans entering St. Adalbert made of Poland's black virgin, Our Lady of Częstochowa? Or the popular St. Jude shrine at St. Pius?[72] The familiar saints at St. Francis felt like home to mexicanos. For generations St. Francis would stand as "el refugio de los mexicanos."[73] Overall, in the 1950s the archdiocese and the Pilsen parishes did not offer viable spiritual homes for the growing multitude of the Mexican faithful. As much as possible, immigrants turned to St. Francis. Had the established Mexican parish not existed, perhaps the process of change in Pilsen would have occurred more quickly than it did.

■ ■ ■

After 1960 ethnic succession quickened in Pilsen. Father Kaspar remembers the striking transformation at St. Pius this way. As a newly ordained priest, he coached sports at the school: "The first year I coached, the spring of 1961, in the eighth grade there might have been perhaps one or two Hispanic kids. The rest were whatever . . . European descent." Within five years that "completely reversed. There might have been two or three that weren't Hispanic. It just kind of changed dramatically." Grace Gonzalez reflected that for Mexican Americans who settled in Pilsen in the mid-1950s, "at first it seemed to be the influx of all these people from the old neighborhood coming into our neighborhood. It was English speaking, an extension of Taylor and Halsted."[74]

Trusted businesses moved from the Near West Side to Pilsen. Francisco and Celia Bonilla operated El Nopal Bakery for six years on the Near West Side. As their Mexican clientele faced dislocation, they closed shop and followed their customers to Pilsen. In 1961 they purchased the Ace Bakery from the Fritz family. At the transfer of ownership, Father Raymond Bianchi, CMF, pastor at St. Francis, blessed the new El Nopal Bakery. Francisco Bonilla proudly carried his baby son, who had been baptized at St. Francis. The Bonillas soon filled the empty shelves with Mexican bread and *pan dulce*, including their heart-shaped *hojarasca*® cookies. No one could miss El Nopal Bakery ("El Pan de Su Hogar"), with its huge prickly pear cactus sign looming over Blue Island Avenue; inside, an image of San Martín Caballero, universal among shopkeepers in Mexico, hung on the wall behind the cash register.[75] The bakery's makeover from the Ace to El Nopal exemplifies the exit of old-time Pilsen residents as the new Mexican neighborhood took form.

In the 1960s most newcomers arrived straight from Mexico. As Loretta Jaimes described, "They were from small towns, from border towns, where people were extra poor." She took on the role of an apologetic Mexican American intermediary, uneasy with her ethnic connection to the Mexican

FIGURE 15. Taking ownership of El Nopal Bakery, Pilsen, 1961. Fr. Raymond Bianchi, CMF (*center*); to his right, new owners Celia and Francisco Bonilla; Bonilla family and friends. Courtesy of Francisco Bonilla, Jr. Used by permission.

newcomers. "I would tell these Polish ladies, 'These people don't have an education. That's why they're doing things that shouldn't be done. That's because they're not educated. They just don't know how to behave.'" The neighborhood's language shifted as well. Jaimes, who was English dominant, noted of the newcomers, "They were speaking in Spanish. Everyone was speaking in Spanish."[76] Suddenly you could purchase Mexican magazines and tamales, have your taxes prepared, and get your washing machine repaired—*en español*. Pilsen, the iconic Mexican barrio known today, began to take shape.[77] Curtains flew out of windows; gangs began to plague the streets and alleys. Settled Mexican American families began to question the advisability of remaining in Pilsen. "These people decided, 'We gotta move on, we gotta better ourselves, we have to move on to a better neighborhood' and started moving out. . . . Just like the whites had started leaving before that."[78] There was change on the streets, on the teams, and the Spanish language was everywhere. By 1962 the neighborhood celebrated Mexican Independence

Day with its own parade. Flag-bearing *charros* led the way down 18th Street, right past St. Procopius and the J. J. Strnad real estate office, advertising "CASAS DE VENTA. ENGANCHE $500" (Homes for sale. Down payment $500).[79] From the corner of Blue Island and 18th Street, Pilsen was hardly "a city of Czechs." The area's quickening transformation finally instigated active responses within the once-reluctant parishes.

At St. Procopius 1960 marked a clear turning point. While Father Mizera continued to lament the parish's evolving membership, he also resolved to adapt for the laity's sake and so opened a door to change. That summer he again reported to his superior that "the good people are all moving out to the suburbs," referring to the Czechs. But he also acknowledged, finally, a dedicated Mexican laity: "The Mexican people are beginning to realize that they have something to bother about. . . . [S]ome 15 good families . . . contribute generously. The moment I notice that they will be interested, I will try and master the Spanish language for their sake." Still, Mizera's familiar complaints continued: "It's nothing but invalid marriages among them [Mexicans] that I have to contend with." The priest worried that he lacked the time to devote to Mexican parishioners. At St. Procopius "it's just like running two parishes simultaneously."[80] He struggled to reconcile the changing nature of his pastorate. Unease certainly lingered between the priest and his new flock. Nevertheless, by the fall Mizera had resolved to "have the Mexicans observe the feast of St. Mary Guadalupe."

This Mass in December 1960 was the first such celebration in Pilsen. While Guadalupan devotion at St. Francis followed the Mexican model (a novena, followed by a dawn Mass on December 12), Mizera made a simpler and less traditional plan for St. Procopius. He scheduled the Mass for noon on December 11, a Sunday. Mizera put his assistant pastor, Matthew Herda, in charge; the sisters would have the Mexican schoolchildren take a note to their parents.[81] Mexican parishioners must have been gratified by the inclusion of their day at the church that they attended, even if it veered from the traditional form. Soon Herda was off to Mexico to improve his Spanish. The following year saw the inauguration of the Mexican Social Club. In 1962 a Mass designated for Spanish speakers became a regular part of St. Procopius's schedule; with hymns and the homily in Spanish, mexicanos could now participate more fully. By 1963 Mizera had proposed adding a second Spanish Mass, noting the popular noon Mass, "during which P. Matthew speaks to them in Spanish."[82] Grudging acceptance of Mexicans turned to open courting of the newcomers, creating changes that characterize the parish today. This first Guadalupe Mass in Pilsen signified the local clergy's increasing spirit of collaboration. Similar initiatives popped up in several parishes in the early 1960s. Efforts to include Spanish-speaking clerical staff became standard in the parishes that survived in subsequent decades.

■ ■ ■

Father Mizera's pastorate reflects how clerical attitudes toward Mexicans could evolve with prolonged interaction. He arrived at St. Procopius in 1950 and, within a year or two, noted the small Mexican presence. For almost a decade he described the new parishioners in mostly negative terms. Mexicans, the priest felt, were indolent and undependable people; their very Catholicism deserved question. He steadily complained that the parents neglected their school tuition bills. Perennial lateness bothered the priest as well. Mizera opined, "Mexicans are unreliable. Their weakness is this—they come at any time—very late in the evening—after 9 p.m. They arrange baptisms at very odd times on Saturday because their godparents are always coming from some distance. After arrangements are made with reluctance, they fail to come. Others come late and . . . into baptisms of others on Sunday."[83] The priest's displeasure may have been plain on these occasions, possibly driving many parents to schedule baptisms at St. Francis.[84] Because he assumed that Mexicans were unreliable, the priest selected European American children to take part in processions. As one St. Procopius School alumna painfully recollected decades later, "For the May Crowning it was always the Polish kids, never—not once ever—the Spanish kids. You knew you would never get picked." But as Czech families grew scarce and the parish's future uncertain, Mizera had little choice but to call upon Mexicans. For a procession to the parish's Lourdes chapel in May 1959, for example, he told the sisters to "get such as can be relied upon even if they are Mexicans. Just girls dressed in white."[85] Schoolchildren noticed how ethnicity played into these selections.

By the late 1950s, Father Mizera had softened his tone somewhat. He argued that Mexicans had a weak religious foundation due to a small number of clergy in Latin America, many of whom "are inferior in training and education." Thus, "people left to themselves in religious matters soon deteriorate into weak sentimentality and dangerous superstitions." He urged the teaching sisters to "do whatever we can for these poor neglected Spanish speaking."[86] Mizera's ensuing adaptation cannot, however, be equated with the more holistic Hispanic inculturation efforts that would emerge eventually.[87] While he came to accept his Mexican parishioners and acknowledged their needs, cultural barriers remained. Nine years into his pastorate, the pastor would muse why Mexican parents did not attend Mass on Christmas Day or bring their children on Easter Sunday. He noted their excuse: "They go to San Francisco [St. Francis of Assisi]."[88]

Mizera was undoubtedly critical, condescending, and driven to stereotype. Bear in mind that he had no contact with Mexicans until he was nearly sixty years old. Yet a sense of priestly duty compelled him not to turn Mexicans away, and gradually he gained some sense of Mexican culture. Even in his darker moments with Mexicans, he accepted them, reminding himself and the sisters that the newcomers' poverty deserved charity. Undoubtedly, Mizera realized the fact that Mexican Catholics (as opposed to most African Americans, as Protestants) could become part of the parish's structure. If they developed loyalties to the fading Czech parish, if they enrolled their children at the school, if they dropped a dollar into the weekly collection, then Mexicans would enable St. Procopius to keep its doors open.

This Chicago parish well exemplifies McGreevy's assertion that European American Catholics in northern cities proved more accepting of Latinos than African Americans.[89] Mexicans' growing importance to the parish is plain in the increasing number of baptisms at St. Procopius around 1960 (returning to pre–World War I levels).[90] But Mizera had a narrow view of change. A Spanish language homily was one thing, but he was reluctant to integrate Mexican devotion in fundamental, ongoing ways. In 1963 Mizera still worried that "it will take a long time for the immigrants to accustom themselves to *our way* of practicing the Catholic religion."[91] While this Czech American priest can be credited with initiating Spanish-language worship at St. Procopius, he did not want to adapt in substantive ways.

▪ ▪ ▪

Spanish Mass had become a regular fixture at St. Procopius, St. Pius, and Providence of God parishes by the mid-1960s. Still, a sense of responsibility to the outgoing ethnic groups lingered. At St. Procopius, clergy maintained ties with the Czechs and Czech Americans who were leaving or had already departed. In addition to the original ethnic mission of the national parish, the parish budget relied heavily on the Czechs' more regular and more substantial envelopes and donations. The older parishioners, more established than their younger Mexican counterparts, simply had the money and desire to support "their parish."[92] Parish efforts to integrate the arriving Mexicans were hampered by the original national group, whose identity was often reinvigorated by Cold War arrivals from Eastern Europe. Nonetheless, a corner had been turned: the future lay with the Mexican majority at the parishes. Priests and sisters grew more familiar with the needs, desires, and distinct devotional styles of the Mexican laity.[93]

A new modus operandi emerged: ethnic coexistence with separate Masses and activities. Mexican groups established themselves, and the old-timers persisted with their own sodalities, albeit with shrinking numbers. The existing groups hardly beckoned the Mexican newcomers. Providence of God, for example, took pride in its six distinct Lithuanian societies. St. Procopius had a number of societies with Czech names and older members. Most parishes had a Holy Name Society for men and an Altar and Rosary Society for women, but the clubbish, exclusive nature of these societies did not call out to Mexicans. The obligations of time and money may have been a barrier to young Mexicans, burdened with young children and lower-paying jobs.[94] Julia Rodríguez knew the Czech members of the Ladies' Social Club, but they did not invite her to join (she reasoned it was "because I had children, who I had to take care of"). In essence, she reflected that in the 1960s, "the Poles, the *güeros*, they had their own sodality. Just middle-class whites."[95] By 1963 the Club Social Mexicano and the *guadalupanas* had established themselves at St. Procopius, and Julia joined both. Her children no longer seemed to be a barrier to participating at the parish.

Rather than join Lithuanian societies, *mexicanas* established their own Sociedad Guadalupana at Providence of God Church in 1961. By 1963 the new group was actively supporting the parish in a variety of ways. They took part in the Forty Hours Devotion ("on the final evening the procession included members of the Guadalupana Society") and served breakfast to the first communicants in the church hall. The women worked with the Lithuanian teaching sisters to have the parochial school children participate in December 12 festivities. The guadalupanas soon had a public presence heading efforts to close a noisy tavern on 18th Street.[96] This Mexican lay society assumed a visible role, often advocating for their children's health and safety in a neighborhood acutely challenged by expressway construction.

New and older parishioners, despite many divisions, began to mix and cooperate on activities such as fund-raisers.[97] Julia Rodríguez remembers her first carnivals at St. Procopius when potato pancakes were a staple. The Czech women held fast to the parish kitchen, only allowing mexicanas to assist "un poquito."[98] Interethnic cooperation remained problematic in the late 1960s. A priest recalls little interaction there and even open hostility from the old-timers: "They used to run the bingo, the Bohemians. I went over there one time to help out." The old-time parishioners warned the priest away, insisting they needed no "help from your Goddamn Mexicans. Get 'em outta here." As Czech parishioners became familiar with their new neighbors, hostilities lessened.[99] In time, tostadas, tacos, and other Mexican snacks dominated the kitchens and the outside booths; eventually, the carnivals assumed the name *kermés* (as church fairs are commonly known in Mexico). That mexicanos so renamed and reshaped existing activities and parish spaces was one thing.

FIGURE 16. *The Mother of the Americas*, by painter Edward O'Brien, 1972. St. Pius V Church. Photo by Cesar Garza.

With greater self-confidence, they would create new spaces that reflected Mexican identity and piety.

The increasingly attuned clergy initiated some new spaces and practices. In the 1950s Our Lady of Fatima had been the focus of Marian devotion at St. Procopius, but about 1962 an image of the Virgin of Guadalupe gained a permanent place inside the sanctuary.[100] At St. Pius, Fr. Bart Joerger, OP, and parishioners conceived of the need for a Guadalupe shrine. The result was an elaborate niche inaugurated in 1972 with a one-of-a-kind mural, *The Mother of the Americas*. On a curved wall, Edward O'Brien painted Guadalupe centering a tableau of Mexican history, from the conquest to the expressways of Chicago. Juan Diego gazes at the Virgin on one side, while the members of a Mexican American family, rosaries in their hands, likewise contemplate her image. Parishioners showed their appreciation with bountiful offerings.[101] Timothy Matovina's research on "Guadalupe and her faithful" in San Antonio helps explain the 1960s shift at key Pilsen parishes: "Recognizing Guadalupe's power among congregants," clergy "tended to engage Guadalupan devotion as a form of Marian piety that fortifies Catholic allegiance and deters Protestant proselytizers."[102] Even Pilsen-area priests open to Mexican devotions tried to direct the laity's inclinations and aimed to confine worship within the church sanctuary. Increasingly, promotion of Mexican piety would arise from the laity, who had their own views of where and when devotion should take place.

■ ■ ■

Matovina argues that Latinos have followed a "national parish dynamic" that is similar to Pilsen's earlier European groups, if in an unofficial capacity: "Latinos attempt to establish and nurture structures of Catholic life that enable them to move from, at best, feeling hospitality in someone else's church to a sense of homecoming in a church that is their own."[103] To make Chicago churches their own, the Mexican faithful began their own initiatives and carved out their own spaces and activities apart from historic European American ways. The Cursillo movement played a crucial role in this process of making parishes Mexican.

The Cursillo movement reached Chicago in 1962, just as the composition of Pilsen parishes was shifting, and inspired many Mexicans to become more active Catholics. This program of lay education and faith building palpably impacted Mexican laymen and laywomen. The Cursillo de Cristianidad developed in Spain, took root in South Texas, and soon made its way to Chicago. The three-day-long Cursillo retreats targeted men, encouraging a deeper reflection of belief and propagating lay leadership. Later, separate Cursillos invited women to leave home and family and deepen their own commitment to Christ and the church community.[104] The retreats provided an opportunity to get to know peers from St. Francis and elsewhere in Chicago, even mexicanos living in other states. Although hesitant to leave home for this strange retreat in Indiana, the *cursillistas* returned to Pilsen parishes with new convictions and a voice.

Initially, the Cursillo retreats led to modest change at St. Procopius, but soon the cursillistas would claim the parish as their own. At first "they [the priests] let us cursillistas" hold meetings and dances at the parish. After the initial retreat, they met weekly for follow-up Ultreyas and gathered to pray the rosary and to "sing to the Virgin."[105] These humble gatherings were the parish's first ongoing Spanish-language popular devotions. For Julia Rodríguez, this lay fellowship allowed her to regain a sense of community and devotion that she missed from earlier days in Texas. The men took on leadership roles; some would become lectors or permanent deacons.[106] Kristy Nabhan-Warren underlines that "for these first-generation Mexican-descent cursillistas and immigrants, their involvement and leadership in the Cursillo movement was

FIGURE 17. Virgin of Guadalupe, garden, St. Procopius Church, 2016. Photo by the author.

the first time they were able to assert authority and autonomy in a pre–Vatican II Catholic Church."[107] At St. Procopius male cursillistas organized a Santo Nombre, or Holy Name Society: "The cursillistas and the Santo Nombre were one and the same."[108]

The Santo Nombre members began to reshape the parish both spiritually and physically, making San Procopio a more Mexican place. These men decided that the church yard that fronts 18th Street needed a shrine for Our Lady of Guadalupe. (The parish already featured a Guadalupe image inside its sanctuary.) Santo Nombre members and their wives organized the initiative, raised money through raffles and dances, and convinced the pastor to allow alteration of the church's public face. They built the substantial niche. By 1966 the Mexican Virgin was ensconced for all to see, whether passing by on foot or on the bus; she remains there today, her image rendered in a colorful mosaic. The men of the Santo Nombre created a new and unrestricted place to express their *fe guadalupana*, thus inviting others to do so also. Even those mexicanos who would not or could not enter St. Procopius's walls—rushing to work, shepherding their kids to school, gathering with their gang for the night—would be reminded of their Mexican and Catholic identity. The outdoor shrine included them all and provided the opportunity to express their devotion with a murmured prayer or a quick sign of the cross.

■ ■ ■

The initial decades of ethnic coexistence would challenge all concerned. The European American laity reluctantly shared space, both sacred and mundane, with their Catholic brothers and sisters of Mexican heritage. Just before Spanish-language Masses were added at St. Pius, parish leaders declared, "The Mexicans . . . are taking up residence in our territory, placing their children in our school, and attending our church."[109] This proclamation could have sounded from any of Pilsen's parishes, and it demonstrates the limits of true inclusion by the older European American parishioners. Looking back at contested spaces such as parish kitchens and carnival cashboxes, the transitional years proved difficult for all involved.

The experiences of Matías "Matt" Almendarez and Lupe (née Parra) Almendarez vividly show what many newcomers faced in Pilsen. Born and raised in Laredo, Texas, Matías followed relatives to Chicago in search of better work. Coming from the relatively homogeneous world of Anglo and Mexican Texas, the young *tejano* was surprised by Chicago's diversity; in workplaces he encountered individuals of different backgrounds, including African Americans and "a lot of DPs." Of his years working at Western Electric, he recalled, "You learn how to get along . . . make friends." Like other tejanos during the postwar period, he lived in the Near West Side Mexican enclave and attended Mass at St. Francis, reminiscent of home. Matías also played baseball with St. Francis teams. There he met Chicago-born and -raised Lupe Parra, the daughter of Mexican immigrants. In 1955 they married at St. Francis and later baptized their children there. But given the Near West Side's precarious future, they found their first apartment in Pilsen on a block with just one other Mexican family.[110] Eventually, the Almendarez family settled close to St. Ann Church. With children nearing school age, the family began, in fits and starts, to make the long-time Polish parish their own.

St. Ann's was established in 1903 as an offshoot of St. Adalbert, Pilsen's enormous Polish parish. In the 1920s St. Ann School overflowed with thirteen hundred children (and literally could not fit another six hundred, who had to attend public schools). The parish mounted Polish-language plays on religious topics. In the interwar years, St. Ann's active societies included the Polish Roman Catholic Union, Polish National Alliance, and Polish Women's Alliance. During World War II the parish priest headed the Aid for Poland drive among Chicago's Poles. The nationalist impulse persisted as St. Ann's members joined the one hundred thousand people who took part in the Polish Millennium at Soldier Field in 1966. The lack of religious freedom under Soviet rule added to Chicago's fervent celebration of Poland's conversion to Christianity in AD 966.[111] The church choirs recorded albums that included Polish folk songs, along with "Ave Maria" and "America the Beautiful." St. Ann's, like many Polish American parishes, retained many Polish religious customs well beyond the immigrant generation.[112]

Mexican entry to Polish St. Ann's began on a discouraging note: a petition was circulated to block the Almendarez family's rental on 21st Street. The signature gathering deterred neither the young family nor their elderly Polish landlord. The family moved into the apartment without incident, making them the first Mexican family on a street of Poles and Bohemians. Despite the initial tension, this was a far cry from the "intermittent terror activities" that African Americans faced as they moved to new blocks on Chicago's West Side.[113] Matías and Lupe enrolled their children at St. Ann School, and that became their parish for the next three decades. Nevertheless, as the petition drive portended, being one of a few Mexican families in this Polish parish brought challenges.

Lupe Almendarez's involvement at her new parish began at the Mothers' Club, where she initially mingled with the mothers without incident. As more mexicanas appeared, however, even simple traditions became contested among the parish women. The mothers recognized each other's birthdays by singing "Happy Birthday." When new members from Mexico revised the custom by singing "Las mañanitas," one long-standing club member challenged, "What are you singing?" Lupe stepped in, responding, "Americans have 'Happy Birthday'; the Polish sing 'Sto lat, sto lat.' Don't gimme the business 'what are you singing?' We sing 'Las mañanitas.'"[114] As she did in many situations, Lupe found herself speaking for the Mexican newcomers.

Lupe and Matías assumed the role of cultural intermediaries at the parish, although their neighbors from Mexico often dismayed them. Even Laredo-raised Matías felt the Mexican immigrants were unlike them, politely offering, "Different cultures, different ways." Mexican Americans like themselves spoke English beyond the home, but the newcomers stuck with Spanish. The Almendarez family raised eyebrows when mexicanos disturbed neighborhood customs with public consumption of alcohol and loud music in the street or when they failed to shoulder responsibilities at parish functions. Still, Matías and Lupe, uniquely positioned as bilingual and bicultural people, gained their pastors' respect and encouraged the parish's integration. At church functions, the Mexican newcomers put themselves on the side. Lupe urged new parishioners to mingle and sit among the others parishioners. The mexicanos hesitated, saying, "No nos quieren" (They don't like us). And Lupe countered,

"¿Como los van a querer si no se dan a conocer?" (How are they going to like you if you don't let them get to know you?). The Almendarez parents persisted in their efforts to include all. Lupe, for example, translated at the Mothers' Club meetings. While the Mexican American Almendarez family struggled to integrate themselves into the Polish parish, the immigrant wave simultaneously forced them to reevaluate their own identities.[115]

For Lupe Almendarez, the real battle between old-timers and Mexican newcomers took place in the parish kitchen. In the weeks preceding the annual St. Ann's festival or St. Joseph's Table, Lupe appeared in the kitchen, ready to prepare food.[116] The old-timers put her stuff on the side and told Lupe, "You're for the Mexicans, and I'm for the Polish." This snub frustrated her, but Lupe persisted, declaring, "I just work for the parish. I didn't know it was a nationality function or whatever. I'm here for the parish." The Polish women tried to maintain control of this corner of the parish. In the modest kitchen, Lupe found it hard to ignore when they made faces at her actions there: "They had the stove, and I had to cook on the side." Lupe worked where she could, thinking to herself, "I ain't gonna start no war here." Anticipating their criticism, she "always used to go in on the weekends and clean the kitchen, top to bottom." Lupe would tell the Mexican women who also volunteered, "Make sure everything is kept nice. It's bad enough they don't like us. I don't want them to think we're dirty."[117]

The menu for the parish festivals became a point of contention. St. Ann's festival sold hot dogs, pizza, and Polish sausage. Lupe wanted to serve the tacos and tostadas that she grew up with at St. Francis events. As she prepared the refried beans for tostadas, the old-timers apprehensively asked about her dish: "You never had pinto beans? These are pinto beans, but they're smashed." She offered samples on a piece of a tostada, cautioning, "You don't like it, there's the garbage can." "Oh, not bad," the women responded. Soon, Lupe smugly recalled, "that's all they wanted. The tostadas, the Mexican food. The Polish stuff didn't go as much." By 1975 St. Ann's was inviting people to the St. Joseph's Table to enjoy "Latin American and Intercontinental Foods!"[118] Yet, as Lupe tells it, she and other Mexican women endured years of hostility in the kitchen; she worked hard for the parish and tried to keep the peace between the two populations at St. Ann's.

Her husband, Matías, volunteered as well and endured similar discomfort in his first decade at St. Ann's. Like other married men, he considered joining the Holy Name Society. But among its members was the man he suspected of leading the petition drive to block the family's move to 21st Street, so he did not seek membership. Still, it rankled Matías that he was not a member of the Holy Name. Members would invite him to join, but with the caveat that he needed a sponsor. He countered, "Why should I need a sponsor? I tell you, I want to join your Holy Name Society. Most of you guys know me." Their insistence on sponsorship stung. The Almendarez couple's liminal status at St. Ann's well exemplifies the practices across Pilsen: parish societies and sodalities remained the domain of European Americans well into the 1960s. In his early years Matías gladly accepted an invitation to help at the parish festival, but he met suspicion from the cashbox holders: men from the Holy Name Society. Eventually, when these old-timers no longer wanted the chore, the parish priest asked Matt (as he was usually called) to take over the festival and its nightly cash collection. He bore this responsibility for over a decade. He looks back ambivalently on his decades of involvement at St. Ann's. While those were "good years there," his desire to fully belong—for example, in the Holy Name Society—would be tainted as long as his foe lived.[119]

Changes in the late 1960s opened the way for the Almendarez family to deepen their parish involvement. In a three-hour interview this devout family never mentioned Vatican II by name, but clearly the changes wrought by the council dovetailed with ethnic succession in Pilsen to create conditions for change. St. Ann's long featured Masses for Polish and English speakers, but the growing Mexican membership wanted Mass in Spanish. The 18th Street Team—a coalition of nuns and priests who worked across parish lines to provide Spanish-speaking liturgy and other services across Pilsen—helped instigate these changes at St. Ann's.[120] When the long-time minister left the parish, the Almendarez family joined others who requested a Spanish-English bilingual pastor. The clergy acknowledged their desires, but the archdiocese could not meet the demand as the Mexican and Puerto Rican population expanded throughout the city. The pastor invited Matías to serve as a Spanish lector. The ritual at first made him nervous, but soon he grew more at ease in this leading role at the parish.

The installation of the Virgin of Guadalupe at St. Ann's took place around 1970 and marked a turning point. Another Mexican family at the parish donated the image: "It came from Mexico, with papers and all." Lupe and Matías Almendarez were selected to carry the image, joining the couple that donated it, through the nearby streets. (Matías constructed the little stretcher.) The two couples proudly carried the Virgin of Guadalupe on a two-block procession, led by a priest, before entering St. Ann's sanctuary. For decades the image remained prominently displayed by the main altar, parallel to Our Lady of Częstochowa. Taking part in the procession and installation felt "beautiful." Soon after, Mexican parishioners purchased a Mexican flag to place by the Virgin's side. The installation of the Mexican Virgin marked

FIGURE 18. Procession bringing the Virgin of Guadalupe to St. Ann Church, ca. 1969–70; (*right*) Lupe and Matías Almendarez. From the Almendarez family collection.

a change to Mexicans and Poles alike. Daughter Lisa Almendarez reflected, "The Polish people realized that you weren't going anywhere."[121]

When the newcomers sought a Spanish-English-speaking priest, some Poles and Polish Americans chimed, "Why? They're coming to take over our parish." Matías summarized: "There was a lot of conflict with those people. Until now they claim they own the parish." But the Almendarez family, like other Mexican families, came to claim the parish as well. The unfolding of the Vatican II reforms, with a greater emphasis on lay involvement and leadership, proved a vital change for them, with Matías serving as an officiant and daughter Lisa as a teen playing guitar at folk Masses. She continued to play for liturgy in the years since. Matías's leadership went beyond his parish, as he took part in Pilsen's first Via Crucis in 1977 (see chapter 5). St. Ann's, despite its many troubled episodes, presents a story of relatively successful ethnic integration within a parish.

Not every parish opened its doors. Apparently, Mexicans understood they would not be welcome at St. Stephen, a Slovenian parish, although the school enrolled their children. Mexican Catholics recall hostile reactions from priests and ushers in Slavic parishes in nearby Little Village in the late 1950s and 1960s. A priest apparently told one woman, "Go to your own church."[122] St. Joseph, a Slovak parish, accepted the newcomers, but the pastor did not pursue a Mexican congregation; as the Slovaks quickly exited Pilsen, St. Joseph's numbers dwindled, and the parish closed in 1968.[123] St. Adalbert, the large Polish parish, similarly took a passive approach to Mexicans. Its school had enrolled Mexican children (but not African Americans) since the 1950s, but the parish offered little attraction to Spanish-speaking adults.[124] Parish rolls, buoyed slightly by recent Polish immigrants, kept slipping in the 1960s. Mexicans chose instead to frequent more welcoming churches, St. Vitus and St. Pius, both within a few blocks.

■ ■ ■

Observing Pilsen closely, from its first Mexican residents making lone professions of devotion in 1947 to the ubiquitous and hyperpublic demonstrations of Mexican Catholicism in area churches and streets in recent decades, this transformation clearly accelerated in the 1960s. Before that, European American residents were not necessarily hostile to the Mexicans moving in next door, but the parishes hardly welcomed the newcomers. As the sacred homes to two generations of Poles at St. Ann's or three generations of Czechs at St. Procopius, these churches and their parishioners and clergy were wary of any change in the pews, programs, and parochial school of "our church." At St. Ann's, as we have seen, increasing arrivals and inclusion of Mexicans faced resistance. Lisa Almendarez suggests that this was understandable for the Polish families who believed that "this was our parish first. The grandparents were here." Polish American parishes, with their pronounced ethnic solidarity, language retention, and nationalism, proved reactive to ethnic change in many US cities. Anthropologist Paul Wrobel wrote of Detroit Poles who, in the wake of Vatican II, found it hard to accept changes in the church. But for them "the Catholic religion remains a guiding light, a way of ordering one's life. Despite new forms of worship and the disappearance of some familiar rituals and symbols, a parish member can still go to confession and hear Mass in Polish." At one Polish Detroit parish in the 1970s, laypeople worried that "those Albanians are gonna take over this place. Why, you go to church on Sunday, and they're all over. They speak this strange-sounding language that doesn't sound nothing like Polish, and I don't know, they're just different from us Poles. . . . This has been our community for over fifty years now, but soon it'll be over."[125] Racism and xenophobia did not always explain European Americans' reactive stance in their changing parishes. Rather, a sense of community and pride in an ethnonational identity motivated the desire to protect the status quo.

Changes came slowly, often grudgingly, in all the Pilsen parishes, as if blind to the undeniable realities of ethnic succession. Some parishes simply refused to change and closed. The magnetic draw of St. Francis of Assisi diluted the kinds of pressures that Mexicans made on Pilsen parishes in the 1950s. Priests had to wonder: Was a Spanish Mass really needed on 18th Street if the young families seemed happy to take the bus to St. Francis every Sunday? Only in the early 1960s would some of the Mexican faithful demand something different at their local parish, often where their children attended school. By the late 1960s the clergy's ambivalence and condescension had lessened, and they began to encourage and integrate Mexican membership, at least in those churches that survive today.[126]

Crucial to parish acceptance was the fact that old-time Pilsen residents and business owners preferred Mexican newcomers to the African American population that dominated other West Side neighborhoods in the same decades. In July 1966, just blocks north of Pilsen at Roosevelt and Throop, an African American neighborhood erupted in riots. Violence spread across the West Side; over the next week, over $2 million in property was destroyed.[127] But Pilsen, just south of the viaduct, remained untouched.

Pilsen-reared author Stuart Dybek (born in 1942) evocatively conjures a scene from the transition years. At a semifictional parish in "an old Slavic neighborhood that had become Spanish," the Polish priest could celebrate the Mass in Spanish. Mexicans' initial reluctance to participate in the local parish was partially a reaction to the slights, small and large, they experienced there. When Mexicans sponsored Mass intentions, the parish bulletin often misspelled their names. European American parishioners acted peeved by the newcomers' many young children. European Americans, as Dybek reminds us, looked askance at the Mexican kids with "their poor-looking gym shoes sticking out from black cassocks."[128]

When parishes finally recognized the needs of Mexican Catholics, significant change transpired due to the efforts of the new laity, including those emboldened by their Cursillo training, such as the Santo Nombre members who envisioned the outdoor shrine to Our Lady of Guadalupe. Father Mizera had fretted about the difficulties of assimilating his new parishioners to US Catholic ways ("It will take a long time for the immigrants to accustom themselves to our way of practicing the Catholic religion"). In the end, St. Procopius and other parishes accustomed themselves to a Mexican way of practicing Catholicism. After 1960, despite foot-dragging by priests and European American parishioners, mexicanos, in concert with those clergy who acknowledged their distinct needs and strengths, made the parishes their own.

The first steps to making Mexican parishes and, moreover, to promoting a Mexican Catholicism in Pilsen preceded the almost simultaneous emergence of the Chicano movement and Vatican II.[129] Both movements undoubtedly accelerated the almost radical change that soon unfolded in Catholic Pilsen.

5. Pilsen *Católico*

1970s and Beyond

In many ways I feel that the entire Pilsen area is a re-creation of the world that we had at St. Francis of Assisi. We have now re-created the Christian, Catholic atmosphere which we once called home but now I am part of that home.
—Esperanza Delgado Godínez, "Mexicanidad: An Oral History"

A STIFF WIND hit Matías Almendarez as he stepped out of his car at 18th Street and Union, literally under the expressway. The weather was unseasonably cold that Friday, April 8, 1977: Viernes Santo, Good Friday. After some thirty years in Chicago, Matías knew that weather could vary a great deal during Semana Santa. Walking toward Providence of God Church, he worried that the extreme cold might sabotage the day's plans. He passed a light post with the flyer announcing the Via Crucis Viviente (Living Way of the Cross) and hoped the best for the day ahead. Given that St. Ann's, his parish, stood over a mile away, Matías had seldom visited this church. He searched for and found the door and then descended into the basement. The cavernous room, long the site of Lithuanian church suppers and dances, was abuzz with *mexicanos* from Providence of God and many other Pilsen parishes, even a few *compadres* from St. Ann's. Some of the only Anglos were neighborhood priests, including Father Jaime and Father Terence. Matías joined the men dressing as Roman soldiers in red-and-white costumes. They chatted in Spanish and English, awaiting the start. The room filled with hundreds of people. When the narrator took the stage, quiet overtook the basement. All those present made the sign of the cross and recited the Padre Nuestro.[1]

As rehearsed, the performers enacted the first station of the cross: Jesus condemned to death. As a crown of thorns was forced on his head, (fake) blood dripped down his face. Then Roman soldiers, Christ bearing his heavy

FIGURE 19. Via Crucis, Pilsen, year unknown. Photo by Peter Rodriguez, CMF. Courtesy of the Claretian Missionaries Archives USA-Canada.

wooden cross, and others ascended the stairs, leaving the basement's warm enclosure, and made their way outside. The centurion mounted his horse. Ten lanes of traffic from the Dan Ryan Expressway roared above them. Matías, the costumed actors, and the crowd crossed the narrow sidewalk, stepped down from the curb, and literally occupied 18th Street with a tableau from another time.

Hundreds of onlookers, bundled up for the cold, watched, along with a TV crew. Most followed the assemblage, walking in the street, westward. They passed by old factories, empty lots, and taverns and over the Burlington rail line. Along the way they paused to watch the reenactment of the stations of the cross and to pray. Mechanics stepped out of their garages, older people looked on from their stoops, and children ran alongside to see this most unusual event in their barrio. As the crowds grew, the police became "visibly upset about not being able to control the crowd nor keep traffic flowing. They [made] repeated attempts to keep one lane of the street open for traffic but soon [gave] up the effort." Soon the crowd and the pageant filled the width of 18th Street.[2]

For the fourth station (Jesus encounters his mother), the Via Crucis stopped outside of St. Procopius at the Guadalupe grotto, erected a decade earlier by the Santo Nombre members. The ever-growing procession turned south on Throop to Holy Trinity—the Croatian parish, but these days Mass was celebrated in Spanish, English, and Croatian. Narration of the sixth station and prayers sounded from a police squad car's loudspeaker in those three languages. Returning to 18th Street, the faithful paused at Blue Island, where in 1973 protesters had dumped garbage to denounce poor sanitation service in Pilsen. They stopped again at Ashland, a major intersection, where in 1972 Chicano protestors had commandeered a bus as part of the campaign for more Chicago Transit Authority (CTA) jobs for Latinos.[3] The procession again veered from 18th Street, heading south two blocks to St. Pius V, Pilsen's largest Mexican parish. While passing St. Vitus, once a Czech parish and in 1977 the center of radical Chicano Catholic activity, the children's *coro* sang.[4]

The Via Crucis arrived at its westernmost point, Harrison Park, the penultimate station. At noon, upon the park's small hillock soldiers nailed Christ to the cross. Thousands of people, the devout and the curious, looked on. "There are no cries from the Christ character, but the crowd gasps at the sound of the blows. Several people can be overheard asking if the soldiers are really nailing Christ to the Cross." From there, an elderly "Czech lay deacon led the procession off towards St. Adalbert's slowly beating an old drum he had borrowed from his local VFW post."[5] The crowd squeezed into narrow 17th Street, pausing at the sites of recent deadly house fires.

The people entered the Italian marble sanctuary of St. Adalbert Church for the final station: Jesus laid in his tomb. St. Adalbert's pews could seat two thousand worshippers, but in the 1970s those pews mostly sat unfilled. (Most Poles had moved to other neighborhoods, and many local mexicanos seemed to prefer nearby St. Pius and St. Vitus.) Only on Good Friday, during the Via Crucis, did the sanctuary fill: now with the Mexican faithful, not the Poles of earlier generations. With the final station and prayers, the lights dimmed in the incense-filled sanctuary. The costumed actors and others came to the communion rail and knelt "down to pay their respects just as they would in any wake service."[6] The faithful quietly filed out of St. Adalbert's. In time, only the reenactors remained, removing their costumes in the old Polish church's basement.

Matías and other lay leaders talked; they considered the day's events a success. Despite the cold (a TV camera crew said it felt like twenty below with the wind), the Via Crucis had attracted crowds of young and old, of Mexican Americans and newly arrived immigrants. Some older Poles and Czech Americans watched as well. The Pilsen parishes had truly banded together, and priests and laity had collaborated in creating a new kind of Catholic ritual for Chicago. This Via Crucis harked back to colonial Mexican rituals and simultaneously reflected the urban Chicano experience.

Now a tradition for four decades, the Via Crucis requires that traffic be diverted off 18th Street for half a day, and the CTA reroutes the number 18 bus.[7] As Mexican Catholics literally take over the streets to walk together with Jesús, the event epitomizes the aims of post–Vatican II inculturation, which strives "to create a form of worship that is culturally suited to local assembly." Apt liturgy and rites promote the laity's active participation in a "fuller experience of Christ" as "revealed in the people's language, rites, arts, and symbols."[8] The Via Crucis epitomizes the flowering of a Hispanic liturgy that draws upon devotional practices with deep roots in Mexico's religious life. At the same time, these practices have been adapted to reflect the realities of immigrants and Mexican-descent Chicagoans. In the words of Chicago-reared priest and theologian Fr. Arturo Pérez-Rodríguez, collectively these faithful "incorporate, embody, enflesh worship."[9]

A decade earlier Matías Almendarez had worked for his family's inclusion in their new parish, St. Ann's. Initially in the 1960s they sought membership and respect within the historically Polish parish: in the Holy Name Society and the Mothers' Club. By 1970 they had successfully lobbied to place the Virgin of Guadalupe in the sanctuary. When Matías as a Roman soldier marched down 18th Street in the first Via Crucis, he found a new way of being mexicano and católico in Chicago. Almendarez became part of the Via Crucis coordinating team. Beginning with a postprocession evaluation, the organizers met regularly throughout the year and ramped up their frequency with rehearsals in the winter. On Good Friday he woke at 4:00 a.m. to prepare the crosses in his garage and to oversee the arrival of a horse to Providence of God. Year after year, Matías was motivated in this work because he saw the involvement of new people and the growing number of spectators, including the youth, whose presence "asegura el futuro de esta forma de evangelización, o sea, esta forma de dar a conocer a Jesús" (assures the future of this form of evangelization or this way of getting to know Jesus).[10]

With the launch of the Via Crucis and its subsequent growth and perseverance in Pilsen, the Mexican spiritual conquest of the neighborhood was complete. As shown in the preceding chapter, the first steps to promoting a Mexican Catholicism in Pilsen came before the near simultaneous emergence of Vatican II and the Chicano movement. Both movements accelerated the radical changes that would unfold in Pilsen.

Some Mexican-descent residents of Pilsen in attendance recalled the Good Friday rituals at St. Francis in the "old neighborhood." As detailed in chapter 2, there, as darkness settled in, crowds converged outside and witnessed the procession that began at St. Francis School and made its way to their church. The St. Francis procession commanded less than a block of Newberry, the side street that linked the convent and school to the church itself, before entering the sanctuary. The event was relatively circumscribed: the reenactors belonged to St. Francis parish.[11] The annual devotion belonged to a pre–Vatican II parish that sought primarily to create a stable, attractive religious home for Mexican immigrants and their children.

What unfolded on 18th Street in 1977 evoked those solemn displays, but Pilsen's Via Crucis was a grander action. It involved seven parishes and required planning and collaboration between Pilsen's many priests and the increasingly vocal lay leaders.[12] It boldly appropriated 18th Street and Harrison Park, sacralizing a broad swath of urban spaces well beyond the churches. The procession flew in the face of the Vatican II conciliar reforms (1962–65) that minimized devotional rituals. The act of walking with Jesus and the deed of witnessing the stations drew in thousands of people and encouraged them to feel their faith in a collective and open setting. The flyer announcing the first Via Crucis stressed the public and communal aspect: "Nos unimos en un acto Público" (We unite in a Public act).[13] By mounting most of the stations outdoors, it united the parishes, and it aimed to unite the barrio. The Via Crucis reminded immigrants of the outdoor celebrations and processions in their hometowns in Mexico, bringing up emotional memories of home. For many new immigrants, the scale of Pilsen's event evoked Mexico's largest and best-known Via Crucis in Iztapalapa. The massive reenactment on the edge of Mexico City, launched in 1843, draws millions of visitors each year.[14] Even for mexicanos who have never visited, the Iztapalapa event is televised live all day on Viernes Santo.

The Via Crucis proclaimed Pilsen as a Mexican and Catholic space in a neighborhood dominated just fifteen years earlier by Poles, Czechs, and

Lithuanians. Unprecedented, the 1977 Via Crucis reflected lofty goals of engaging issues of social justice and embodied an identity at once Catholic, Mexican, and Chicano. For Esperanza Godínez, raised at St. Francis, the Via Crucis presented a distinct and emotional way of demonstrating faith in community. In her master's thesis, Godínez reflected that Pilsen came to re-create "the world that we had at St. Francis of Assisi." In these immersive Mexican Catholic surroundings, she was home. Still, Godinez acknowledged that the Via Crucis as it unfolded in Pilsen was new to her; she learned of it only as an adult living in Pilsen.[15] This chapter demonstrates how a committed Mexican laity, partnering with sympathetic European American clergy, indelibly stamped Pilsen as católico, Catholic, *and* Mexican.[16]

■ ■ ■

Pilsen became Chicago's first Mexican majority neighborhood precisely in the decade preceding the 1977 Via Crucis.[17] Emblems of the one-time "Little Bohemia" grew scarce, little more than hieroglyphics for most people walking by the grand but empty Plzensky Sokol, the longtime Czech gym and community center that loomed over Ashland Avenue.[18] Mexican children and parents entering St. Procopius School thought little of the mysterious letters carved over the entryway: "Nechte malickych prijiti ke mne" (Let the little ones come to me).

Fewer taverns advertised *zimne piwo*, and every year more signs read *cerveza fría*. Mexican music—polkas and *norteño*—played on jukeboxes in those bars and social clubs and drifted into the streets. The modest Milo movie theater became Teatro Villa and showed Mexican movies. *Librerías* sold Mexican movie magazines and *novelas*, the flimsy paperback romances. Dads took their kids to buy the newspaper from Mexico and maybe an *elote* or a Polish sausage. Grocery stores smelled of fresh tortillas and cilantro. Piñatas hung from the ceilings over merchandise such as traditional Mexican mortars and pestles (*molcajetes*), bottles of mole, and votive candles emblazoned with the Virgin of San Juan de los Lagos and the Santo Niño de Atocha.[19] Sales staff spoke Spanish at the three-story Leader Department Store on 18th Street. The neighborhood weeklies (*Lawndale News*, *West Side Times*) carried ads in Spanish.

When a newcomer walked Pilsen's side streets, she noted that the small homes and modest apartment buildings, some of Chicago's oldest, were generally cared for. In warmer months, people sat outside on their stoops or on folding chairs on the swept sidewalks and talked while kids played in front. The streets, never vacant, came alive as people returned from work. Neighbors talked and children ran to the store for the evening tortillas or pop. Corner stores readily extended credit to frequent shoppers, who viewed the local storeowners as friendly and helpful, ignoring the higher prices.[20] On summer evenings, the melody of an approaching ice cream truck mingled with the sounds of Mexican radio stations. Upstairs, amid the secondhand furniture or matching sets from local discount outlets, many families maintained an *altarcito* often featuring la Guadalupana "surrounded by plastic flowers, votive candles, and crucifix or rosary beads." Many people in Pilsen had close family nearby. A young wife reflected at the time, "I've always lived close to my family. My married sister lives around the corner, my parents live on the next block, I have six aunts and uncles within five blocks, and my husband's family mostly lives around here."[21] Pilsen in the 1970s overall exhibited energy and communitas.

Yet streetscapes also revealed troubling decline in the early 1970s. When Cristina Vital, a young Chicana activist raised on the north side, first visited Pilsen, the "crowded, deteriorated, and dirty" neighborhood "shocked and terrified" her.[22] Too many of the old wooden structures were firetraps. Vacant lots had rubble and broken glass. Walls that gave way to open spaces bore spray-painted graffiti of the local "clubs," as the gangs called themselves. When the clubs formed in the early 1960s, they engaged in low-grade hostilities. As one member described the early years, it was "like the rumbles in West Side Story"; "we would humbug [fight] but no one got killed." But violence grew more serious: "In the mid-sixties, the guys started using guns, and that changed things a lot. . . . [E]veryone started packing. . . . [P]eople started getting killed."[23] Pilsen residents in the 1970s suffered "poor medical care, lack of garbage service, poor press, poor schools, lack of political clout, and minimal recreational facilities." Further, "the gangs are everywhere." Despite the neighborhood's vigor, media representations of Pilsen stressed the neighborhood's miserable conditions.[24]

Citywide, systemic economic ills challenged new immigrants to Chicago. Deindustrialization hit less-educated workers hard. The economic crisis of the early 1970s greatly affected Latinos. In 1975 alone the unemployment rate among Latinos increased from 9.3 to 13.2 percent. Many of the new arrivals in Pilsen lacked legal documentation. The effects on neighborhood young people were acute. "Close to one-third of Pilsen's households were headed by a single parent," which meant that many youth went unsupervised.[25]

Pilsen's public schools had become famously overcrowded and inadequately staffed to meet the needs of large numbers of English-language learners. The high school dropout rate hovered at 77 percent. Efforts to improve the quality of education for Pilsen's youth had been under way for a decade. Jaime Alanis well documents student organizing at Harrison High School. Mexican parents met at St. Procopius School in October 1968 to review the situation at their children's high school. (The Chicago Police Department's Red Squad infiltrated the meeting and reported on the Spanish-language proceedings.) Four days later over four hundred Latino students walked out of Harrison in protest.[26]

A great deal of community organizing had its roots in the Pilsen Neighbors Community Council (PNCC), which had actively sought to combat neighborhood malaise since 1954. The PNCC followed Saul Alinsky's tenets for community organization, quickly integrated Mexican-descent people among its leaders, and partnered with local churches of different denominations.[27] Activist Monsignor John Egan wholly supported the PNCC and repeatedly encouraged Pilsen's Catholic pastors to collaborate. The PNCC had a history of documenting and publicizing Pilsen's problems, petitioning the city for attention, and building community programs such as a credit union, tutoring programs, and block clubs. From the late 1950s, Mexican women and men had a hand in all of these activities. The PNCC laid solid groundwork in training Latino leadership years before the Chicano movement.[28]

A new generation of Chicano leaders took to the streets to raise awareness and seek socioeconomic justice as the neighborhood's problems worsened in the late 1960s and early 1970s.[29] In 1967 activists, some of whom had splintered off from the PNCC, protested overcrowding and other conditions at neighborhood schools and pushed for more Mexican representation at Howell House and in the PNCC. Mexicans in Pilsen gained a new awareness of the Chicano movement flaring up in the southwestern United States. In 1969 some young Chicagoans went to the Chicano Youth Conference in Denver. As one activist recalls, "We had a bus full of guys, and that conference blew their minds." Returning from Denver, they brought the movement to Pilsen and "began to turn other people on, talking about racism, oppression, and Chicano power."[30] Even the decision to call oneself Chicano was a political act; for Mexican Americans, it meant allegiance with mexicanos and a devotion to struggle.[31]

In the 1970s Pilsen turned into an epicenter of both Mexican immigrant life and the new currents of the Chicano movement. The old school at St. Joseph's (the Slovak parish, which closed in 1968) now housed El Centro de la Causa. The once-Czech settlement house, Howell House, became Casa Aztlán in 1970. There enthusiastic young people picked up paintbrushes and covered the once nondescript exterior with bright murals that glorified Aztec deities and warriors, the United Farm Workers (UFW) black eagle, and inspirational sayings from Benito Juárez. Ray Patlan, the center's first artist-in-residence, recalls, "The Brown Berets began to have activities there, the folklorico began to do dances there, arts and crafts, photography, and other Raza activities."[32] A large Mexican flag defiantly flew in front of this "Mecca of the Chicano Movement in Chicago."[33] The local movement connected to national trends. The young stars of the Chicano movement, Rodolfo "Corky" Gonzales and José Angel Gutiérrez, visited Pilsen in 1972.

Protests took place over issues far and near. Chicanos and allies protested against the Vietnam War, championed the UFW, and mounted a prolonged struggle to establish a public high school in Pilsen. Seeking more CTA jobs for Latinos, activists (including clergy from St. Vitus) converged at the busy intersection of Ashland Avenue and 18th Street on Sunday, September 26, 1972. There they stopped two CTA buses, and "women sat down in front of the buses." People chanted, "¿Que queremos? ¡Trabajo! ¿Cuando? ¡Ahora!" (What do we want? Work! When? Now!). Protest turned into clashes with police and resulted in injuries and thirty-three arrests. In December 1973 St. Vitus parishioners joined other Pilsen residents at 18th Street and Blue Island, dumping garbage into the intersection to protest the city's poor sanitation service.[34] The use of these public thoroughfares as protest venues remained vivid in community memory for many years.

The lack of city services in Spanish moved from annoyance to tragedy in Pilsen. In the midst of a family Christmas Eve party in 1976, fire broke out. Firefighters arrived, but, unable to communicate with the Mexicans trapped in the burning building, their efforts proved futile. The fire killed ten children and two mothers. Most neighborhood parishes took part in planning the funeral; Pilsen priests concelebrated the Mass that took place at St. Vitus. Less than a week later, another fire in Pilsen proved deadly on New Year's Day. Local people blamed the many deaths on the firefighters' inability to communicate in Spanish.[35]

With the charred buildings in plain view and fresh memories of small white coffins, in the spring of 1977 Pilsen Catholics envisioned, organized, and executed the neighborhood's first Via Crucis. The Good Friday tableau and procession literally and symbolically incorporated these recent local troubles and struggles. In the following decades, the Via Crucis stopped at a tool factory to reflect on the workers' suffering, at several cantinas to call out their bad influence, and at the El station to highlight the CTA's high fares, among other pointed themes.[36] This Catholic procession linked the sorrows of a condemned Christ with those of a struggling people. Decades later, the Via Crucis continues to meld both biblical and present-day realities.

■ ■ ■

In the larger story of an emerging Chicago católico, the Via Crucis epitomizes the growing confidence and vision among Pilsen's majority Mexican laity: they would increasingly influence their priests. In the 1970s the neighborhood had twelve Catholic parishes, most of which had clergy who spoke Spanish. As more and more parishes offered *misa en español*, what did Mexican immigrants seek from a new church? Some people simply chose the closest church, often where their children went to school. But others considered joining a parish a few blocks farther away. What drew people to select a new parish? Providence of God and St. Vitus evolved into centers of activism, hosting organizations and meetings for workers' and immigrants' rights. St. Pius developed diverse service programs to meet the needs of the immigrants and the poor, including food and clothing aid. St. Procopius, meanwhile, ran a municipally funded Neighborhood Youth Corps, with its attendant three hundred summer jobs. Scholar Robert H. Stark categorized these types of parish activities as protest, service, and patronage. Each type of orientation and outreach, he argued, attracted parishioners.[37] Remarkably, Stark (himself a priest) barely considered how traditional devotions also impacted personal allegiances to a specific parish.

Fostering devotions, whether of Mexican origin or otherwise, did create interest and even ongoing connections to a church. Our Lady of Guadalupe made an early arrival at many Pilsen parishes, for example, in the St. Procopius shrine and in the devotional niche at St. Pius. Other popular devotions came more slowly. Amid the aggiornamento and radicalization of Pilsen's churches in the late 1960s and 1970s, an array of traditional devotions—beyond the Virgin of Guadalupe—quietly drew in Mexican Catholics and helped to make Chicago feel more like home.[38]

Consider the Santo Niño de Atocha, a much-beloved image of the Christ child that emerged out of the fringes of colonial Mexico. Although the Santo Niño devotion is not recognized by the Catholic hierarchy, images of the Santo Niño proliferate in northern Mexico and New Mexico and among Mexican immigrants to the United States. Many believe that the Santo Niño has special abilities to intercede on behalf of sick or lost children, travelers and migrants, and even soldiers and prisoners: all "children" or sojourners, like the Santo Niño himself, alone without a mother. At his largest shrine in Plateros (in the Mexican state of Zacatecas), immigrants to the United States have a huge presence as they return to thank the Santo Niño for his aid in their journeys and travails.[39] Since the 1990s the Santo Niño de Atocha has graced one corner in St. Procopius's sanctuary, while the Holy Infant of Prague stands in another.

Back in the 1960s the Santo Niño had no place in Chicago's churches. The closest thing was the image of another Christ child: the Holy Infant of Prague. At St. Procopius, the Czechs venerated Our Lady of Fatima, but according to Julia Rodríguez, they truly favored the Holy Infant of Prague.[40] Mexicans also came to express devotion to this Bohemian Holy Child. In the 1990s the Jesuit priests at St. Procopius considered placing a figure of the Santo Niño de Atocha in the sanctuary. The head pastor asked Julia, then a parishioner of forty years, which Holy Child she preferred in the church, the Holy Child of Atocha or the Holy Child of Prague? Julia considered and responded, "Padre, well, the one from Prague has always been here. And the *tejanas*, *mexicanas* always said that that Child brought many blessings to the neighborhood, to everything, to Pilsen." Both images of the Christ Child, Julia opined, were "the same."[41] Some Mexicans grew to embrace a Czech icon as their own.

Tales of the Santo Niño also illustrate how Mexicans' popular piety could influence their American priests. In 1967 Fr. Terence Fitzmaurice, OSB, began two decades of ministry at St. Procopius after a short time in Mexico to learn Spanish. He worked mainly with the parish youth, helping to diffuse gang activities, getting young men out of jail, and overseeing summer free lunch programs.[42] The priest learned about the Santo Niño from Raúl, a young immigrant from Mexico. The seventh grader told Fitzmaurice how the Santo Niño had saved his life after a medical emergency in the Mexican countryside. Fearing for young Raúl's survival, the family made a *promesa* to the Santo Niño and walked nine kilometers to the shrine at Plateros.[43] Raúl was cured. The story of this miracle made a great impression on Fitzmaurice, who shared it with me in great detail thirty years later. Soon after hearing Raúl's story, the priest went to the hospital to baptize a dying baby. He told parish boys about the sad situation, and Raúl piped up, "He won't die. We'll make a promesa." Fitzmaurice reminded him that their church had no Santo Niño de Atocha, but the boy countered that they did have the Holy Infant of Prague. The group returned to the church and the statue of the Czech Christ Child. At the church "we all knelt down. Raúl and I made a promesa. The other kids just prayed. We made a promise for that kid, and sure enough, he lived." This episode again shows Mexican immigrants substituting the Holy Infant of Prague for their more familiar Santo Niño. Soon the priest, raised in Illinois, would propagate this Mexican devotion among his Pilsen parishioners, urging prayer to the Santo Niño de Atocha on behalf of gravely ill children.[44]

Fitzmaurice's memories exemplify how American priests might embrace a more Mexican way of practicing Catholicism. Moreover, this priest took pride in promoting more Mexican features of Catholic worship. He arranged for *mariachi* Masses and joined organizers of Pilsen's first Via Crucis. Fitzmaurice took credit for orchestrating the visit of a large image of the Virgin of San Juan de los Lagos to St. Procopius in 1982, which spawned outdoor novenas of five thousand faithful. People who had made vows to the Virgin of San Juan de los Lagos but could not travel to her shrine in Mexico to thank her flocked to St. Procopius to make good on their promesas. The schoolyard at 18th and Allport Streets, with its makeshift outdoor altar, became a sacred and Mexican space, albeit temporarily.[45] Joseph Bernardin, just installed as the archbishop of Chicago, joined Mexicans there. (That day the Chicago Police Department sent multiple squads to help with traffic and crowds.) He helped carry the visiting statue at St. Procopius, and he gave a homily in Spanish. He began, "Brothers and sisters, like you, I come here as a pilgrim to ask for the Virgin Mary's intercession under the title of 'Virgen de San Juan de los Lagos.'"[46] Two decades earlier that very schoolyard was a place where Mexican American pupils whispered to each other in Spanish, fearing a scolding from the sisters. Now the archbishop addressed the faithful in Spanish. That temporary visit evolved, in time, to make St. Procopius Chicago's shrine to the Virgin of San Juan de los Lagos.

■ ■ ■

While most local parishes' hostility toward Mexicans had waned by the mid-1970s, ethnocentric holdovers persisted.[47] Some parishes moved slowly. St. Adalbert's, historically Polish, was the last of the major parishes to include Spanish-language Mass in its weekly schedule. St. Procopius instituted this option in 1962. Only in 1975, with two decades of Mexican families on parish rolls, did the clergy at St. Adalbert add a Spanish Mass. An image of the Virgin of San Juan de los Lagos gained a place in the sanctuary in the same year. In 2000, with hardly any Poles residing in the neighborhood, Our Lady of Częstochowa still reigned over the sanctuary. The single Sunday Mass in Polish brought in a few dozen faithful, but they drove in from other neighborhoods.

Refusal to engage with Mexican coreligionists persisted in Pilsen's southwestern edge, the Heart of Chicago neighborhood.[48] At St. Stephen's, a Slovenian parish (one of just two in the city), parishioners aimed to further stamp their church and surroundings as Slovenian through the 1970s.[49] While other churches just blocks away added a Spanish-language Mass, St. Stephen's held firm to its Slovenian identity. When Mexicans organized and executed the first Via Crucis, the Heart of Chicago parishes (excepting St. Ann's, the Almendarez family's parish) barely engaged their new neighbors from Mexico. At the Italian parish, official history reported in 1980: "Although Mexicans live in the neighborhood, few belong to St. Michael Church."[50] A few Pilsen parishes doggedly held fast to the founders' ethnic identity, denying the face of change. The need for Spanish Mass increased, while the attendance at Slovenian and Polish Mass shrank every year. Of the five Heart of Chicago parishes, only one remains open in 2019.

Even with the fuller inclusion of Mexicans at most Pilsen parishes, people continued to return to St. Francis in the 1970s. Some went regularly, drawn by its legendary status as Chicago's "Mexican cathedral." Reportedly, some four thousand people attended Sunday Masses there. For many newly arrived immigrants, St. Francis was simply where they had first continued their Catholic devotion in Chicago. For others, the old Near West Side church had special memories as the site of family weddings, baptisms, and funeral Masses. While many people became members of churches in Pilsen and beyond, they often returned to St. Francis for certain festivities and family sacraments.[51] With the politicization of Mexican-descent people in the late 1960s and 1970s, St. Francis Church also became a center of mobilization. For example, many Chicago Mexicans became "very supportive of the farm workers movement, the boycott of lettuce and grapes. So, when Cesar Chávez came to Chicago, we were there at the rally at St. Francis of Assisi Church."[52] Fr. Peter Rodriguez, CMF, attracted many immigrants in the 1960s and 1970s as he directed the Juventud Obrera Cristiana (popularly called JOC), an offshoot of Catholic Action. He regularly spoke out and took action for workers and immigrants. Even stripped of its residential neighborhood, St. Francis retained its magnetic place for Chicago Mexicans.

■ ■ ■

In recent decades Pilsen resident have mounted numerous sites of public devotion, from yard shrines to murals with Catholic themes, to spots commemorating deceased priests and police officers. The Santo Niño de Atocha looks down from a third-story window on Loomis Avenue. People pass the modest shrine to the late Fr. David Staszak, OP, a St. Pius priest, in front of a home on 19th Street. One of the *botánicas* on 18th Street features a hand-painted sign, "Tenemos vestidos y sillas para su Niño Dios" (We have clothing and chairs for your Christ Child).[53] At Panadería del Refugio (which promises "el verdadero y auténtico sabor del pan estilo Acambaro") a large framed image of the Virgen del Refugio graces the front window, enhanced by the glowing red neon open sign. Street vendors sell brightly colored friendship bracelets and scapulars on pastel pink and blue threads; iridescent rosaries and key chains with medals of St. Jude and the Virgin of San Juan sparkle in the Chicago sun. Visible from half a mile away, a four-story-high mural looms over busy Ashland Avenue and vividly depicts the Virgin of Guadalupe protecting immigrants crossing the Rio Grande. As pedestrians walk by the mural (entitled "increible las cosas que se ven"), many look up and cross themselves.[54] A makeshift memorial with candles, flowers, and a cross appears on a parklet on Blue Island. The next summer, just the cross remains; notably, the sanitation workers have let it be. Some doors bear the modest stickers that proclaim "Este hogar es católico" (This home is Catholic), with the Virgin of Guadalupe. The stickers further warn any would-be proselytizer, "No aceptamos propaganda protestante ni de ninguna otra secta" (We don't accept Protestant propaganda nor from any other sect).[55]

People take over the streets for seasonal processions, including, most prominently, the Via Crucis. For neighborhood residents and participants in the Via Crucis, the locations of the fourteen stations become landmarks where memories of the religious event, that year or in the time of Christ, may surge whenever passed throughout the year.[56] One crucial sacred space has disappeared: the hill that served as the Calvary in the Via Crucis. The Chicago Park District flattened the hill (ca. 2013), making way for another soccer field in Harrison Park.

In the summer since at least 1986, two Pilsen parishes have conducted a series of evening street Masses (*misa en la calle*).[57] A parishioner hosts the Mass in front of his or her home. Traffic is shut down for the duration of the Mass, with a parked car or trash cans at the block's ends. In addition to parishioners, family members and neighbors may attend, taking seats lined up in rows astride the street. People arrive with a bag or a cart on their way home from the grocery store. Strollers and walkers easily find a place as a small crowd convenes. A priest presides behind a makeshift altar, a folding table covered with a white cloth. Attendees take part in the sacrament, as well as the fellowship with food and drink that follows. Elderly neighbors with limited mobility sit at their doorstep and witness the Mass, maybe taking Communion when the priest and servers walk along the block. People sing hymns *en español*. The Mass concluded, people join in on "De colores," the song of the *cursillistas* and Charismatics. For an hour or two on a hot summer evening in the nation's third largest city (plagued by gang violence and a stubbornly high homicide rate), a block of South Miller or West 23rd feels peaceful, like a *pueblito* or rancho of blessed memory.[58]

Be it with street Masses, a faded palm frond on a door, beloved saints in a garden, or a hurried sign of the cross from people walking past a church, ubiquitous and visual reminders of Catholic faith abound in Pilsen. This neighborhood became a place where, to borrow Robert Orsi's words, "religion cannot be neatly separated from other practices of everyday life."[59] Even the neighborhood's most visible community and housing organization today, The Resurrection Project, has a strong Catholic identity and roots in multiple parishes. The organization promotes "good housing, solid family relationships, [and] strong economic growth" in Pilsen, all from its offices in the former St. Vitus parish.[60] A mural including the Virgin of Guadalupe, surrounded by colorful Mesoamerican glyphs, adorns the exterior of the old St. Vitus School.

The Mexican Catholic devotions that flourish in Pilsen have rippled far beyond, influencing the Archdiocese of Chicago in recent decades. During Holy Week in 1995 at least four other Chicago parishes mounted a Via Crucis in addition to the Pilsen original. In 2016 twelve distinct Via Crucis processions took place in Chicago and its suburbs.[61] The Via Crucis reverberates beyond Chicago. Milwaukee began its procession three decades ago. More recently, Latino Catholics have mounted a Via Crucis in Grand Rapids, Michigan; Peekskill, New York; Opelika, Alabama; and elsewhere. Laypeople are at the forefront of these public mobilizations of Catholic faith. Fr. Charles Dahm, OP, a longtime pastor at St. Pius, maintains that in the Via Crucis "the official and the popular church meet. . . . [C]hurch officials walk with the people."[62]

Following the Mexican-descent people who have raised their voices and made public their faith, the institutional church often speaks for new immigrants, acknowledging their difficult journeys and lives in the United States. In 2015 Pilsen celebrated its thirty-eighth Via Crucis; the new archbishop, Blaise Cupich, addressed the faithful at the final station in St. Adalbert Church in Spanish and English. "We know who they are in our neighborhoods, our families, those who come to us in need, but also in our city, in our country, who pick our vegetables, who lack papers, who do the kind of work no one else wants to do."[63] Where for generations St. Procopius nurtured the Czechs and St. Ann's nurtured the Poles, these churches barely paused in being immigrant churches.

■ ■ ■

On a summer afternoon in 2004 I sat with Julia Rodríguez in her small living room in a sunken "English basement" in Pilsen, listening to her stories about growing up in rural Texas and her life in Chicago. It was our first meeting. Almost all of my oral histories had been conducted in English. But as we began the process, Julia confided that she would prefer to tell me about her life in Spanish. At age seventy-one, Julia was a lively talker, and I enjoyed her

FIGURE 20. Julia and Rubén Rodríguez (*standing*), Mayor Richard J. Daley (*sitting*), and children from St. Procopius parish, December 1976. Courtesy of Concepción Rodríguez, from the collection of the Rodríguez family. Used by permission.

rural, *tejano* way of speech. After five decades in Chicago, Julia felt much more comfortable in Spanish than in English. This fact ran counter to the expected patterns of immigrant assimilation; moreover, Julia was born and raised in the United States. Her preference for Spanish reflected the all-encompassing Mexican enclave that formed in Pilsen when Julia raised her children, did her shopping, and became a member of St. Procopius. Julia laughed often as she reflected upon her life. I turned off the recorder, and Julia asked me to go into her bedroom: there was something there she wanted to share.

Atop her bed, I found an eight-by-ten glossy black-and-white photo: Julia, her husband, and several children dressed in *folklórico* costumes, with a framed print of the Virgin of Guadalupe, stood around a smiling Mayor Richard J. Daley. The group portrait took place in the mayor's office; the city flag and seal are visible behind them. Clearly, this photo was special to Julia as, prior to my arrival, she had left it to share with me. Given her impoverished childhood picking cotton and just a bare-bones education, this photo expressed an adulthood of stability, respectability, faith, and belonging. Here Julia stands proudly as a Mexican American Catholic with the pinnacle of her adopted city, the mayor, himself a Catholic. With her husband, Rubén, and the parish children, she represented St. Procopius.[64] Two decades earlier she hesitated to attend Mass there ("¡Los polacos como que no!"); in 1976 St. Procopius was home. Chicago had usually been willing to give a chance to Mexicans, fellow Catholics, who, like the Irish, Czechs, Poles, and Lithuanians, also expressed their devotion to the Virgin Mary.

Julia's prized photo, the St. Procopius parishioners with the mayor, was taken in December 1976. In April 1977 the first Via Crucis took over 18th Street. These events differed greatly in tone and message, but both showed the rise of a Chicago católico.

Epilogue

I wanted to go to church to remember my grandmother and to ask God to give me the chance to make my father proud. . . . As soon as we opened the door, I became intoxicated with the smells of incense, melted wax, and flowers. All of a sudden, I was back in Iguala. I was back with my sweet grandmother. We took a seat in a back pew and listened to mass while surrounded by the saints and Christ, wondering if Abuelita Chinta was at church in Iguala at that very moment, looking up at the face of Jesus, as we were doing now.

—Reyna Grande, *The Distance Between Us*

There are fancier churches and richer churches, bigger churches and fuller churches, but what we have in our little parishes here in Pilsen is just as sacred as any other and extra special in its own quiet, stoic, dignified, and almost secret way.
#DelPueblo
#PilsenKid
#Catholic

—Roberto Montaño, post on a now-defunct Facebook group, 2018

JULIA RODRÍGUEZ'S PORTRAIT with the mayor and Pilsen's Via Crucis both expressed a strong Mexican and Catholic identity in 1970s Chicago. Both events were unimaginable in the 1920s, when Elidia Barroso, Ignacio Valle, and other Mexicans first arrived in Chicago. By the start of the twenty-first century, Chicago was the second-largest Mexican metropolis in the United States, home to "a new urban mestizo culture with an identity that spans two nations."[1] This book has highlighted how making Mexican parishes helped generations of immigrants create new homes and identities: first, at St. Francis of Assisi and, in the past half century, at parishes across Pilsen. Mexican people remade more than specific parishes. They transformed entire neighborhoods and have impacted the entire archdiocese, resulting in a Chicago *católico*.

By numbers alone, the surge in the Archdiocese of Chicago's Latino laity is indisputable. Mexican people—together with the Claretian Missionary Fathers and Cordi-Marian Sisters—made the city's initial Latino parishes before World War II. In subsequent decades, parish after parish in innumerable neighborhoods added Spanish-language Mass for the Mexicans, Puerto Ricans, and Cubans who settled nearby. More recently, Guatemalans, Ecuadorans, and their children joined them in the pews. Latino Catholics today are an increasingly diverse mix of national groups and generations.[2] In 2018 *misa en español* was celebrated at 130 parishes (or 38 percent of the 336 that comprise the Archdiocese of Chicago).[3] Driving across the city's southwest side from Marquette Park to Pilsen, I pass miles and miles of neat little bungalows, all of them majority Mexican today. An abundance of Catholic parishes, once dominated by specific European ethnic groups, punctuate the neighborhoods: St. Nicholas of Tolentine, St. Turibius, St. Gall, St. Clare of Montefalco, St. Joseph, Holy Cross, to name just some. The northwest side is similarly speckled with parish after parish offering Spanish Masses.

The growing Latino Catholic population is also a suburban story that parallels Pilsen's transformation decades ago. New Latino residents include people moving from older inner-city neighborhoods such as Pilsen along with newcomers from Michoacán and Zacatecas. In some places, Latinos encountered the elderly founding ethnic groups of postwar parishes and faced uneasy meetings on the streets and in the pews. David Badillo examines Mexican entry into parishes in Melrose Park, Cicero, and Berwyn. There he found that "parishes resisted racial change with incoming African Americans, but they have proved versatile and flexible community institutions for Mexicanos."[4] When I visited Our Lady of Mount Carmel in 2001, this Italian parish already celebrated two Sunday Masses in Spanish and was preparing for its 108th annual *festa*, a well-attended multiday event that features a procession with Our Lady of Mount Carmel that winds its way through the streets of Melrose Park. The parish bulletin included this note: "Están todos invitados para llevar en procesión la imagén de la Virgen de Guadalupe" (All are invited to carry the Virgin of Guadalupe in the procession).[5]

Across the nation, Latinos are becoming a significant force in historically European American parishes. In Grand Rapids, Michigan, St. Francis Xavier Church (established in 1914) bustled at midcentury but was in serious decline by the 1980s, leading to the school's closing. With a priest from Mexico at the helm, the parish began to stabilize and attract Latino parishioners.[6] In 2002 Mexicans with their priest brought the Virgen de los Migrantes, an eight-foot tall, richly colored, wooden statue of Our Lady of Guadalupe designed in Mexico City. The image traveled north on a flat-bed truck for a three-week, eighteen-stop pilgrimage that began in Mexico, crossed the border at El Paso, and continued north along the migrants' historic route to the Great Lakes (including Denver, Iowa, and Chicago). On a sunny and hot September afternoon I joined the festive, almost entirely Mexican crowd that gathered at her penultimate stop at a Wyoming, Michigan, parish. We then accompanied the image on foot to her new home. Grand Rapids police on bikes controlled the procession route, headed by the archbishop of Mexico and the Knights of Columbus, as the faithful sang Guadalupan hymns. From their front porches, African Americans watched the procession with surprise. A young Anglo family in the procession pushed their kids in a stroller; the parents told me that they wanted to support the new people joining their parish. We arrived at the St. Francis Xavier schoolyard. Awaiting the evening outdoor Mass, Mexican American youth from Holland, Michigan, danced as Aztecs and immigrant parents lifted their toddlers to touch the Virgin's robes. Volunteers distributed roses to be placed before the *virgencita*. The schoolyard felt more like Guanajuato or Jalisco than western Michigan.

The parish old-timers stood by and watched the procession's arrival. Shamrocks still adorned the old gym, harking back to a long-ago time when many parishioners' families came from Ireland. Most of them recalled the grand dedication of the current church building when they were children, as well as the installation of a lovely but small Holy Infant of Prague and the school's additions in the 1960s—all prayed for and paid for by their parents' hard-earned donations. That, however, was when the parish was all white. The St. Francis Xavier old guard revealed to me some discomfort with the Mexicans' rejoicing. Would the Mexican priest watch out for them and their family memories? Would they be squeezed out from their own parish? This meeting of two ethnic groups echoed the Pilsen stories from St. Procopius or St. Ann's in the 1960s. Today the Grand Rapids parish is now the Shrine of St. Francis Xavier and Our Lady of Guadalupe: on Sundays, Mass is celebrated once in English and twice in Spanish, one of which is Charismatic.[7] As theologian Hosffman Ospino puts it, "Thanks to Hispanics, in many parts of the country U.S. Catholicism is de facto a bilingual reality." This saga of Latinos reshaping—often revitalizing—parishes plays out all over the United States.[8]

In Chicago the archdiocese aims to include and embrace Mexicans and other Latinos. In 1985 the archdiocese began to publish a monthly paper, *Chicago Católico*, in addition to the biweekly *Catholic New World* (published since the 1890s).[9] Francis Cardinal George joined other Chicago pilgrims to Tepeyac, on the northern edge of Mexico City, in 2000. He became the first

US prelate to celebrate Mass in the basilica there on December 12.[10] The low number of US Latino priests has been a sore point for generations in Chicago. In 2018 the archdiocese claimed 121 active Latino priests, yet 84 percent of them are foreign-born.[11] (The archdiocese only had three Mexican American priests in 2014.) Beyond these clergy the number of Spanish-speaking priests is substantial.[12] Latinos make up 44 percent of the Catholic laity in the archdiocese. Chicago offers a preview of the emerging majority Latino US Catholic Church.[13]

But in Pilsen, with its pioneering and rich tradition of Mexican Catholic life, the mosaic of parishes has diminished. Consider the numbers. In 1977, the Via Crucis's first year, Pilsen had twelve parishes. By 2015 the number had decreased to seven as a result of parish closures and consolidations. As of 2019 just three parishes remain in the entire Pilsen neighborhood: St. Procopius, St. Pius V, and St. Paul.[14] Preceding the most recent closings, parish leaders hustled to preempt their community's demise. At Providence of God, parish stalwarts organized Zumba classes and Latin Oldies nights in the church basement.[15] Former students from Mexican and Lithuanian families attended all-year school reunions: the profits are bound for the church. At St. Adalbert's, parishioners considered renovating its long-vacant convent for use as Airbnb rentals. St. Adalbert's had the further challenge that its towers (185 feet tall), a soaring Pilsen landmark, became structurally unsound. In 2015 the archdiocese had the towers covered in protective scaffolding at significant cost. To "Save the Towers" parish loyalists started a GoFundMe campaign. The archdiocese tried to sell the church to a music school, arguing that at least the magnificent marble sanctuary—built by working-class Polish parishioners a century ago—would be preserved. In 2016 the archdiocese directed the six extant parishes in Pilsen to participate in a reorganization plan. The seemingly bottom-up, collaborative process ended with the archbishop's top-down "decree of suppression" to close St. Ann, Providence of God, and St. Adalbert.[16]

Many people in Pilsen view the string of parish closings as a symptom of gentrification or the "whitening" of their barrio. Home values rise, the population has diversified—Latinos may comprise only 80–85 percent of Pilsen currently, which marks a significant decrease in the past twenty years.[17] 18th Street has emerged as a destination for tourists and hipsters, now seeking black truffle and foie gras fondue and craft cocktails. Many longtime Pilsen residents fear that they are losing the barrio that is home. As one Mexican American member of a three-generation family at St. Procopius posted on her Facebook page in 2017:

CHART 2. Timeline of Pilsen Parishes

Parish	Year established	First Spanish Mass	End
St. Pius ("territorial")	1874	1963	Present
Sacred Heart ("territorial")	1874		1959[1]
St. Adalbert (Polish)	1874	1975	2016
St. Procopius (Bohemian)	1875	1962	Present
St. Paul (German)	1876	c.1975	Present
St. Vitus (Bohemian)	1888	1969–80	
St. Stephen (Slovenian)	1898		1996
St. Michael Archangel (Italian)	1903	c.1980	2003
Providence of God (Lithuanian)	1904	c.1967	2016
St. Joseph (Slovak)	1906		1968[2]
Our Lady of Vilna (Lithuanian)	1906		1985
St. Ann (Polish)	1906	c.1971	2016
Holy Trinity (Croatian)	1915	c.1970	2015

Timeline axis: 1870, 1880, 1890, 1900, 1910, 1920, 1930, 1940, 1950, 1960, 1970, 1980, 1990, 2000, 2010, 2020

Year established

First Spanish Mass

[1] Closed after fire. Merged with Providence of God

[2] Merged with Providence of God

> The Passion of Christ procession starts tomorrow at 9am at Providence of God Church and procession goes down 18th Street to Harrison Park for the Crucifixion ends at St. Adalbert Church. Friends and neighbors please support this Pilsen Neighborhood procession so many things are being taken away from US; our faith, traditions and barrio . . . in the last years they have closed our churches (Holy Trinity closed, St. Adalbert, St. Ann and Providence churches are now worship sites) and closed schools; with the gentrification going on in Pilsen please don't let this beautiful tradition of the Passion of Christ be part of OUR past! It's free and is supported by Nuestra Gente!!!! . . . It is run by volunteers of our local parishes still opened!!! See you all there.[18]

Clearly, for many in Pilsen the notions of home, ethnicity, neighborhood, and faith are intertwined. In an odd twist of demographic fate, it has fallen to Mexican people to fight to preserve the neighborhood and its structures, including the churches built by Lithuanians, Czechs, and Poles.

The Pilsen church closings fit within larger patterns facing US Catholics, whether in the Archdiocese of Boston, Detroit, or New York. Faced with shifting and declining Catholic populations and a diminishing pool of clergy, parish consolidations have been standard policy since the 1980s. I began this research precisely when the news hit of widespread clerical child sexual abuse. I heard many people blame the continuing closings on the legal costs and settlements. John McGreevy, author of *Parish Boundaries: The Catholic Encounter with Race in the Twentieth-Century Urban North*, recently reflected that "the diminishment of the Catholic subculture—is obvious now."[19] In many Latino neighborhoods (and in Latin American–sending countries), the growth of evangelical Protestant churches certainly erodes the number of Latino people who identify as Catholic.[20] One Mexican American parishioner blamed her church's closing on a decline in "family values": she saw fewer people willing to make the church a priority. The explanations for Pilsen's church closings are multiple.

As a historian, I take the long view. A century ago, no one imagined that the tides from Lithuania, Poland, Bohemia, or Croatia would end. A century ago, with just a few hundred Mexican men working in the city's railroad yards, no one could ever imagine that Pilsen would become a 90 percent Mexican neighborhood. The thirteen parishes established before 1915 to harbor nine different ethnic groups—often just blocks apart—were not made for a neighborhood with just one prevailing ethnic group. The Johnson-Reed Act of 1924 severely curtailed immigration from southern and eastern Europe. As a result, by the 1950s Pilsen parish memberships had decreased. Parish closures are an outcome of local ethnic succession, which, in turn, reflects changes in national immigration policies and global patterns. With fewer clergy, aging buildings, decreasing church membership, and archdiocesan budget problems, parish closings have rolled across the city in several waves since 1990.[21] That year Isabel Wilkerson reported on a final Mass in Chicago's Bridgeport neighborhood, where "too many aging, unfilled church buildings . . . had once been virtual village halls for European immigrants but whose worshipers have long since dispersed."[22]

The overarching story of parish closings, however, muffles laypeople's feelings of loss and anger with each closure. When St. Ann's final Mass was announced in June 2018 for three weeks hence, Lisa Almendarez worried about what would happen to the saints, including the Virgin of Guadalupe, introduced by her parents, Lupe and Matías, together with other pioneering Mexican families, in 1970. The final Mass was publicized by word of mouth, Facebook, and TV. The descendants of Polish immigrants, the parish founders, and Mexicans of different generations nearly filled its modest sanctuary on a stifling summer evening. Bishop John Manz delivered the homily in Spanish and English, acknowledging the feelings of sadness that come with closing a parish, akin to the death of a loved one: "A parish is meant to be a living thing." Chicago today, the bishop explained, simply had "menos parroquias, menos sacerdotes" (fewer parishes, fewer priests), adding that "the Cardinal is the one who makes the final decision." He stressed that the church is *people*, not a building.[23] Yet clearly, the building and its spaces did matter, as people, some teary-eyed, recalled sacraments, family events, and repeated prayers carried out in this humble, "almost secret" church, during decades recent and long past.

As the final Mass concluded, people made their way to beloved spaces in the sanctuary. A middle-aged Mexican man went straight to the Virgin of Guadalupe, first kneeling before the stand of votive candles. He moved closer, prostrating himself on the step just below her altar. A middle-aged Polish American woman took a photo of Our Lady of Częstochowa as she explained the devotion to her teenage son. A young couple from Mexico, an infant in tow, made their way to the church's back corner to show their devotion to St. Toribio Romo, protector of immigrants in distress. Many past and current parishioners then went to St. Ann's School for a reception in the gym, where they filled plates with quesadillas, potato salad, *pan dulce*, and chocolate chip cookies. They reminisced about old times at the church and school, and they took pictures with the Sisters of the Holy Family of Nazareth, their former teachers. The next day, parishioners moved the five-foot wooden statue of St. Ann from the main altar, placed her on a decorated litter, and carried their patroness in a procession the half mile to her new sanctuary at St. Paul's.

Even with fewer parishes, the public Mexican devotionalism of Pilsen remains noticeable. As people walk by the outdoor Guadalupe niche at St. Procopius, they cross themselves. At the end of every October, the Guadalupe garden becomes a makeshift cemetery as St. Procopius parishioners engage in a range of Día de los Muertos customs, both inside and outside the church walls. Julia Rodríguez's daughter brings her late mother's personal stash of copal; the priest obliged her request to use it to incense dozens of family-made altars assembled for the occasion.[24] As another summer approaches, parishioners at St. Pius and St. Procopius plan their summer kermés. With *banda* or house music blasting, women (and a few men) will prepare and sell endless plates of tostadas and enchiladas: the very foods that caused turf battles for the first Mexican women in Polish and Czech parishes of yore. Parishioners will block off side streets for the scheduled open-air street Masses, as will St. Agnes of Bohemia, farther west in the Little Village neighborhood.

In recent decades, Chicago has seen striking immigrant-driven expressions of devotion, often beyond the more controlled spaces of a US parish. Since the 1980s *peregrinos* who describe themselves as "muy sanjuaneros" (very devoted to the Virgin of San Juan) walk as a group fifteen miles from suburban Blue Island to St. Procopius, to fulfill *promesas* or simply to demonstrate their devotion. On an August Sunday the group bears their standard of the Virgin across the hot, humid streets of the South Side. As they march up Western Avenue, people in the neighborhoods show "mucho apoyo" (much support) by honking horns, crossing themselves, and offering water. At St. Procopius's door, a priest welcomes the sweaty, worn-out Blue Island pilgrims, sprinkling them with holy water. Many drop to their knees, crawling toward the Virgin. St. Procopius *guadalupanas* offer sandwiches and *aguas frescas* to the pilgrims while also tending to their busy enchilada stand at the kermés taking place outside. The faithful soon take the statue out of the sanctuary on a litter. Led by the parish priest, a procession winds its way down 18th Street and through residential blocks, where people have decorated their yards in blue and white to honor the Virgin. People set off fireworks and launch blue and white balloons, which fly upward; they can be seen from blocks around. The faithful chant, but some lament the lack of *tamborazo* music (a variant of banda).

On the eight evenings preceding the pilgrims' arrival, a novena in the Virgin's honor takes place at St. Procopius. Each night, people in the pews listen as their neighbors' intimate prayers of intention are read aloud (nearly all in Spanish); they call upon the Virgin of San Juan to help deceased family members and to cure the sick. Others thank her for blessings received. Sharing the forty-some intentions links the community together in their personal histories and their shared devotion to the virgencita. While Chicago-area devotees might prefer to go to San Juan de los Lagos in Mexico to complete their *manda*, issues of distance, cost, and in some cases undocumented status make that too difficult. According to Rev. Sean O'Sullivan, SJ, pastor at St. Procopius (2009–16), "San Procopius was made a sanctuary of San Juan de Los Lagos, so it's the same thing. It means the same thing."[25] For over a century, beginning with a lost and overwhelmed Matías Lara in 1918 (see figure 3), Mexicans in Chicago have expressed their faith in the Virgin of San Juan.

Well beyond Pilsen, Mexican devotionalism is evident in Chicago católico: from Waukegan to Blue Island, from Holy Name Cathedral to the western suburbs. The Virgin of Guadalupe appeared to her faithful on a tree in the Far North Side neighborhood of Rogers Park. As Elaine Peña masterfully describes, the cult grew, the faithful fashioned a makeshift chapel, and devotion took place for several years without any clerical leadership. Similarly, an open-air replica of Tepeyac arose in the western suburb of Des Plaines, now the sprawling Santuario de Nuestra Señora de Guadalupe, creating a massive pilgrimage site on December 12 and throughout the year.[26] People visit this Tepeyac in Illinois monthly, often as family groups; they worship, leave bouquet after bouquet of roses, chant the rosary, attend Mass, visit the gift shop, and take family photos in front of the *cerro* (hill). The grotto adjoining the cerro fills with row after row of votive candles, its walls plastered in notes, *trenzas*, graduation photos, and ultrasound images. Some families drive there every week because *la abuela* insists on it. The shrine claims to be one of the world's most popular pilgrimage sites. On the other hand, the suburban sanctuary's draw impacts parishes: some members choose to attend novenas and Misa de Gallo in Des Plaines and neglect the December preparations and events in their local parish.

Devotions, like parishes, continue to evolve. Our Lady of Bistica, long venerated by the Croatians at Holy Trinity Church, processed around Pilsen for the final time in 2015.[27] At St. Pius, the statuette of the Holy Infant of Prague is now flanked by the Santo Niño de Atocha and el Divino Niño, a rapidly growing devotion in the United States with roots in Bogotá. At St. Francis, administered by an Argentine missionary order, the still-majority Mexican parishioners remain devoted to el Nazareno, the Virgin of San Juan, and Our Lady of Guadalupe. In 2016 in the vestibule, I met Amparo, a middle-aged woman from Mexico. She was returning a small Fatima image (with a guide to saying the rosary) that her family took home for the week. (The church has a lending system, encouraging the Fatima devotion.) She reflected, "Es bonito tener la Virgen en la casa" (It's nice to have the Virgin at home). Previously, her family attended St. Callistus and Precious Blood, but both parishes have closed.

In 2017 "las reinas de Jalisco"—Our Lady of Zapopan, Our Lady of the Rosary of Talpa, and Our Lady of San Juan de los Lagos—visited Chicago. In the violence-rattled Back of the Yards neighborhood, St. Joseph Church hosted the queens of Jalisco as part of a Walk for Peace.[28] The historically Polish parish (today trilingual) brought the Virgins from Jalisco, a major sending state to Chicago. As parishioners carried the statues through the streets, the procession drew crowds. This event at St. Joseph marked the surrounding neighborhood as Mexican and Catholic space. It further affirmed the strong transnational allegiances of Mexican people in the United States. Now more than ever, homeland directly impacts worship in Chicago católico.[29] As scholar Peggy Levitt puts it, "American religious life is no longer just American."[30]

Prior to Vatican II, priests generally determined or mediated the addition of Mexican devotions, as seen with Fr. Thomas Matin at St. Francis and Fr. Peter Mizera at St. Procopius. In our times, immigrant Catholics, often working together in a hometown association, drive the creation of new spaces and devotions in the United States and Mexico.[31] The emergence and development of Mexican and Catholic devotional spaces large and small, permanent and passing, might be expected today, given Chicago's great Mexican population.

The making of Mexican parishes started nearly a century ago when a small stream of Catholic immigrants from Mexico, including Elidia Barroso, settled in Chicago. Elidia sought Catholic worship to express her faith, continuing the devotions that surrounded her childhood on *ranchos* and in the city. Participating in the sacraments helped her connect with family left behind in Mexico and Texas, as well as welcoming a new generation in Chicago. Immigrants continue to arrive in Chicago and its suburbs, and they seek churches, in part as *refugio* in a strange city. They also seek churches to remain connected with family across the continent, sharing a devotion to the Virgin of San Juan or "looking up at the face of Jesus" just like a grandparent back home. They share these devotions with their children: the demographic future of the US Catholic Church. The geography and forms of religious life continue to evolve in Chicago. If fewer in number, these enduring parishes certainly continue to anchor community, ethnic identity, and the very present spiritual lives of Mexican people in the United States.

Notes

Introduction

1. *Blessed Agnes Parish 75th Anniversary 1904–1979*, CSAGSI. Blessed Agnes remained largely Czech until 1972. A Spanish-language Mass was added in 1973. The church is now called St. Agnes of Bohemia.

2. Models include McGreevy, *Parish Boundaries*; McMahon, *What Parish Are You From?*; Matovina, *Guadalupe and Her Faithful*.

3. On Chicano scholars' reluctance to address religion, see M. García, *Católicos*, 13, 278; Gutiérrez, "New Turn," 111–13. The first wave of Chicano scholarship on the Midwest exemplified this pattern with its heavy labor studies slant. See Valdés, *Al Norte*; J. García, *Mexicans in the Midwest*; Vargas, *Proletarians of the North*.

4. Sánchez, *Becoming Mexican American*, 165, 11. In fact, a dozen Mexican parishes opened in Los Angeles during the 1920s. Matovina, *Latino Catholicism*, 32.

5. Unnamed author, "With Chicago's New Mexican Church," folder 4, box 134, Burgess Papers, UC.

6. Calls for more cautionary reading include Young, *Mexican Exodus*, 37–38; Espinosa, "History and Theory," 20–22; Sanguino and Tenorio, "Orígenes de una ciudad mexicana."

7. Menchaca, *Mexican Outsiders*, 44.

8. Davalos, "Real Way of Praying," 59; Acuña, *Occupied America*, 203.

9. Gutiérrez, "New Turn," 125; Ruíz, *From Out of the Shadows*, 108.

10. Treviño, *Church in the Barrio*, 13–14, 43.

11. Valerio-Jiménez, Vaquera-Vásquez, and Fox, *Latina/o Midwest Reader*, 2. Recent monographs on Latino Chicago history include Arredondo, *Mexican Chicago*; L. Ramírez, *Chicanas of 18th Street*; Rúa, *Grounded Identidad*; Innis-Jiménez, *Steel Barrio*; Fernandez, *Brown in the Windy City*; Necoechea, *Parentesco, comunidad y clase*; J. Flores, *Mexican Revolution in Chicago*.

12. P. Taylor, *Mexican Labor*, 51; Limón, "*Al Norte*," 47. Anti-Mexican sentiments became more pronounced after 1950 as Chicago's Latino population quickly grew, including new arrivals from Puerto Rico. Fernandez, *Brown in the Windy City*.

13. McGreevy, "American Catholic Century," 4.

14. Exemplary works include Matovina, *Guadalupe and Her Faithful*; M. García, *Católicos*. Badillo, *Latinos and the New Immigrant Church*, provides a comparative view across the nation. Treviño's study of Houston is best on the Church and the Chicano movement. Dissertations that make important contributions include S. González, "'I Was a Stranger'"; Heisser, "Thanks to the Virgin"; Kelliher, "Hispanic Catholics"; McCarthy, "Which Christ Came"; Pitti, "To 'Hear about God.'"

15. On national trends, see Pew Research Center, "How the U.S. Hispanic Population Is Changing," http://www.pewresearch.org/fact-tank/2017/09/18/how-the-u-s-hispanic-population-is-changing/. The surge in Chicago's Latino population was widely reported in 2017. For example, "Latinos Have Become Chicago's Second-Largest Ethnic Group," *Economist*, https://www.economist.com/blogs/democracyinamerica/2017/10/chicaganos-rising.

Chapter 1. Paths to Chicago

1. For the diary's full transcription and translation, see Kanter, "Faith and Family."

2. Ibid., 24, 27.

3. Sánchez, *Becoming Mexican American*, 56.

4. Kanter, "Faith and Family," 25.

5. On female immigrants and fictive kin networks, see Ruíz, *From Out of the Shadows*, 7.

6. Of San Antonio, Jesús Garza reflected, "I like that city because it is pretty and there are many Mexicans. But the wages are very low there and work is very scarce" (Gamio, *Mexican Immigrant*, 18).

7. Sánchez, *Becoming Mexican American*, 31.

8. Kanter, "Faith and Family," 26. Elidia noted beginning at the factory on Holy Monday.

9. Matovina, *Guadalupe and Her Faithful*, 109, 116; Badillo, *Latinos*, 33–37.

10. *Dipo*, a Hispanicized version of "depot," is the diary's only English word.

11. Kanter, *Hijos del Pueblo*.

12. A. Jones, "Conditions Surrounding Mexicans," 41; Gamio, *Mexican Immigrant*, 68–69. Mexicans comprised 77.3 percent of San Antonio's population in 1920.

13. Kanter, "Faith and Family," 26.

14. Ibid., 27.

15. McCarthy, "Which Christ Came," 142, 151, 214; Jirasek and Tortolero, *Mexican Chicago*, 94–96. Just a year earlier this Spanish-language wedding would not have been possible. The church's first Mass for Spanish speakers took place on December 8, 1923.

16. McCarthy, "Which Christ Came," 242–43; Kelliher, "Hispanic Catholics," chap. 2. St. Francis of Assisi celebrated its first Mass for Spanish speakers on January 19, 1926.

17. Journalist John Drury visited Valle's shop in 1930. Folder 552, box 18, John Drury–Marion Neville Papers, NL. Information on Valle's family drawn from 1930 and 1940 censuses.

18. Silvano R. Ramos (1889–1943) was born in Celaya. He performed and recorded in Chicago from 1927 to 1931, including in the light opera *Marina* in 1930. Ramos composed the song "Rancho grande," immortalized in the 1936 film *Allá en el rancho grande*.

19. Jones and Wilson, *Mexican in Chicago*, 7.

20. Sánchez, *Becoming Mexican American*, 177–78. Gamio presented songs from his 1926–27 fieldwork. The phrase "el sistema americano" appears in "Los enganchados," which he heard in Chicago. *Mexican Immigration*, 85–86.

21. Lyrics and translation from P. Taylor, "Songs of the Mexican Migration," 228.

22. Ibid.

23. Anthropologist Robert Redfield interviewed Valle in 1925. Valle joined Carranza's forces and then fought briefly under Obregón. Robert Redfield, April 7 entry, "The Mexicans in Chicago," folder 20, box 57, Redfield Papers, UC. Valle's first child was born in 1920 in DePue, a small railway hub in central Illinois. Obituary of Louis Sosa Valle, *CT*, May 10, 2018.

24. Valle managed the Rialto's busy Mexican department. By 1924 the store had "already built up a business on Mexican records alone." *Presto-Times: The American Music Trade Weekly*, http://presto.arcade-museum.com/PRESTO-1924-2000/PRESTO-1924-2000-25.pdf; http://mtr.arcade-museum.com/MTR-1927-85-5/13/; http://mtr.arcade-museum.com/MTR-1924-79-20/MTR-1924-79-20-10.pdf.

25. Folder 552, box 18, Drury-Neville Papers, NL. Valle promoted the Banda Mexicano de Chicago and the zarzuela (starring Silvano Ramos). Valle often appeared in Chicago's liberal paper *México*. On *México*, see J. Flores, *Mexican Revolution*, 27.

26. Between 1918 and 1922, an average of 137 Mexicans who entered the United States annually gave Illinois as their intended destination. A. Jones, "Conditions Surrounding Mexicans," 30, 33; J. Flores, *Mexican Revolution*, 25.

27. Mexicans comprised almost two-thirds of track laborers in the Southwest, Great Plains, and Midwest between 1880 and 1930. Garcilazo, *Traqueros*, 34; Valdes, *Al Norte*; Mapes, *Sweet Tyranny*. On boxcar life, see Garcilazo, *Traqueros*, chap. 5; Ruíz, *Out of the Shadows*, 10, 22–23.

28. P. Taylor, *Mexican Labor*, 35; Vargas, *Proletarians of the North*, 18; A. Jones, "Conditions Surrounding Mexicans," 33–35.

29. Jirasek and Tortolero, *Mexican Chicago*, 23.

30. Lara eventually went to San Juan de los Lagos to thank the Virgin. His 1918 *retablo* recounts the incident. Durand and Massey, *Miracles on the Border*, 144–45.

31. R. Jones and L. Wilson summarized reports: "In Chicago feuds among Mexicans and Poles are well-known among all social workers" (*Mexican in Chicago*, 19). See also Guglielmo, *White on Arrival*, 47–48.

32. P. Taylor, *Mexican Labor*, 3; A. Jones, "Conditions Surrounding Mexicans," 62.

33. Innis-Jiménez, *Steel Barrio*; Jirasek and Tortolero, *Mexican Chicago*.

34. Berkow, *Maxwell Street*, 289. Grove and Kamedulski, *Chicago's Maxwell Street*.

35. Grove and Kamedulski, *Chicago's Maxwell Street*, 62. A Mexican grocer near Hull House explained that Mexicans not only liked purchasing Mexican goods but also frequented these *tiendas* knowing they "can order in their own language, be understood without repetition, and then exchange a few words of gossip or news" (P. Taylor, *Mexican Labor*, 169).

36. Single men comprised 53.2 percent of Mexican employees at the Chicago-Calumet area's largest employers in 1928. P. Taylor, *Mexican Labor*, 52; 1930 menu, folder 552, box 18, Drury-Neville Papers, NL. On Mexicans and banking, see A. Jones, "Conditions Surrounding Mexicans," 74–75; Innis-Jiménez, *Steel Barrio*, 72–73.

37. Entertainment businesses played a crucial role in a "network of interdependency and mutual support" (Gunckel, *Mexico on Main Street*, 43).

38. Ganz and Strobel, *Pots of Promise*. Anglo-run organizations in the Near West Side consistently ran "fiestas" as fund-raisers, signifying Chicagoans' attraction to exotic Mexico. Ganz, *1933 Chicago World's Fair*, 130–33; McCoyer, "Darkness," 242; Perez, "Color of Youth," 54.

39. Dyja, *Third Coast*, 7.

40. Shanabruch, *Chicago's Catholics*.

41. F. Hinojosa, *Latino Mennonites*, 18–20. The mission became La Iglesia Menonita Mexicana in 1942. On early Mexican Pentecostalism, see D. Ramírez, *Migrating Faith*.

42. Ganz and Strobel, *Pots of Promise*; McCoyer, "Darkness," 126. The website Urban Experience in Chicago: Hull-House and Its Neighborhoods, 1889–1963 offers rich resources. http://hullhouse.uic.edu/hull/urbanexp/contents.htm.

43. The Marcy Center occupied 1335 Newberry Avenue from 1896 to 1930. It focused on outreach to Jews with a kindergarten, vacation Bible school, and mission work. Elizabeth C. Harvey, "Looking Backward," box 7, MNA, UIC; Aldrich, *Open Door*.

44. "Inauguration of a Mexican Social Center," *El Nacional*, October 24, 1931, CFLPS, http://flps.newberry.org/article/5423405_2_0459. On Methodists' collaboration with Mexican liberals at the Centro Social, see J. Flores, *Mexican Revolution*, 34–36.

45. Jirasek and Tortolero, *Mexican Chicago*, 52.

46. *Marcy Messenger*, 1932 newsletter, box 71, MNA, UIC.

47. With shrinking clientele, the Chicago Hebrew Institute (modeled on Hull House) moved to Lawndale in 1926; the Marcy Center likewise moved to Lawndale in 1930, abandoning its building. Grove and Kamedulski, *Maxwell Street*, 51–54; Aldrich, *Open Door*.

48. McCoyer, "Darkness," 119. Mexicans living in the Near West Side faced less violent resistance than in other neighborhoods.

49. Grove and Kamedulski, *Maxwell Street*, 60.

50. Sánchez, *Becoming Mexican American*, 55–57.

51. McCarthy, "Which Christ Came," 118–20, 236. These efforts preceded the founding of Our Lady of Guadalupe Church by a decade. On proselytization efforts at an El Paso Methodist settlement house, see Ruíz, *Out of the Shadows*, 43–44.

52. *Claretians in America*, 11, 17. Following the Mexicans' movements along the railway lines, the Claretians set up a mission church in Dodge City, Kansas, in 1913. The order's Mexican province fled the revolution and relocated in San Antonio in 1914.

53. Kelliher, "Hispanic Catholics," 71–72; *Claretians in America*, 25. Saldívar stressed that "it is not our intention to establish in Chicago a parish-church exclusively for them [Mexicans]." Instead, he proposed that Claretians might serve in "English-Spanish congregations" of special utility to "those of the Spanish race."

54. In 1928 the parish moved to a new Classical Revival building, where it remains today.

55. In one such assault, a Mexican fled his Italian attackers and sought refuge in Ignacio Valle's store. "More Mexicans Attacked," *El Nacional*, May 20, 1931, CFLPS, http://flps.newberry.org/article/5423405_1_0807.

56. Kelliher, "Hispanic Catholics," 97; Shanabruch, *Chicago's Catholics*, 134.

57. McCarthy, "Which Christ Came," 245.

58. Robert Redfield noted that newly arrived Mexican men "wore a clean suit of overalls for Sunday clothes, but later they came to see that wasn't the thing, and wore ordinary clothes" (November 16, 1924, entry, "The Mexicans in Chicago," folder 20, box 57, Redfield Papers, UC). The Sociedad Mutualista was an East Chicago–based Catholic organization. See J. Flores, *Mexican Revolution*, 56–63.

59. "Church of St. Francis D'Assisi—Chicago," June 3, 1928, folder 46, box 11, Paul S. Taylor Collection, Bancroft Library, University of California, Berkeley. I thank Michael Innis-Jiménez for this reference. In 1930 men outnumbered women two to one. Arredondo, *Mexican Chicago*, 28; McCoyer, "Darkness," 72.

60. Saldívar arrived in the United States in 1909. From 1918 to 1928 he served as the provincial of the Claretian order in the United States and Mexico. In this role, Saldívar created seminaries with the goal of forming American vocations. Provincial Bulletin, July 1946, CMA.

61. Shanabruch, *Chicago's Catholics*, 181, 211; Cohen, *Making a New Deal*, 83–86; McCarthy, "Which Christ Came," 243–44; Badillo, "Catholic Church," 252.

62. Kelliher, "Hispanic Catholics," 97.

63. Koenig, *History of Parishes*, 284–85. At its height as a German parish in 1894 St. Francis celebrated 285 baptisms. Baptisms declined to 89 in 1910, to 46 in 1917. Shanabruch, *Chicago's Catholics*, 116; Kelliher, "Hispanic Catholics," 97n48; McCarthy, "Which Christ Came," 240, 246. Mexicans comprised 33 percent of St. Francis students in 1927.

64. McCarthy, "Which Christ Came," 241, 256.

65. United Charities case report of Placida [*sic*] and Severna Gonzales, February 17, 1929, folder 21, box 57, Redfield Papers, UC.

66. On the guadalupanas, see Pitti, "To 'Hear about God,'" 26. I attended a meeting of the Santo Nombre at St. Francis in 2003 where shouts of "¡Viva Cristo Rey!" harked back to Mexico's Cristero rebellion.

67. "Chronicles of St. Francis Church, Chicago," 1939 entries, CMA; "Tour Topics," January 4, 1938, in Clipping File, Ethnic Groups, Mexican, CHM; Pérez interview.

68. Lillian Gregory, "St. Francis of Assisi Church," box 81, Illinois Federal Writers' Project Papers, Illinois State Historical Society Library, Springfield.

69. Parish annual reports, AAC. Continued high revenue from votive candle sales is especially striking in 1930; all other parish revenues dropped.

70. Gamio, *Mexican Immigration*, 4–5.

71. Arredondo, *Mexican Chicago*, 63; Innis-Jiménez, *Steel Barrio*, 4.

72. McCoyer, "Darkness," 110.

73. Matovina, *Latino Catholicism*, 32; S. González, "Interethnic Catholicism." In the 1920s Mexican immigrants acted with dioceses to create Mexican parishes in midwestern cities, including Detroit, Milwaukee, and Toledo.

74. Wright-Rios, *Revolutions*, 89, 130; Taylor, *Shrines*, chap. 6. On religious life in western Mexico, see L. González, *San José de Gracia*; Butler, *Popular Piety*; Murillo, "La Vela Perpetua."

75. After the Barroso family emigrated, Catholic stalwarts erected a statue to Cristo Rey atop El Cubilete, a mountain near Silao. Calles ordered the monument's destruction in 1928.

76. Young, *Mexican Exodus*, 36. On diasporic religion, see Tweed, *Our Lady*, 138–42.

77. J. Flores, *Mexican Revolution*.

78. Matovina, *Guadalupe and Her Faithful*; Badillo, *Latinos*; Perales, *Smeltertown*; Treviño, *Church in the Barrio*; Young, *Mexican Exodus*.

Chapter 2. *La catedral mexicana*

1. The *Chicago Tribune* described Guízar as a "dream caballero" who "when he sings he is the personification of all the gay romance of Mexico . . . all that is strong and great and good to look upon in our colorful neighbor to the south" (March 14, 1943). The title song for Guízar's 1936 movie *Allá en el rancho grande* was written by Silvano Ramos. Guízar joined the parade of stars on WGN television's first broadcast in 1948. Rafael Guízar y Valencia, bishop of Veracruz, was Tito's uncle; he was canonized in 2006.

2. *SFC*, January 1946.

3. In Chicago Fr. Thomas Matin (born Matischok) was known as Father Thomas or padre Tomás. He signed letters to the Chancery as Thomas Matin. When discussing his work in Chicago, I will generally follow this preference.

4. SSF, 1945–46. Some grades reconvened in the rectory, others in the Boys' Club a block away.

5. SSF, August 18, 1946. Folkloric dress helped foster a positive display of Mexicanness in Chicago. McCoyer, "Darkness," 203–4.

6. P. J. Miranda, undated report [ca. 1956], folder 10, box 88, CAP, CHM; Father George Ruffalo, CMF, personal communication, May 25, 2001.

7. Innis-Jiménez, *Steel Barrio*, 148–49; McCoyer, "Darkness," 194–95; Bada, *Mexican Hometown Associations*, 15. Reardon, "Americanization of the Lunas," discusses multiple branches of a Chicago family during the Depression. On the repatriation figures nationally, see Balderrama and Rodríguez, *Decade of Betrayal*, 150–51.

8. S. Lopez, *El Poche*, 31–32; Cohen, *Making a New Deal*, 221.

9. McCoyer, "Darkness," 228. The Century of Progress Fair also created popular positive images of Mexicans, especially females.

10. *Jane Addams News*, January 7, 1939, December, 15, 1939, folder 2, box 6, WSCC.

11. Folder 6, box 14, WSCC. *CT*, May 27, 1938, featured Dante's multiethnic adult students.

12. Folder 6, box 14, WSCC.

13. Frank X. Paz estimated that the railroads employed up to two thousand Mexican American men. "Mexican-Americans in Chicago," 1948, folder 4, box 147, WCMC; advertisement, *ABC*, December 21, 1946. Marshall Field & Co. also advertised for busboys and dishwashers.

14. Scholarship on the Bracero Program includes D. Cohen, *Braceros*; L. Flores, *Grounds for Dreaming*; Loza, *Defiant Braceros*; and Rosas, *Abrazando el Espíritu*. Amezcua highlights the *indocumentados* who found work in wartime Chicago. "Second City Anew," 34–38.

15. All from advertisements in *ABC*, December 21, 1946. Armando Almonte published this Spanish-language newspaper. García, *Luis Leal*, 33.

16. "Smaller Firms Thrive with Loyalty, Quality Tortillas Became 'a Miracle' for an Immigrant," *CT*, May 6, 1993. El Milagro has become a multistate business.

17. *ABC*, December 21, 1946. A report from the 1950s stressed that even Jewish-owned stores displayed Spanish signage. "Mexicans in the Chicago Area" [undated report, likely 1957], folder 190, box 12, IAF. The 1940 census lists Ignacio Valle as "merchant of retail food store."

18. Amezcua, "Second City Anew," 95.

19. The Globe, located at Blue Island and Roosevelt, occupied the old Glickman's Palace Theatre, a Yiddish-language theater that operated from 1918 to 1931.

20. M. García, *Luis Leal*, 23.

21. F. Hinojosa, *Latino Mennonites*, 18–20, 23–24; Felter, "Social Adaptations," 43–44. Some *menonitas* formerly attended the Pentecostal church. Two dozen Mexicans worshipped at St. Mark's Church, held at the Congregationalist-affiliated Firman House and at the First Mexican Baptist Church, part of the Aiken Institute. Felter believed that "the Mexicans in the neighborhood [Near West Side] are not tied as closely to the Catholic church as are those in the parish of Our Lady of Guadalupe [South Chicago]" ("Social Adaptations," 44).

22. Fernandez, *Brown in the Windy City*; Rúa, *Grounded Identidad*.

23. Prieto, *Harvest of Hope*, 66–67, 87.

24. File 77–81, 1948, Miriam R. Tyler Papers, UIC; "Mexicans in the Chicago Area," undated report [likely 1957], folder 190, box 12, IAF.

25. Amezcua, "Second City Anew," 112–16; J. Flores, "Deporting Dissidence"; Hernandez, *All They Will Call You*.

26. Amezcua discusses the Mexican Civic Committee, the Mexican Social Center, and most thoroughly the Mexican American Council. "Second City Anew," 59–64, 69–72, 116–21.

27. Felter, "Social Adaptations," 26; Frank X. Paz, "Mexican-Americans in Chicago,"

1948, p. 22, folder 4, box 147, WCMC; P. J. Miranda, undated report [ca. 1956], folder 10, box 88, CAP. Scholars and students affiliated with the Chicago School of Sociology often emphasized the disorganization of specific ethnic groups or neighborhoods.

28. Jirasek and Tortolero, *Mexican Chicago*, 39, 57; Frank X. Paz, "Mexican-Americans in Chicago," 1948, pp. 14–15, folder 4, box 147, WCMC. The Centro Social Mexicano took over the Vorwaerts Turner Hall, a German athletic and social club, at 2431 W. Roosevelt Road. It became a popular place for club meetings, events, dances, and *quinceañera* and *posadas* parties.

29. Felter, "Social Adaptations"; Frank X. Paz, "Mexican-Americans in Chicago," 1948, folder 4, box 147, WCMC.

30. At the AAG I read dozens of personal letters to Archbishop José Garibí y Rivera from laypeople in Detroit, Houston, Colorado, and California between 1940 and 1964. Few such letters came from Chicago.

31. When Archbishop Garibí visited Chicago, he chose to stay at the St. Francis rectory. His nephew was a member of St. Francis.

32. Matin's 1961 book promoted the "stigmatic" Therese Neumann of Konnersreuth, Germany, whom he first visited in 1928. He reported seeing her "in bed bathed in her own blood, following her suffering Savior . . . bloody tears trickled unceasingly from her eyes" (*Mystery of Konnersreuth*, 12–13). On the "culture of suffering" among US Catholics, see Orsi, *Between Heaven and Earth*, 22.

33. Religious Communication Men Claretian, folder 2, box 2, RG06, correspondence box A765, Archives of the St. Louis Archdiocese. Daniel Gonzales generously shared this note.

34. Thomas Matin, St. Francis Xavier Church, El Paso, to Claretian Provincial, Los Angeles [undated, among 1943 correspondence], and Thomas Matin, St. Francis Xavier Church, El Paso, to Apostolic Delegate, Washington, D.C., May 26, 1944, CMA. Matin wanted to serve as a US Army chaplain, partly to escape disagreements with his Claretian superiors and to allow him to leave the "Mexican environment in which I am stuck [*metido*] ten years already." He wanted to improve his English before returning to his German province but worried that he would not achieve this goal as long as he remained in El Paso. Matin's German roots may have blocked his plan to serve as military chaplain. In 1944 he sought the Apostolic Delegation's permission to leave the US Claretians altogether, claiming in part that he could not work with the Spaniards of his current province.

35. Expediente 1953–6, caja 3, Gobierno: Otras Diócesis: Estados Unidos: Varias: 1953–58, AAG. By 1954, for example, he described his work as "18 hours daily with *los mojados*."

36. File 10, box S–T, Samuel Cardinal Stritch Papers, Chancery Correspondence 1946, AAC. Broadcasts began on April 6, 1946. The cardinal was pleased with the initial broadcast but warned Matin "to keep the talks centered on things which are strictly within the competence of the Church and not give any occasion for gossip."

37. By 1948 the program was renamed *Hora Católica Hispano-Americana*, perhaps reflecting outreach to Puerto Ricans. Rangel had performed at Mexican festivities in the Midwest since the 1930s. Dr. Galindo practiced near St. Francis Church; he was

the president of soccer club Necaxa S.A.C. The radio show netted $671.48 in 1949 and $3,250 in 1956. Parish Annual Reports, AAC.

38. McGreevy, *Parish Boundaries*, esp. chap. 1; Skerrett, "Sacred Space." L. Cohen argues that early radio "promoted ethnic, religious, and working-class affiliations" (*Making a New Deal*, 135).

39. "Mexicans in the Chicago Area" [undated report, likely 1957], appendix D, folder 190, box 12, IAF.

40. St. Francis was the largest Claretian-run parish in the United States. (In 1948 runner-up parishes were Phoenix with ten thousand and two Los Angeles churches with eight thousand souls each.) A Chicago-reared Mexican American priest told me, half jokingly: "Just about any Mexican over a certain age was baptized at St. Francis."

41. Parishes in nearby Pilsen struggled to meet expenses as fees from baptisms and weddings decreased. This decline continued after the war. Kanter, "Making Mexican Parishes"; Pacyga, *Chicago*, 321. On the postwar decline of white urban parishes, see McGreevy, *Parish Boundaries*, chap. 4.

42. An all-male Sociedad de Nuestra Señora de Guadalupe formed. *SFC*, June 1944; SSF, May 18, 1944.

43. Felter, "Social Adaptations," 47.

44. On increased Mass attendance among mid-twentieth-century US Catholics, see Tentler, *Seasons of Grace*, 171, 173, 403–5; O'Toole, *The Faithful*, 115–19; McMahon, *What Parish Are You From?*; Samors and Williams, *Old Chicago Neighborhood*, 40.

45. *SFC*, December 1945; Jaimes interview, May 14, 2002.

46. Dolan, *In Search*, 52; O'Toole, *The Faithful*, 135–36; McMahon, *What Parish Are You From?*, 63–64.

47. "The name of the person for whom the Holy Hour is to be offered, is read over WGES [radio station] on the Hora Azteca" (*SFC*, February 1944). See also SFC August 1945, November 1945; S. Lopez, *El Poche*, 58.

48. Tentler, *Seasons of Grace*, 409–12; McMahon, *What Parish Are You From?*, 61.

49. The Friday noon Mass and novena drew mostly Americans who worked near St. Francis. See *SFC*, April 1944; Kane, "Marian Devotion," 95–97. The largely Irish St. Sabina's held a Mother of Sorrows novena seven times on Fridays. McMahon, *What Parish Are You From?*, 61.

50. *SFC*, 1947.

51. McMahon, *What Parish Are You From?*, 62.

52. L. González, *San José de Gracia*, 50, 111.

53. *SFC*, January 1944; SSF, January 6, 1948, February 22, 1950.

54. SSF, April 1950. On the Living Stations of the Cross at an African American parish, see Neary, *Crossing Parish Boundaries*, 56–58.

55. SSF, May 7, 1950.

56. *SFC*, June 1946.

57. This text comes from a contemporary source, but its essence fits mid-twentieth-century ceremonies. http://www.catholicculture.org/culture/liturgicalyear/prayers/view.cfm?id=1086.

58. Kane, "Marian Devotion," 98.

59. *SFC*, January 1944.

60. McMahon, *What Parish Are You From?*, 64.

61. Parra, also a musician, advertised in the *Crier*; see November 1945. Hernández's funeral Mass was announced in *SFC*, April 1945.

62. *SFC*, February 1944, March 1944. On bracero deaths and burials, see Driscoll, *Tracks North*, 117–18; Rosas, *Abrazando el Espíritu*, 92. Communication of bracero deaths to family in Mexico was often delayed, even obstructed.

63. Prior to 1960, burials of immigrants took place in Chicago. On the growing practice of sending the deceased for interment in Mexico, see Sarah Lopez, *Remittance Landscape*, 238–41.

64. Parish annual reports, AAC. Fr. George Ruffalo, CMF, described St. Francis as "a candle place." Personal communication, May 25, 2001.

65. On votive offerings in Mexico, see W. Taylor, *Shrines & Miraculous Images*, 175.

66. Mrs. Irene Belman, personal communication, August 5, 2001. On immigrant parents' influence on children's devotion, see Heisser, "Thanks to the Virgin," 58. The fiesta de Cristo Rey was celebrated at St. Francis on October 30. *SFC*, January 1944.

67. A small Spanish-language ad in *SFC*, January 1946. In 1956 the parish spent $5,365 to stock its store with religious items; it took in $7,049 in sales. Parish Annual Report, Saint Francis Assisi, 1956, AAC.

68. Expediente 1953–6, caja 3, Gobierno: Otras Diócesis: Estados Unidos: Varias: 1953–58, AAG. The archbishop did not send the statue. The pastor who suceeded Matin seemed uninterested in acquiring the image the following year.

69. Heisser, "Thanks to the Virgin," 5.

70. St. Francis maintained a Perpetual Adoration society since at least 1937. Notice in *El Ideal Mexicano* paper. Sixty people took part in the society in 1941. *Provincial Bulletin of the Province of the United States Claretians* 6, no. 2 (February 1942), CMA. When Matin returned to Los Angeles in the late 1950s, he avidly participated in Perpetual Adoration at La Placita. One layman wrote admiringly of "an elderly priest, Fr. Matin (who never sleeps) at the Old Plaza Mission downtown" (William C. Williams to Fr. Donanzan, St. Peter Church, May 22, 1957, St. Peter Church [Italian] files, ADLA).

71. On Mexicans' devotion to Christ, see Hughes, *Biography of a Mexican Crucifix*; W. Taylor, *Shrines & Miraculous Images*, 64; Goizueta, *Caminemos con Jesús*. Espinosa and García, *Mexican American Religions*, explores the multiplicity of devotions.

72. Vela Perpetua was often the only pious association in Michoacán parishes, and it was common throughout the Bajío, primary sending areas to Chicago. Murillo, "La Vela Perpetua," 96; Chowning, "Catholic Church."

73. *Bulletin of the Province of the United States of America Claretian Missionaries* 7, no. 2–3 (March–April 1949), and 10, no. 5 (May–October 1952), CMA.

74. In 1947 the *guadalupanas* had sixty-eight members at St. Francis. The Archconfraternity of the Immaculate Heart of Mary had only twenty-seven members. *Bulletin of the Province of the United States of America Claretian Missionaries* 7, no. 2–3 (March–April 1949), CMA. Likewise, the Saint Jude devotion, introduced by the

Claretians in 1929 at Our Lady of Guadalupe Church, spread widely throughout the United States but gained limited interest among the parish's Mexican majority. Orsi, *Thank You, Saint Jude*, 83.

75. Father George Ruffalo, CMF, personal communication, May 25, 2001.

76. Various receipts in the CMA from 1950 and 1951 show shipments of Claret relic pictures, medals, and estampitas to St. Francis of Assisi. It is unclear if these were meant for the parish store or if Claretian priests distributed these to parishioners.

77. Amelia Zúñiga, personal communication, June 7, 2015.

78. Castillo interview.

79. Fr. James Tort, CMF, described similar assistance to "Brazeros" at the mission church in Back of the Yards. *Provincial Bulletin of the Province of the United States Claretians* 6, no. 3 (March 1948), CMA.

80. Chancery correspondence, 1949, unprocessed papers, AAC. Ed Kantorwicz brought this document to my attention.

81. Felter considered that St. Francis's active social program was "partly motivated by the presence of Protestant settlements and churches in the area" ("Social Adaptations," 43). Priests at St. Francis sought to establish the social service agency in 1942–43. *Provincial Bulletin of the Province of the United States* 7, no. 2 (February 1943), CMA; folder 6, box 89, CAP. After Saravia returned to Mexico around 1948, the MWC declined and apparently disbanded in the early 1950s.

82. "Mexicans in the Chicago Area" [undated report, ca. 1957], appendix D, folder 190, box 12, IAF.

83. Prieto, *Harvest of Hope*, 64–65. In 1964 Prieto tried to open a child development center in Guadalajara. See "1965—Los Ángeles y Otras," caja 5, Gobierno: Otras Diócesis: Estados Unidos: Varias, AAG.

84. P. J. Miranda, undated report [ca. 1956], folder 10, box 88, CAP.

85. Fernandez, *Brown in the Windy City*, 76. This paralleled policy in New York. Díaz-Stevens, *Oxcart Catholicism*, 99–101.

86. File 675, NWSCC.

87. Diamond, *Mean Streets*, 198, 200–201. Chicago Mexicans exhibited similar tendencies.

88. Mahon interview; "Report on Ministry among Puerto Rican in Chicago," in *¡Presente!*, 115–16. Kelliher, "Hispanic Catholics," offers a good overview of the CCSS and Puerto Rican ministry.

89. Photos of the novena, record group 600, subgroup 605.16, CMA.

90. Rúa, *Grounded Identidad*, 116–20. Social announcements in the magazine *Vida Latina* show that St. Francis was Puerto Ricans' preferred location for weddings through the early 1960s.

91. No other parish claimed more than six hundred attendees. "Work among the Spanish-speaking in the Archdiocese of Chicago" [undated], Albert Cardinal Meyer Papers, AAC.

92. "Spanish Language Training Program," May 25, 1966, CCSS file, John Cardinal Cody Papers, AAC. The archdiocese noted St. Francis's pull, as priests throughout the

city were confounded that "none of the Mexican-Americans living in these parishes are in their church societies or attend Mass there." From a 1955 Catholic Charities report, cited in Kelliher, "Hispanic Catholics," 242.

93. Devotion to the Virgen de la Nube began with her apparition in Azogues, Ecuador, in 1696. Grupo Virgen de la Nube, a lay group at St. Francis, has a Facebook page with over fourteen hundred friends in 2018.

94. Since 2008 St. Francis has been staffed by an Argentine order, Instituto del Verbo Encarnado (IVE).

95. Prieto, *Harvest of Hope*, 67. Of the fifteen social service agencies in the Near West Side utilized by Mexicans in 1945–46, the largest number frequented the Cordi-Marians. "Description of the Near West Side . . . 17 Group Work Agencies" (1949), folder 4, box 92, WCMC.

Chapter 3. Red, White, and Blue and Mexican

1. *SFC*, January 1945, March 1945. I also draw upon the 1943 movie *Guadalcanal Diary*, featuring a Mexican American GI (played by Anthony Quinn), and Richard Tregaskis's book of the same name.

2. Teófilo Arévalo and Lupe Murillo married at St. Francis on July 22, 1945. *SFC*, August 1945.

3. Pvt. Norbert Torres López shared the *Crier* with his sergeant, a Mexican from California. *SFC*, April 1944. Manning details how servicemen "craved their reading. Army newspapers and magazines, such as *Stars and Stripes* and *Yank, the Army Weekly*, were in high demand. When each set of popular domestic magazines arrived, they were snatched up, pored over, and passed on to the next guy" (*When Books Went to War*, 62).

4. *SFC*, March 1945.

5. *SFC*, August 1944. When these boys ("the Cain Gang") bought their first draped suits, "they pledged never to change style until they would all be given tailored made [*sic*] GI drapes." In Chicago, wartime concerns over zoot suits and juvenile delinquency focused on African American youth. Diamond, *Mean Streets*, 138, 142; L. Alvarez, *Power of the Zoot*.

6. St. Justin Martyr, an Irish American parish, produced a newsletter (*Just-In-Passing*) for its members in the service. Frisbie, *Alley in Chicago*, 35.

7. Mario García highlights the emerging leadership, especially political, in the Mexican American generation that surfaced in Texas and the Southwest. In contrast to their immigrant parents, Mexican Americans were urbanized, more educated, and more likely to work in industry. García, *Mexican Americans*, 16. Note that this new generation faced less discrimination in the urban Midwest.

8. L. Cohen, *Making a New Deal*, 145.

9. Jesse Galvan, the *Crier*'s business manager and printer, so explained its launch in the first issue. *SFC*, November 1943; S. Lopez, *El Poche*, 57. The *Crier* had antecedents in two short-lived Mexican American youth papers, *The Comet* and *The Crown*.

10. *SFC*, November 1945.

11. López visited the *Crier* office after his discharge and brought the photo. *SFC*, February 1946. Non-Mexican servicemen from Chicago enjoyed the *Crier*. John W. Gough of Presentation parish wrote, "Your paper is that little bit of Heaven that all Chicago boys treasure" (*SFC*, August 1945).

12. *SFC*, November 1945. The *Crier* referenced *ABC* but wanted a paper that spoke to its generation, such as the prewar *Comet* and *The Crown*.

13. Hull House clipping file, 1940–41, folder 7, box 6, WSCC; Rivera, "Re-inserting Mexican-American Women's Voices," 126–27.

14. Sánchez, *Becoming Mexican American*, 255, 263.

15. These socials offered a welcoming alternative to the USO centers downtown. Los Angeles had Mexican American Señoritas USO. Escobedo, *From Coveralls to Zootsuits*, 117–18.

16. Eleven Mexican Americans were awarded the Congressional Medal of Honor in World War II. Foley, *Mexicans in the Making of America*, 117. On historical debates over Manuel Pérez Jr. and identity in Mexican Chicago, see David Fremon, "Mexican Standoff: What's in a Street Name?," *Chicago Reader*, April 9, 1987.

17. SSF, October 19, 1946; *SFC*, November 1946. Johnny played on the Murrietas baseball team (likely named for Joaquín Murrieta, the Mexican "Robin Hood" of 1850s California).

18. Pupil record cards, St. Francis Assisi School, AAC. Of the twenty-two pupils born elsewhere in the United States, half listed their birthplace as Texas. In 1940 only 10 percent of neighborhood residents had been born in Mexico.

19. Dante School graduation booklet, 1939, folder 5, box 14, WSCC. On negative experiences of some Spanish-speaking students, see Rivera, "Re-inserting Mexican-American Women's Voices," 113–14.

20. Galvan interview.

21. Laura Vasquez, personal communication, July 5, 2004.

22. At San Antonio's majority Mexican Lanier High School, activities "were firmly grounded in the traditions of mainstream American culture" (Noboa, "On the West Side," 83).

23. Pérez interview; Rivera, "Re-inserting Mexican-American Women's Voices," 177.

24. The Sisters of St. Francis had little to do with the Mexican Cordi-Marian Sisters who lived nearby. When fire destroyed the school and damaged their convent in 1946, the sisters sought refuge with the block's few German families. The nuns enjoyed parties with the Friends of St. Francis, European American school alumnae who formed in 1937 to support the sisters and persisted through the 1950s.

25. In 1946 "Miss Lupe, a Mexican lady" taught the kindergarten class. In May 1950 the sisters let a volunteer teacher take "charge of all pupils who just came from Mexico recently." In 1956 early grades were divided into English-speaking and non-English-speaking classes. SSF 1946, 1949, 1956.

26. SSF, November 12, 1943, 1947. At the archdiocesan celebration of the Claretians' centennial as an order, St. Francis School pupils again processed at the cathedral. SSF, October 22, 1949.

27. SSF, December 10, 1950; Neary, *Crossing Parish Boundaries*, 9.

28. Photo, St. Jude Police League, March 7, 1948, record group 700, subgroup 740, accession #2897, CMA.

29. *Chicago Police Newsletter* 2, no. 15 (1961); SSF, 1947. Car rides as remembered in a tribute entry on McPolin's on-line obituary, August 20, 2012.

30. SSF, March 16, 1950.

31. SSF, August 1948. The sisters described Fatima's twenty-four-hour visit, during which "loving clients of Mary paid her homage by reciting the Holy Rosary, singing hymns and touching the statue with religious articles and reverently kissing her image. . . . [I]n spite of terrible heat, a continuous stream of people approached her."

32. SSF, 1946, 1948, 1951.

33. McDannell, *Spirit of Vatican II*, 25.

34. Godínez, "Mexicanidad," 5. The slur ("dirty Mexican") does not typify my findings.

35. For the Our Lady of Guadalupe novena, Father Martin taught pupils Spanish-language songs, which they sang at the novena for nine evenings. SSF, December 3, 1943.

36. SSF, June 12, 1944.

37. *SFC*, March 1946. I did not find any Chicago Mexican American women who donned zoot-suit styles. On this defiant look, see Escobedo, *From Coveralls to Zoot-suits*, 18, 26.

38. *SFC*, November 1944.

39. Such movies "brought Catholics into the mainstream of American culture." McDannell, *Spirit of Vatican II*, 30.

40. *SFC*, June 1945, February 1946. The Girls' Club also held socials to raise money for St. Francis School. The Roller Bowl became Oprah Winfrey's Harpo Studios.

41. The Chicago-wide Mexican beauty queen pageant was in place by 1940. Amezcua, "Second City Anew," 165, 175.

42. McGurn, *Yank*, 117–23.

43. *SFC*, July 1945, September 1945.

44. Foley, *Mexicans in the Making of America*, 75–76.

45. *CT*, August 15, 1945; *SFC*, August 1945.

46. *SFC*, August 1945, September 1945, October 1945.

47. *SFC*, January 1944.

48. The fashion columns covered mainstream trends. In an exception, the *Crier* told of neighborhood girls who admired Emily Zúñiga's white jacket, "embroidered with different designs that came from Mexico" (*SFC*, June 1945). The *rebozo* (Mexican shawl) became a fashion accessory circa 1950. Amezcua, "Second City Anew," 161–64.

49. Escobedo, *From Coveralls to Zootsuits*, 112. On chaperonage, see Perales, *Smeltertown*, 203.

50. *SFC*, November 1946.

51. Mike García quoted in Jiraesk and Tortolero, *Mexican Chicago*, 77.

52. *SFC*, November 1945, February 1946.

53. *SFC*, August 1944, July 1944, December 1944, June 1945. Travel to Mexico was also detailed in *The Broadcast*, the Mexican Civic Committee's youth magazine. Amezcua, "Second City Anew," 89.

54. *SFC*, September 1944, December 1945, July 1944.

55. They married in Mexico, returned to Chicago, and started their family. López, interview. See also Jirasek and Tortolero, *Mexican Chicago*, 45.

56. The Mexican team included Henry Bellagamba, a Monterrey native, who became a popular Spanish-language radio announcer. Jirasek and Tortolero, *Mexican Chicago*, 123.

57. Cisneros, *Woman Hollering Creek*, 13. P. J. Miranda noted the cross-generation attraction to the Spanish-language movies. Undated report [ca. 1956], folder 10, box 88, CAP.

58. *SFC*, November 1946. Likely a reference to the 1945 romantic comedy *Me he de comer esa tuna*. Amezcua notes the popularity of Mexican movies in "Second City Anew," 103, 135.

59. *SFC*, February 1944, May 1944, November 1943, September 1944.

60. The *Crier* used the occasion to award a trophy to local athlete Henry Silva; two Claretian priests took part in the ceremony. *SFC*, January 1945, February 1945, March 1945.

61. *SFC*, January 1945, January 1944, December 1944.

62. When Trio Atotonilco played Chicago's 16th of September festivities, they were billed as "estrellas de la estación radiodifusora XEW de la Ciudad de México" (*SFC*, September 1944).

63. Lyrics to this "Song of the Month" were printed in Spanish and English. *SFC*, June 1944, May 1944.

64. *SFC*, July 1944.

65. Macías, *Mexican American Mojo*, 4.

66. Rivas-Rodriguez, *Legacy Greater Than Words*; Foley, *Mexicans in the Making of America*, chap. 4; Harrison, *Ghosts of Hero Street*; Álvarez Curbelo, "Color of War."

67. *SFC*, May 1944, May 1945.

68. *SFC*, May 1944. This popular phrase translates as "Mexico, stand firm" or "Mexico, don't surrender."

69. Readers were reminded that Roosevelt and Churchill supported religious influence among soldiers. *SFC*, December 1944. Mexican American soldiers also expressed devotion to the Virgin of San Juan de los Lagos, continuing immigrant parents' practices. Heisser, "Thanks to the Virgin," 58.

70. *SFC*, November 1944.

71. *SFC*, January 1944, May 1946. Decades later, Ramon Barba compiled the World War II–era issues of the *St. Francis Crier* into a single volume.

72. *SFC*, November 1944, February 1945. The Honor Roll included two women: Aurelia Valtierra and Nancy Marcione.

73. "Public Schools to Open Tomorrow," *CT*, April 13, 1945.

74. Marling and Wetenhall, *Iwo Jima*, 73, 107, 109.

75. The Soldier Field event featured celebrities including Humphrey Bogart and Lauren Bacall. Samuel Cardinal Stritch addressed the crowd. *CT*, May 20, 1945, May 21, 1945.

76. The "Mighty Seven" also featured John Garcia, then stationed in Europe, and Tino Vasquez, an Army Air Corps radio technician and sergeant. *SFC*, May 1945.

77. *SFC*, June 1945; Jirasek and Tortolero, *Mexican Chicago*, 84.

78. *SFC*, June 1945, November 1945, May 1946, August 1945.

79. "Description of the Near West Side . . . 17 Group Work Agencies" (1949), file 4, box 92, WCMC.

80. SSF, 1948–49; Jaimes interview, May 14, 2002.

81. The parish souvenir album included Stritch's speech in Spanish. "Alocución del eminentísimo Sr. Cardenal Stritch, Arzobispo de Chicago, durante la benedición de nuevo gimnasio mexicano de Chicago, el 1 de agosto de 1948," *St. Francis Assisi School and Gym Dedication Souvenir*, CMA.

82. The West Side Community Center—CYO operated a mile away in 1943–61, but few Mexicans took part in the Italian-dominated programs (closely linked to Our Lady of Pompeii Church). File 77, NWSCC; Sinnott, "West Side Community Center"; "Description of the Near West Side . . . 17 Group Work Agencies" (1949), file 4, box 92, WCMC.

83. P. J. Miranda, undated report [ca. 1956], file 10, box 88, CAP.

84. González interview; Jaimes interview, May 14, 2002.

85. Almendarez interview.

86. Santos interview.

87. Julie Byrne underlines the pleasure and the Catholic identity expressed by female basketball players in *O God of Players*.

88. *SFC*, March 1946. Mexican American girls played on Harrison High's volleyball team. Amezcua, "Second City Anew," 88–89.

89. In *From Coveralls to Zootsuits* Escobedo stresses how World War II, with its challenges to the family and rise in better-paid work, created opportunities for Mexican American women.

90. Pescador, "Héroes del Domingo."

91. Santos interview.

92. Elena Durán interview; quotation from Castillo interview.

93. González interview.

94. Fr. Patrick McPolin, CMF, began the glee club in 1946. *SFC*, October 1946.

95. P. J. Miranda, undated report [ca. 1956], file 10, box 88, CAP.

96. Minutes, Maxwell Street Citizens' Committee, July 16, 1958, file 4, box 92, WCMC; Diamond, *Mean Streets*, 211–14.

97. File 1, box 111, CAP.

98. Santos interview.

99. Diamond, *Mean Streets*, 121; Fernandez, *Brown in the Windy City*, 100. Chicago's black population increased by 77 percent in the 1940s.

100. "Mexicans in the Chicago Area" [undated report, likely 1957], appendix C, file 190, box 12, IAF.

101. Almendarez interview. On the staying power of positive memories, see Perales, *Smeltertown*, 259.

102. Eastwood, *Near West Side Stories*, 222.

103. On a national level, by law Mexicans were deemed Caucasian. Yet in many spheres of daily life, as Guglielmo argues, Mexicans were "a truly in-between people, neither black nor white, and truly disadvantaged" ("Fighting for Caucasian Rights," 1216).

104. SSF, March 19, 1945, May 1946. The sisters noted in September 1947 that a ten-day carnival drew "colored people galore."

105. SSF, September 1952. The St. Joseph's Mission School, opened in 1933, "was a part, but a separate part, of the large Jesuit parish of Holy Family" (Hoy, *Good Hearts*, 93).

106. Despite the archdiocesan shift to interracialism in the 1940s, "in the day-to-day affairs of local parish schools, there was little indication that a movement away from segregation and toward integration was under way." The archdiocese mandated an end to racial segregation in 1960. Hoy, *Good Hearts*, 98, 107.

107. *SFC*, December 1944; Diamond, *Mean Streets*, 132. P. J. Miranda describes Mexican boys' "contempt and respect" toward Italians. Undated report [ca. 1956], file 10, box 88, CAP.

108. *SFC*, March 1945.

109. Reindl interview.

110. In 1946 dozens of Mexican families sent their teen sons to Camp Reinberg, a county-run outdoor facility touted as "interracial" that year; it was a postwar experiment bringing black and white children together. The Manuel Pérez Post and the MWC organized this opportunity. Mexican American men (many St. Francis veterans) accompanied the fifty boys as counselors. The boys bunked mainly with other Mexican American boys. *SFC*, September 1946.

111. Fr. Patrick McPolin, CMF, served as the post's chaplain. By 1954 the post operated out of the Mexican Social Center, two miles away.

112. *SFC*, July 1946.

113. Foley, *Mexicans in the Making of America*, 140–43; SSF, September 10, 1954.

114. Fernandez, *Brown in the Windy City*, 54–56; Amezcua, "Second City Anew," 113–15.

115. Rúa, *Grounded Identidad*, 116. On the emergence of a Latino ethnic identity in Chicago, see Padilla, *Latino Ethnic Consciousness*.

116. Robert Loerzel, "Displaced: When the Eisenhower Expressway Moved In, Who Was Forced Out?," https://interactive.wbez.org/curiouscity/eisenhower/.

117. "Report on the Feasibility of Rehabilitation in the Near West Side," 1958, p. 902, file 230, NWSCC.

118. Fernandez, *Brown in the Windy City*, 108. Fernandez masterfully recounts the urban renewal schemes and neighborhood resistance. See also Rosen, *Decision-Making Chicago-Style*.

119. SSF, 1961–62. Cardinal Meyer returned for a Mass in May 1962; he addressed the schoolchildren in Spanish. The SSF Annals did not mention fireworks in other years suggesting that this display was tied to the parish's imminent peril.

120. SSF, 1963–64.

121. Castillo interview.

122. Eastwood, *Near West Side Stories*, 298.

123. Infante headlined a fund-raiser for St. Francis. Jaimes interview, May 14, 2002.

124. As described on the website of University Village Maxwell Street, http://uvmaxwellstreet.com/.

125. Ecuadoreans hosted the fiesta for the Virgen de la Nube in the gym's old basketball court in the mid-2000s.

Chapter 4. Making Parishes Mexican

1. *Chicago Dominican*, November 9, 1947, G.06, DPA; Heisser, "Thanks to the Virgin."

2. Kaspar interview; Kelliher, "Hispanic Catholics," 267. By 1970, 80 percent of St. Pius V School students were Latino.

3. Deck, *Second Wave*, 58; Matovina, *Latino Catholicism*, 50–51.

4. Protestant churches had a limited role in Pilsen.

5. On the Pilsen parishes, see Dahm, *Parish Ministry*, 9–10. Pilsen's national parishes exemplify "Catholicism, Chicago Style." Skerrett, Kantowicz, and Avella, *Catholicism Chicago Style*. On Pilsen's geography, architecture, and history, see National Register of Historic Places, "Pilsen Historic District, Cook County, Illinois" and fuller documentation: https://www.nps.gov/nr/feature/hispanic/2010/pilsen_historic_district.htm.

6. Tentler, *Seasons of Grace*, 403.

7. McGreevy, *Parish Boundaries*, 10.

8. O'Toole, *The Faithful*.

9. Lorraine Bartolozzi, "Community Study of the Lower West Side," folder 11, box 1, LWSCC, CPL; *Wojciechowianin / St. Adalbert's News*, January 1926, archive, PMA; Norbert Blei, "Take Me to Your Leader," *CT*, January 20, 1974.

10. Ehrenhalt, *The Lost City*, 97; Wrobel, *Our Way*, 46.

11. Paul Nemecek, "History of Dvorak Park, Pilsen Neighborhood Chicago," *KORENY* 9, no. 3 (June 2005).

12. On Nemecek's connections to St. Procopius, see Pero, *Chicago's Pilsen Neighborhood*, 74–75.

13. Gertrude Ray, *Howell Neighborhood House: Its Forty Years, 1905–1945* (Dubuque, IA: Telegraph Herald Publishers), folder 270, box 39, BHNC, UIC; Sternstein, *Czechs of Chicagoland*, 23.

14. Howell House hosted the Czech-language comedic play *Mrs. Kutilova Finds a Wife for Her Son. West Side Times*, November 19, 1940, folder 266, box 39, BHNC.

15. Kolin, *Pilsen Snow*, 4.

16. The Catholic Central Union, a national organization, embodied the strong interplay between Catholic and Czech identity. *Catholic Central Union Diamond Jubilee* (1952), CSAGSI; Barton, "Religion and Cultural Change."

17. Laura Brade suggested these translations. Even the younger, Chicago-born and -raised membership of the Immaculate Conception Society included only Czech-surnamed women. "Diamond Jubilee of St. Procopius Parish, Chicago, Ill. / Diamantové Jubileum Osady Sv. Prokopa," Chicago [1950], SPAA; *St. Procopius Church 1875–2000 125th Anniversary* souvenir book, n.d. The annual meeting of the Zdruzeni Jednot drew one hundred women in 1959. Peter Mizera to Abbot, December 30, 1959, PMP.

18. Rodríguez interview. Linked to anticommunism, the Fatima devotion resonated especially with Eastern European Catholics. Zimdars-Swartz, *Encountering Mary*; Kselman and Avella, "Marian Piety"; Avella, *This Confident Church*, 68.

19. Two-flats (and three-flats) were classic Chicago immigrant housing, especially in early Czech neighborhoods: the owner often occupied one unit, renting out the other to cover the mortgage and create income.

20. "Solemn Re-dedication of St Procopius School," October 18, 1953, SPAA.

21. From the poem "Pilsen Snow," Kolin, *Pilsen Snow*, 14.

22. Czechs and Poles began moving from Pilsen in the 1920s. Pilsen's population dropped from 85,680 in 1920, to 66,198 in 1930, and to 57,905 in 1940. Hoyt Homer, "Rebuilding Old Chicago—The Lower West Side," *Real Estate*, December 6, 1941, folder 15, box 1, LWSCC; Parish annual reports, AAC. Chicago's population has declined since 1950. Pacyga, *Chicago*, 284.

23. "Conferences given to the Sisters," PMP, SPAA; letters from Peter Mizera to Msgr. Casey, Chancery, May 19, 1952, and July 23, 1952, box M–N, Chancery Correspondence, 1952, AAC.

24. On high rates of Polish parochial school enrollment nationally, see McDannell, *Spirit of Vatican II*, 23; Bukowczyk, *History of the Polish Americans*, 72; L. Cohen, *Making a New Deal*, 85.

25. 202 remained in 1974. Parish annual reports, AAC.

26. L. Cohen, *Consumers' Republic*, 73; Bukowczyk, *History of the Polish Americans*, 96–97; Bukowski, *Pictures of Home*, 41. On Chicago Poles' high rates of prewar homeownership, see Roediger, *Working Toward Whiteness*, 158.

27. Stritch quoted in Avella, *This Confident Church*, 75.

28. At St. Pius V the number of families declined from 815 in 1951 to 600 in 1956. Parish annual reports, AAC.

29. Pacyga, *Chicago*, 321. At the Depression's end, Bartolozzi wrote that Pilsen "isn't as desirable a place to live as other parts of the city, [although] it is by no means the

worst area of the city" ("Community Study of the Lower West Side," folder 11, box 1, LWSCC).

30. Relations between Chicago Polish Americans and Polish refugees could be fraught. Bukowczyk, *History of the Polish Americans*, 95. John Guzlowski, who arrived in Chicago's "Polish Triangle" in 1951, writes: "My parents called the older immigrants *Warsavjaki*. . . . The older immigrants tended to treat the DPs like farmers/yokels/hillbillies, and the DPs tended to look on the older immigrants as effete, pretentious, hi-falutin' urbanites. There wasn't a lot of social commerce going on between the two groups" ("DPs in the Polish Triangle, Chicago, 1950s," http://lightning-and-ashes.blogspot.com/2007/09/dps-in-polish-triangle-chicago-1950s.html).

31. Peter Mizera to Abbot, July 1, 1961, PMP. The revival of Czech hymn singing attracted former parishioners. The American priests found Vit a difficult presence, given his insistence on the Czech language; his Mass served very few Pilsen residents. Some Mexican laity found a kindred spirit in the refugee priest. Fitzmaurice interview. Czech Masses ended in 1981. Charles Kolek to Abbot, August 1981, Kolek Papers, SPAA.

32. *Chicago Dominican*, various issues, G.06, DPA; Skerrett, "Documenting the Immigrant Experience."

33. Barrett, *Irish Way*, 101; Roediger and Barrett, "Making New Immigrants," 183; McGreevy, *Parish Boundaries*, 80; Bukowski, *Pictures of Home*, 64.

34. Pacyga, *Chicago*, 189–91, 267–68; L. Cohen, *Making a New Deal*, 29. Both wars sparked nationalist impulses in Czech and Polish communities.

35. Fernandez, *Brown in the Windy City*, 215. On the origins of the phrase "white flight," see Seligman, *Block by Block*, 3–4. Bigott argues that by the 1910s, "while many Catholics remained loyal to ethnic traditions, a larger number [chose] the exit option willingly." In the postwar decades, "the movement of Catholic populations . . . was ubiquitous. It occurred in many older neighborhoods completely unaffected by racial change" ("Form Followed Culture").

36. Peter Mizera to Cardinal Stritch, September 28, 1953, and Peter Mizera to Msgr. Burke, October 20, 1952, box M–N, Chancery Correspondence 1953, AAC; "Conferences given to the Sisters," PMP.

37. When she was a girl Evangelina Skowronski noticed that Father Mizera "didn't like black people. I was shocked . . . that a priest can do something wrong, not to love everyone. He didn't like it when they were starting to move in" (Skowronski interview).

38. Hirsch, *Making the Second Ghetto*; McMahon, *What Parish Are You From?*, chap. 6; Seligman, *Block by Block*; McGreevy, *Parish Boundaries*.

39. Catholic Charities report, cited in Kelliher, "Hispanic Catholics," 37; McGreevy, *Parish Boundaries*, 104–5.

40. Pilsen Neighbors Community Council (PNCC) formed in 1954 to stabilize Pilsen as its residents diversified. In 1957 PNCC estimated that two thousand African Americans and six to seven thousand Mexicans had moved into eastern Pilsen,

home to twenty-five thousand people total. Folder 190, box 12, IAF. A 1966 article on PNCC estimated that just five hundred African Americans lived there. Folder 9, box 38, JEG, UNDA.

41. Cardinal Stritch proposed a committee on Spanish-speaking Catholics in 1955 but mandated that no "national Spanish churches should be set up to care for these people" (folder 12, box 7, Samuel Cardinal Stritch Papers, AAC). These policies were in line with national trends. Badillo, *Latinos*, chap. 4.

42. In the 1940s Chicago's Mexican population climbed from an estimated seven thousand to a conservative count of twenty-four thousand (or as high as thirty-five thousand). Pacyga, *Chicago*, 390; Valdés, *Barrios Norteños*, 137; Frank X. Paz, "Mexican-Americans in Chicago," 1948, file 4, box 147, WCMC; Kelliher, "Hispanic Catholics," 226.

43. Fernandez, *Brown in the Windy City*, 123–24.

44. Jaimes interview, July 9, 2003. Accompanied by her darker-complexioned husband from Mexico, a Bridgeport landlord told them: "I'm sorry, we don't rent to Mexicans."

45. Pérez interview; González interview. Esperanza Godínez attended St. Procopius High School in the 1950s and recalls feeling poor for the first time. "I can remember feeling ashamed when my schoolmates invited me to partake of their after-school snacks. They always seemed to have spending money" (Godinez, "Mexicanidad," 22).

46. González interview. Homer Hoyt, a real estate expert, similarly compared the two neighborhoods. In 1941 he urged partial demolition of the Near West Side. Pilsen, meanwhile, "has the aspect of genteel poverty. Its structures are crowded close together and playgrounds are sadly lacking but the predominately Polish, Czech and Lithuanian national groups living here have sought to preserve a semblance of neatness in their drab surroundings" ("Rebuilding Old Chicago—the Lower West Side," *Real Estate*, December 6, 1941, folder 15, box 1, LWSCC).

47. Rodríguez interview.

48. Seligman, *Block by Block*, 68–69.

49. González interview.

50. Jaimes interview, July 9, 2003. Roediger notes that European immigrant women "insisted on having white curtains," thus stressing cleanliness, respectability, and whiteness. *Working Toward Whiteness*, 190–91. A Pilsen department store owner reported a great decline in screen sales: "The Bohemians had screens in every window. The Spanish keep the windows wide open" (Norbert Blei, "Take Me to Your Leader," *CT*, January 20, 1974).

51. Bethlehem Center's teams included a mix of Spanish- and Slavic-surnamed boys. *West Side Times*, April 5, 1956, CHM; Stern, "Ethnic Identity," 53. Fernandez stresses hostile, racialized encounters in Pilsen. *Brown in the Windy City*, 215–16.

52. Kelliher, "Hispanic Catholics," 250.

53. Rodríguez interview.

54. Concepción Rodríguez reflects that her mother's light complexion and height explained some of why European Americans favored Julia. As she walked down

Miller Street in the mid-1960s, a stranger called out, "Hey, lady! You looking for an apartment?" (personal communication, August 12, 2015).

55. Skowronski interview; Calderón interview; Fernandez, *Brown in the Windy City*, 216–17.

56. "Conferences given to the Sisters," PMP.

57. Skowronski interview. She also noted the nuns' kindness: when her father was unemployed, the nuns bought her First Communion dress.

58. Godínez, "Mexicanidad," 5.

59. Unnamed source in Stern, "Ethnic Identity," 86. When I asked about Lithuanian language at Providence of God School, alumni offered mixed responses. The Sisters of St. Casimir maintained their convent chronicle in Lithuanian language until 1961. Chronicles of Providence of God Convent, Archive, SSC.

60. On area public schools, see R. Alvarez, "Minority Education," 185–86; Fernandez, *Brown in the Windy City*, 223–24.

61. From a 1955 Catholic Charities report cited in Kelliher, "Hispanic Catholics," 242.

62. Haphazard ethnic labeling was common in my interviews. For older Spanish speakers, the default term for all Slavic people was "polacos."

63. Rodríguez interview; Skowronski interview.

64. Zuñiga interview.

65. Announcement for the special Mass, April 9, 1966, *Prensa Libre*. The Infante family placed the announcement.

66. Rodríguez interview.

67. The regular transfers of diocesan clergy stymied their Spanish-language acquisition. Kelliher, "Hispanic Catholics," 134–35, 208–9, 214; Avella, *This Confident Church*, 223–24. With the exception of New York, US diocesan officials only slowly acknowledged the need for Spanish-speaking clergy. Badillo, *Latinos and the New Immigrant Church*, 81; Pitti, "To 'Hear about God'"; Treviño, *Church in the Barrio*, 120.

68. Kaspar interview.

69. Mizera noted that the diocesan clergy only took the brief Berlitz course. Peter Mizera to Abbot, July 1, 1961, PMP.

70. Skowronski interview. Prior to the Latin liturgy's end with Vatican II, parts of Catholic worship did take place in the vernacular. On novenas, see Kane, "Marian Devotion," 97.

71. Chicago-reared Loretta Jaimes commented, "To me, I don't care who they [Mexican immigrants] want, but I want Virgin Mary. I still pray to Virgin Mary, not the Virgin of Guadalupe. I see her as Virgin Mary" (Jaimes interview, July 9, 2003).

72. St. Jude was not well known in the Mexican provinces, nor for Mexicans at St. Pius. Kaspar interview. Benjamin Arredondo discusses the rise of St. Jude devotion in recent decades in Mexico. "San Judas Tadeo, ¿acaso uno de los cinco santos más venerados en México?," October 28, 2017, http://vamonosalbable.blogspot.mx.

73. Márquez interview.

74. Kaspar interview; González interview.

75. Frank Bonilla Jr., personal communication, July 25, 2018. The Bonillas long donated bread to the Mexican Cordi-Marian Sisters.

76. Jaimes interview, July 9, 2003.

77. Ads from *Prensa Libre*, April 9, 1966; Stern, "Ethnic Identity."

78. González interview. PNCC stressed the challenge of youth gangs. 1965 annual report, folder 9, box 38, JEG. Due to increased criminal and gang activity, the Campos family moved out of Pilsen in 1962. Skowronski interview.

79. Photo by Adalberto Barrios, Estudio Azteca Archives, http://americanhistory.si.edu/many-voices-exhibition/creating-community-chicago-and-los-angeles-1900%E2%80%931965/chicago/pilsen.

80. Peter Mizera, letter, July 28, 1960, PMP.

81. A Mexican priest (Reverend Murio) heard confessions the day before. "Conferences given to the Sisters," PMP.

82. Peter Mizera to Father Superior, March 20, 1963, PMP.

83. "Conferences given to the Sisters," 1958, PMP.

84. "Even though we lived right across from St. Procopius, each one of us was baptized at St. Francis of Assisi" (Skowronski interview).

85. "Conferences given to the Sisters," 1959, PMP; Skowronski interview.

86. "Conferences given to the Sisters," 1959, PMP. Clergy nationally complained of Mexicans' irregular sacramental participation, often ascribing this to weak loyalty to the Catholic Church or superstition. Deck, *Second Wave*, 56; Pitti, "To 'Hear about God in Spanish,'" 34–36.

87. Chupungco, "Inculturation of Worship"; Kanter, "Making Mexican Parishes," 36–37.

88. "Conferences given to the Sisters," February 22, 1959, PMP.

89. McGreevy, *Parish Boundaries*, 104–5.

90. Parish annual reports, AAC.

91. "Conferences given to the Sisters," 1963, PMP, emphasis mine.

92. In 1969 school alumni donated nearly $26,000 to St. Procopius. Parish annual reports, AAC.

93. The archdiocese sponsored a summer "course for priests in work with the Spanish-speaking" in 1964. Except for sessions on Cursillo and Los Hermanos de la Familia de Dios, Latino-specific content seems minimal. Folder 16, box 15, JEG.

94. Ehrenhalt argues, "Holy Name societies functioned as little neighborhood fraternities" (*Lost City*, 116–17).

95. "Puros güeros de la clase media." While European American women never joined the *guadalupanas*, they did attend club-sponsored parties. Rodríguez interview. On her Mexican mother's lack of participation at St. Procopius, Evangelina Skowronski commented, "I don't think there were any Spanish ladies there at any of the activities" (Skowronski interview). Eventually, the Ladies' Social Club included

both Czech and Mexican members. *St. Procopius Church 1875–2000 125th Anniversary* souvenir book, 18. At St. Pius, the Rosary & Altar Society included only European American members in the 1960s. Kaspar interview.

96. *A Look at the History of Providence of God* souvenir book, 2000; Chronicles of Providence of God Convent, SSC; "Concerted Action Shuts Down Rowdy Tavern," *West Side Times Lawndale News,* November 25, 1962, folder 11, box 38, JEG.

97. Alex Kaspar, St. Pius's pastor in the late 1960s, stresses that Hispanics and non-Hispanics did not mix, but "their one common thing was the church. They kind of united around that. It was very nice. The carnival, for example, the bingos—it was a good mixture of both involved in all those things" (Kaspar interview). See also McGreevy, *Parish Boundaries*, 105.

98. Rodríguez interview. Kolin evokes the Czech church carnivals "under the Chicago summer stars, eating potato pancakes (resembling large brown Communion hosts)" (*Pilsen Snow*, 4).

99. Fitzmaurice interview.

100. Providence of God had also installed a Guadalupe image by 1962. Kelliher, "Hispanic Catholics," 262.

101. *Souvenir Book, 1874–1974*, G.03, DPA; Kaspar interview; P. Lopez, *Edward O'Brien, Mural Artist*, 29. The Guadalupe shrine netted $9,121 in donations in 1976. St. Pius V parish annual report, AAC.

102. Matovina, *Guadalupe and Her Faithful*, 16.

103. Matovina, *Latino Catholicism*, 50.

104. Burns, "Mexican Catholic Community," 222–24; G. Hinojosa, "Mexican-American Faith Communities," 116–19; Nabhan-Warren, *Cursillo Movement*; Treviño, *Church in the Barrio*, 71–72; Kelliher, "Hispanic Catholics," 196–97. On the Cursillo's gendered nature, see Nabhan-Warren, "'Blooming,'" 112.

105. Rodríguez interview.

106. On Latinos and the permanent diaconate, see Bautista, "Vatos Sagrados."

107. Nabhan-Warren, "'Blooming,'" 115; Matovina, *Latino Catholicism*, 112.

108. Rodríguez interview.

109. *Program, Fortieth Anniversary of Dominican Fathers at St Pius V Church, 1922–62*, G.03, DPA.

110. During their honeymoon with relatives in Jalisco, the couple visited San Juan de los Lagos. They approached the Virgin on their knees, thus fulfilling Matías's mother's *promesa* to the Virgin of San Juan for his protection as a soldier in the Korean War. Matías and Lupe Almendarez, personal communication, August 15, 2016.

111. Koenig, *History of Parishes*, 68–69; Ford, *Soldier Field*, 224–26. At the Millennium Mass, Cardinal Cody sang in Polish.

112. Wrobel, *Our Way*, 118.

113. Seligman, *Block by Block*, 168.

114. Almendarez interview.

115. David Gutiérrez posits that the central leitmotif in Mexican American history is the divide between long-time Mexican residents and the newly arrived. *Walls and*

Mirrors, 6; McCoyer, “Darkness of a Different Color,” 377–78. On the Chicago slur “brazer,” see Ray Salazar, “Holding a Callused Hand,” September 29, 2011, http://www.chicagonow.com/white-rhino/2011/09/holding-a-callused-hand/; L. Ramírez, *Chicanas of 18th Street*, 80.

116. Many Catholic parishes (especially Italian) celebrated the feast day of St. Joseph with a special altar and parish meal, known as the St. Joseph's Table.

117. Lupe may have been reacting to the “dirty Mexican” stereotype. Her anxiety may also reflect Polish American women's obsession with cleanliness. Wrobel, *Our Way*, 46–47.

118. *Lawndale News*, March 13, 1975, CHM.

119. Wrobel describes a similar Polish American parish in which fierce competition raged among parish clubs. *Our Way*, 97.

120. In 1965 the nuns from eleven (of twelve extant) of Pilsen's convents collaborated in the Urban Apostolate of Sisters. Folder 23, box 17, JEG. Monsignor John Egan pushed the Pilsen priests to meet as a group in the mid-1960s. Folder 10, box 38, JEG.

121. Almendarez interview.

122. Kelliher, “Hispanic Catholics,” 254, 259–60; Dahm, *Parish Ministry*, 16; Koenig, *History of Parishes*, 898. Refusal to offer Spanish-language Mass contributed to St. Stephen's closure as a parish in 1996.

123. Kelliher, “Hispanic Catholics,” 261. St. Joseph declined from 738 to 80 souls from 1964 to 1966. Parish annual reports, AAC.

124. Kelliher argues that Mexicans met their “most hostile” reception by Poles at St. Adalbert. “Hispanic Catholics,” 253. African American parents who lived north of Pilsen tried to register their children at St. Adalbert School; the parish priest reportedly asked if the child spoke Polish and turned them away. Kaspar interview. In Detroit “Polish parishes were slower than those of other groups to lose their distinctive ethnic identity” (Tentler, *Seasons of Grace*, 247, see also 512).

125. Wrobel, *Our Way*, 148, 140.

126. Despite St. Vitus parish's strong efforts to include Mexican worship and leadership in the 1970s, the parish closed in 1990. Stark, “Religious Ritual.” At Providence of God, the teaching sisters of St. Casimir took an avant-garde position, collaborating with Mexican families.

127. Seligman, *Block by Block*, 217.

128. Dybek, “The Wake,” in *Childhood and Other Neighborhoods*, 107.

129. Kelliher, “Hispanic Catholics,” 270–80. On changes preceding Vatican II, see Matovina, *Guadalupe and Her Faithful*, chap. 5; Treviño, *Church in the Barrio*, chap. 7; Burns, “Mexican Catholic Community,” 222; Tentler, “Beyond the Margins.”

Chapter 5. Pilsen *Católico*

1. Unless otherwise noted, my description of the 1977 Via Crucis is based on the Almendarez interview; Stark, “Religious Ritual.”

2. Stark, “Religious Ritual,” 250.

3. Ibid., 179, 177. The CTA protest began as a march on 18th Street. It turned violent, resulting in arrests and injuries.

4. Many St. Vitus parishioners had participated in Cursillos, as well as the Latino male group Los Hermanos. Ibid., 183; Kelliher, "Hispanic Catholics," 194–98.

5. Stark, "Religious Ritual," 266, 220.

6. Ibid., 272.

7. Stark remains the best source on the first Via Crucis. For subsequent years, see Davalos, "'Real Way of Praying.'" Davalos conducted fieldwork from 1989 to 1998. Elsewhere in the United States, see Goizueta, *Caminemos con Jesús*, chap. 2; Pitti, "To 'Hear about God,'" 255.

8. Chupungco, "Inculturation of Worship."

9. Lara, *Christian Texts for Aztecs*, 18, 255; Pérez-Rodríguez, "Toward a Hispanic Rite," 75–76.

10. *El manual del Viacrucis Viviente en Pilsen*, 1994 booklet; Matías Almendarez, personal communication, August 15, 2016.

11. St. Francis of Assisi Church had its own costumed Via Crucis by the 1930s. McCarthy, "Which Christ Came," 377; "Folks of Latin Blood Add Fire to Easter Tale," *CT*, March 30, 1947.

12. The parishes that participated in the 1977 Via Crucis were St. Adalbert, St. Ann, Holy Trinity, St. Pius V, St. Procopius, Providence of God, and St. Vitus.

13. Stark, "Religious Ritual," 159.

14. Trexler, *Reliving Golgotha*. The idea for Pilsen's Via Crucis began with a lay deacon at St. Vitus who had witnessed the event in Iztapalapa. Stark, "Religious Ritual," 210.

15. Godínez, "Mexicanidad," 60. As remembered at Godínez's passing in 2010, "Esperanza's bilingual skills were put to good use as she rode in the procession van and led the rosary in English and Spanish. For about 20 years, Esperanza devoted herself for months in advance of Good Friday to recruiting, training and ultimately executing this faith-filled event" (Sr. Alicia Gutierrez, SH, "An Experience of Being in Communion with a Saint," https://societyofhelpers.wordpress.com/2010/01/06/an-experience-of-being-in-communion-with-a-saint/).

16. Protestant churches had a limited role in Pilsen in the 1970s. Stark, "Religious Ritual," 152. Despite Protestantism's rise among Latinos, a survey of 1990s Pilsen found a scant presence. Hurtig, "Hispanic Immigrant Churches," 38.

17. Hispanic people comprised 85 percent of Pilsen's residents in 1977. Stark, "Religious Ritual," 5.

18. Kolin, "Czech Hieroglyphics," in *Pilsen Snow*, 27.

19. Stern, "Ethnic Identity," 31–33. Gwen Stern conducted ethnographic fieldwork in Pilsen from 1970 to 1972.

20. Stern, "Ethnic Identity," 38; Horowitz, *Honor and the American Dream*, 37, 39. Ruth Horowitz conducted fieldwork in Pilsen from 1971 to 1977, with a focus on youth culture.

21. Stern, "Ethnic Identity," 36; Horowitz, *Honor and the American Dream*, 39. The ethnographic documentary *Mi Raza: Portrait of a Family* (Susan Stechnij, 1972) shows Pilsen in these same years.

22. Quoted in L. Ramírez, *Chicanas of 18th Street*, 111.

23. Stern, "Ethnic Identity," 32–33, 91. Horowitz emphasized the influence of a Mediterranean code of honor in discussing gang violence. *Honor and the American Dream*, 22.

24. Horowitz, *Honor and the American Dream*, 34, 36.

25. Stark, "Religious Ritual," 36, 77. On closures by local employers, see Fernandez, *Brown in the Windy City*, 218.

26. Stark, "Religious Ritual," 81; R. Alvarez, "Minority Education," chap. 5; Alanis, "Harrison High School Walkouts," 117.

27. Horwitt, *Let Them Call Me Rebel.*

28. Due to Egan's cajoling, area priests met on a regular basis by 1966. Egan stressed that "involvement of the total Church, and particularly of its clergy, in the total community becomes a much deeper responsibility to all of us" (Egan letter dated April 8, 1966, folder 9, box 38, JEG). See also folder 25, box 38, JEG. Stern notes that Mexicans involved in the PNCC were "slightly older, more 'middle class.'" She mistakenly conflated PNCC with "Community House," her pseudonym for Howell House. "Ethnic Identity," 96–97.

29. See "Chicago Movement Time Line," in L. Ramírez, *Chicanas of 18th Street*, xxi–xxviii.

30. Stern, "Ethnic Identity," 100; Alanis, "Harrison High School Walkouts," 142–43.

31. Mexican-descent people did not universally accept the term "Chicano" in the 1960s and 1970s. L. Ramírez, *Chicanas of 18th Street*, 24, 90. De Genova, *Working the Boundaries*, 3.

32. Quoted in Jackie Serrato, "Ray Patlan: A Pioneer of Pilsen Muralismo," March 24, 2016, http://gozamos.com/2016/03/ray-patlan-a-pioneer-of-pilsen-muralismo/. The original murals appear in Teena Webb's 1974 documentary *Viva la Causa*. Marcos Raya repainted Casa Aztlán in 1977. When Casa Aztlán closed, a real estate developer painted over the murals in 2016. Under pressure from local activists, the developer commissioned a new, third version of the murals in 2017.

33. Yenneli Flores and María Gamboa, in L. Ramírez, *Chicanas of 18th Street*, 29, 86, 90.

34. Robert Stark, interview in *Rudy Lozano*, 109; Magda Ramírez-Castañeda, in L. Ramírez, *Chicanas of 18th Street*, 138–39; Stark, "Religious Ritual," 174–75, 177, 179.

35. Stark, "Religious Ritual," 196, 199–200, 202.

36. *El manual del Viacrucis Viviente en Pilsen*, 1994 booklet; Davalos, "'Real Way of Praying.'"

37. Fr. James Colleran at St. Vitus and Fr. John Harrington at Providence of God stand out as activists. Magda Ramírez-Castañeda, in L. Ramírez, *Chicanas of 18th Street*, 158–59. On initiatives for Latino parishioners at St. Pius since 1980, see Dahm,

Hispanic Ministry. Holy Trinity and St. Adalbert churches barely engaged in Pilsen's social and political ferment. Stark, "Religious Ritual," 155–56.

38. León emphasizes *guadalupanismo* in the Mexican diaspora. *La Llorona's Children*, 99.

39. Pescador, *Crossing Borders*.

40. The Holy Infant of Prague was also venerated at St. Pius. *Chicago Dominican*, various issues, G.06, DPA. St. Vitus had dual side altars dedicated to the Holy Infant of Prague and the Virgin of Guadalupe. Stark, "Religious Ritual," 130.

41. Rodríguez interview.

42. In 2006 multiple claims of child sexual abuse were made against Fitzmaurice, dating from his time at St. Procopius. On the settlement of claims by the archdiocese and the Benedictine order, see the 2009 report prepared for the Archdiocese of Chicago Office on Child Abuse Investigations Review, http://www.archdiocese-chgo.org/departments/ocair/report_111809/PughReport.pdf.

43. On promesas, see Dahm, *Hispanic Ministry*, 189.

44. Fitzmaurice interview.

45. Fitzmaurice interview. The Virgin of San Juan de los Lagos, in the town of the same name in Jalisco, is the second most popular pilgrimage site in Mexico. Heisser, "Thanks to the Virgin."

46. *Chicago Catholic*, August 1982; Procession in Honor of the "Virgen de San Juan de Los Lagos," August 29, 1982, EXEC/C0500/947#1, Joseph Cardinal Bernardin Addresses and Talks Collection, AAC. The archbishop's remarks, delivered in Spanish, were preserved in English translation.

47. One (unnamed) church was "reputedly hostile to Mexicans where there is no Spanish mass and a largely Polish parish." Additionally, at two parishes the priests "do not speak, or attempt to speak, Spanish." Stern, "Ethnic Identity," 64.

48. Heart of Chicago was a midcentury real estate designation for this section of Pilsen, which encompassed Our Lady of Vilna (Lithuanian), St. Michael (Italian), St. Stephen (Slovenian), St. Paul (German), and St. Ann (Polish).

49. The American Slovenian Civic Alliance led efforts to create Baraga Place. The city named a play lot on Leavitt for Frederic Baraga, the Slovenian missionary-priest.

50. Koenig, *History of Parishes*, 641. Spanish-language Mass was offered at St. Michael by 1980. Mario Gonzales, personal communication, July 15, 2016.

51. Stern, "Ethnic Identity," 64–65. Similarly, in New York City, the dispersed Puerto Rican population returned to La Milagrosa church. Badillo, *Latinos*, 76–77. Also see Orsi, *Madonna of 115th Street*, 66–67.

52. Carlos Heredia quoted in Alanis, "Harrison High School Walkouts," 142.

53. On the domestic and communal rituals of devotion to the Niño Dios in Mexico, see Zárate, *Celebración de la infancia*. In New York, see David Gonzalez, "Figures of an Infant Jesus, Dressed for a Feast Day," *NYT*, January 31, 2011.

54. St. Pius V Church commissioned Jeff Zimmerman's mural in 1999.

55. These stickers were widely posted in Mexico in the 1980s. Mexican blogger

Aaron Benítez reflects, "Era tan natural encontrar la calcomanía católica al visitar a mis amigos, novias y vecinos que como todo lo cotidiano se convirtió naturalmente en algo invisible" (http://www.aaronbenitez.com/).

56. Davalos, "'Real Way of Praying,'" 55–59.

57. Street Masses began at St. Procopius in 1986 under Fr. Ted O'Keefe's pastorate. Concepción Rodríguez, personal communication, July 12, 2016.

58. Based upon my observations in 2004 and 2016.

59. Orsi, "Everyday Miracles," 6.

60. Raúl Raymundo, quoted in Wilson, *Politics of Latino Faith*, 173. Wilson details the Resurrection Project's roots in liberation theology.

61. *Chicago Católico*, May 1995; announcements, *Chicago Católico*, April 2016. Some were small events, mostly held inside a given church. Following the Pilsen model, the four parishes in Chicago's Little Village neighborhood mounted their own Via Crucis in 2014, occupying the business-lined 26th Street. On commerce in Little Village, see Sandoval-Strausz, "Latino Landscapes."

62. Dahm, *Parish Ministry*, 175–76.

63. "Cupich: True Followers of Christ Have Compassion for the Undocumented," April 3, 2015, http://chicago.cbslocal.com/2015/04/03/cupich-true-followers-of-christ-have-compassion-for-the-undocumented/.

64. The Procopius group delivered the Guadalupe image to Mayor Daley December 12 or 13, a week before his death on December 20, 1976. The photo appeared in the local *West Side Times*.

Epilogue

1. Jirasek and Tortolero, *Mexican Chicago*, 50; Bada, *Mexican Hometown Associations*, 3.

2. On the national origins of Chicago's Latino population, see "Hispanic Population and Origin in Select U.S. Metropolitan Areas, 2014," Pew Research Center, http://www.pewhispanic.org/interactives/hispanic-population-in-select-u-s-metropolitan-areas/; Gutiérrez, "New Turn," 114–15.

3. Data from advertising information page, *Católico*, http://www.catolicoperiodico.com/advertise/RatesSpecs.pdf.

4. Badillo, *Latinos*, 34. On the increase and dispersal of Mexicans in suburban Chicago, see De Genova, *Working the Boundaries*, 119–21; Sarah Lopez, *Remittance Landscape*, 215; Matovina, *Latino Catholicism*, 169. On transnational devotional influences in Aurora, Illinois, see Bada, *Mexican Hometown Associations*, 69–70.

5. In 2018 this historic Italian parish celebrated three Masses in Spanish, one in Italian, and two in English. The organizing committee for the 125th Feast, while majority Italian, included about 20 percent members with Spanish surnames (http://olmcparish.org/). The church now features an image of St. Toribio Romo. Bada, *Mexican Hometown Associations*, 18–19.

6. On Grand Rapids' early Latino community, see D. Fernández, "Becoming Latino."

7. Based on my memories from September 7, 2002, together with the website of St. Francis Xavier and Our Lady of Guadalupe, http://sfxolg.org/. Nearly half of parishes with Hispanic ministry include Catholic Charismatic Renewal. Matovina, *Latino Catholicism*, 113–19.

8. Hosffman Ospino, "Ten Ways Hispanics Are Redefining American Catholicism in the 21st Century," *America*, November 13, 2017; Matovina, *Latino Catholicism*; Sam Quinones, "A Church Is Reborn," *Los Angeles Times*, February 10, 2008; Kirk Semple, "Mexicans Fill Pews, Even as Church Is Slow to Adapt," *NYT*, March 25, 2011. James Rutenbeck's 2009 documentary *Scenes from a Parish* explores demographic change in Lawrence, Massachusetts, and attendant challenges for one parish. See also Barber, *Latino City*.

9. *Chicago Católico* recently shortened its name to *Católico*. In 2006 the archdiocese began Polish-language *Katolik* but has since ceased publication.

10. Teresa Puente, "As Faithful Begin Mexico Pilgrimage, Virgin of Guadalupe Becomes Focus," *CT*, December 10, 2010.

11. Statistics from "Key Demographic, Social, and Religious Statistics for the Archdiocese of Chicago," https://vencuentro.org/wp-content/uploads/2018/03/704-Chicago-EN.pdf. In 1987 the archdiocese established Casa Jesús, a discernment program to support Latin American natives with a clerical vocation in Chicago. Casa Jesús aimed to "generate priests who will effectively evangelize the growing Hispanic population" (according to its now-defunct website). Of some 250 Latin American recruits, 53 were ordained over thirty years. In 2016 Archbishop Cupich shuttered the program. Mary Ann Ahern, "Archbishop Cupich Quietly Suspends Program Recruiting Latinos to Priesthood," *NBC Chicago*, September 19, 2016. https://www.nbcchicago.com/news/local/casa-jesus-chicago-archdiocese-suspension-394027211.html.

12. Dolan, conclusion, in Dolan and Figueroa Deck, *Hispanic Catholic Culture*, 449. On the travails of learning Spanish as a young priest in Chicago, see Enright, *Diary*, 6–11.

13. As reported in 2009. Fr. Claudio Díaz, "Latino Catholics in Chicago; One Church, One Body of Christ," *Catholic Chicago* blog, July 20, 2009, www.archchicago.org/Blog/comments.aspx?postid=21. For an optimistic view of Latino Catholics and the future US church, see Dan Morris-Young, "Fr. Figueroa Deck Says the Latino Catholic 'Sleeping Giant' Is Awakening," *National Catholic Reporter*, March 8, 2018, https://www.ncronline.org/news/parish/fr-figueroa-deck-says-latino-catholic-sleeping-giant-awakening.

14. At the archdiocese's behest, in 2016 the six extant parishes took part in a neighborhood-wide reorganization planning process. The clustering process resulted in the closure of three parishes. On the competitive nature of clustering and the decision-making process, see Seitz, *No Closure*, 7. St. Pius V and St. Procopius retain their grade schools, maintain a shrine on some level, and have long had the external resources of a religious order. St. Paul's survival might be explained by the church's singular architecture.

15. José wrote on Yelp about Providence of God in 2013: "This Church is serene

and prayerful but is also fun because they keep it real by holding Zumba classes for the folks who want to exercise too!"

16. St. Ann and Providence of God initially remained "worship sites" with regular Masses but without a resident priest or on-site rectory. Within two years the archdiocese had closed both churches, except for occasional services. St. Adalbert parishioners continue to fight closure there, and as of 2019 it remains a worship site with Sunday Masses in Spanish and English and a monthly Polish-language Mass.

17. Mauricio Peña, "In Pilsen, Churches Are More Than Sunday Mass—and Their Closures Are 'Devastating,'" *Block Club Chicago*, June 8, 2018, https://blockclubchicago.org/2018/06/08/.

18. Concepción Rodríguez, Facebook post, April 12, 2017.

19. McGreevy, "The Author Responds," *Religion in American History* blog, November 18, 2016, http://usreligion.blogspot.com/2016/11/the-author-responds.html.

20. Pew Research Center, "The Shifting Religious Identity of Latinos in the United States," http://www.pewforum.org/2014/05/07/the-shifting-religious-identity-of-latinos-in-the-united-states/.

21. Seitz, *No Closure*, 87. McGreevy comments, "This process of Catholicism becoming a majority Latino church demands further study. But Latinos are generally less tied to local parish structures and have fewer Catholic schools available for them to attend" ("The Author Responds").

22. Isabel Wilkerson, "Catholic Parish Closings Bring Tears in Chicago," *NYT*, July 9, 1990.

23. Author's notes from final Mass on June 30, 2018.

24. I found no evidence of Day of the Dead observances in Chicago prior to 1970. Sandra Cisneros reflects on the lack of Day of the Dead observance during her Chicago childhood. *House of My Own*, 67. St. Francis–raised Esperanza Godínez learned about the mestizo customs from a public television documentary. Celebration of Day of the Dead began in Detroit in the 1970s. Sommers, *Fiesta, Fe y Cultura*, 37, 43–44. In a more secular spin, Pilsen now hosts a 5k Carrera [Run] de los Muertos to promote community health amid "a traditional Day of the Dead setting."

25. Quoted in Ellen Jane Hirst, "Worshipers Make Local Pilgrimage to Honor Sacred Figure," *CT*, August 8, 2013; León, *La Llorona's Children*, 99, 121.

26. Peña, *Performing Piety*. On Guadalupe apparitions in the contemporary United States, see W. Taylor, *Shrines & Miraculous Images*, 138.

27. Pat Butler, "Holy Trinity Building Closed," *Gazette Chicago*, August 7, 2015, http://www.gazettechicago.com/index/2015/08/holy-trinity-building-closed/.

28. Manya Brachear Pashman, "Believers Hope Statues of Mary from Mexico Can Ease Violence," *CT*, October 7, 2017.

29. One woman commented on St. Joseph's Facebook page: "Es la iglesia donde me gusta ir a misa con mis hijos . . . y ahora muy contenta de ver a la virgen de Talpa . . . Talpa de Allende Jalisco que es el pueblo que me vio creser" (This the church where I like to go to Mass with my children . . . I'm now very happy to see the Virgin of Talpa . . . Talpa de Allende Jalisco is the town where I grew up). Some associations have

brought their hometown priest to Chicago. Bada, *Mexican Hometown Associations*, 18; Smith, *Mexican New York*, chap. 7.

30. Levitt, *God Needs No Passport*, 2.

31. Bada, *Mexican Hometown Associations*, 68–69; Sarah Lopez, *Remittance Landscape*.

Glossary

baile folklórico: Mexican folkloric dance, usually highly choreographed.
botánica: Store specializing in religious items and ethnomedicine.
bracero: Male contract worker from Mexico, part of a binational program (1942–64).
Chancery: Administrative offices of a diocese or archdiocese that handle written correspondence.
charro: Mexican horseman with a specific, often elaborate costume.
Claretian: Member of the Spanish missionary congregation, Sons of the Immaculate Heart of Mary, popularly known as the Claretians. These priests and brothers ministered to migrants and the poor globally.
colonia: Neighborhood or community.
comadre (fem.), *compadre* (masc.): Religious godparent, for example, at baptism linking the child's parents and godparent in a unique relationship; also may refer to close friends.
corrido: Ballad of Mexican or Mexican American origin.
Cristo Rey: Christ the King. The term became the touchstone for committed Mexican Catholics in the 1920s, as Catholics wished to recognize Christ's kingship over the country. Allegiance is often reflected in the cry "¡Viva Cristo Rey!" or "Long live Christ the King!"
Cursillo: Catholic retreat program of lay education and faith building that emphasizes a recommitment to Catholicism; participants are *cursillistas.*
enganchista: Labor recruiter.
escapulario: *See* scapular.
estampita: Holy card that usually depicts a specific saint or holy figure; a prayer for the saint's intercession is printed on the obverse.
guadalupanas: Group of laywomen dedicated to the Virgin of Guadalupe.
Hora Santa: Holy Hour, a devotion consisting of the exposition of the Blessed Sacrament for one hour to allow the faithful to meditate before it, sing hymns, or recite prayers.

iglesia: Church.
kermés (or kermesse): Carnival or fair to benefit a church, often held outdoors.
kolachky: Pastry with Central European origins, often filled with cheese or fruit.
la garra: Chicago's Maxwell Street market; literally, "the claw."
la pulga: Maxwell Street market; literally, "the flea."
la Raza: Literally, "the Race." Term signifying ethno-racial pride, often underlining a mestizo identity, commonly used by Mexicans.
Las Posadas: Reenactments of Mary and Joseph's search for lodging; a multiday ritual before Christmas, often with a procession and parties, usually in the evening from December 16 to 24.
manda: Religious promise, usually to a saint or other holy figure. *See promesa.*
mexicanidad: Mexican identity.
milagro: Literally, "miracle." Small metal charm used in votive offerings; often attached to altars in churches and shrines in Mexico. Many milagros come in the form of a leg, an eye, or a heart to represent an injury or illness.
Misa de Gallo: Literally, "Rooster's Mass," Mass held at dawn that is traditionally part of December 12 festivities for the Virgin of Guadalupe.
misa en español: Spanish-language Mass; before Vatican II, a Mass that included hymns and a homily in Spanish.
mojados: Literally, "wets"; undocumented immigrants.
national parish: A church designated to serve a specific linguistic or ethnic group, often continuing the religious practices of the homeland. In contrast, a territorial parish was English speaking.
Nochebuena: Christmas Eve.
novena: Nine consecutive days of private or public prayer, often dedicated to a specific saint or Marian devotion such as Our Lady of Guadalupe or Our Lady of Fátima.
novio: Fiancé or boyfriend.
padrinos de casamiento: Wedding sponsors of the bride and groom; they may subsidize expenses associated with the nuptials.
paisano: Countryman; fellow immigrant.
peregrino: Pilgrim.
polacos: Literally, "Poles." Commonly used Spanish label for Czechs, Poles, Lithuanians, and other Slavic people.
promesa: Promise to perform a religious act if the Virgin or a saint grants a request. The promise is often made while seeking divine intervention in a time of crisis.
ranchera: Genre of traditional Mexican music.
rebozo: Mexican shawl.
recién llegados: Recently arrived people; new immigrants.
rectory: Residence of the priests in charge of a parish, often adjoining the church.
retablo: Painting traditionally made on tin to demonstrate thanksgiving for divine help; ex-voto.
Santo Nombre: Holy Name Society; national organization of Catholic male laity that fosters devotion and reception of Holy Communion.

scapular: Small cloth necklace worn to show devotion, often to the Virgin Mary, and placing oneself under her protection.
Semana Santa: Holy Week. It opens with Palm Sunday and continues with Holy Thursday, Good Friday, and Easter.
sodality: Pious association often at the parish level, typically with same-sex membership.
sokol: Czech athletic clubs dedicated to fitness, community, and culture.
solos: Male immigrants who are traveling without a wife or family.
Su Majestad: Literally, "Your Majesty." The Host or Holy Communion bread.
tejano, *tejana*: Ethnic Mexican person from Texas.
territorial parish: Parish designated to serve a specific neighborhood, regardless of ethnicity. Services are generally provided in English, in contrast to the national parishes, which are dedicated to a specific linguistic or ethnic group.
tienda: Shop or grocery store usually owned by Spanish-speaking immigrants and often featuring merchandise aimed at Mexican clientele.
tilma: Cloak worn by Juan Diego when the Virgin of Guadalupe appeared to him. The cloth is considered essential to the miraculous story.
traque: Work on the railroad or "track." This term was commonly used by early Mexican immigrants.
trenza: Braided hair, plait.
Ultreya: Literally, "Onward." The *cursillistas*' postretreat meetings.
veladora: Votive candle.
Vela Perpetua: Lay society dedicated to perpetual adoration of the Blessed Sacrament twenty-four hours a day.
Via Crucis: Living Way of the Cross, a Good Friday procession.
Viernes Santo: Good Friday.

Bibliography

Abbreviations

AAC	Joseph Cardinal Bernardin Archives & Records Center, Archdiocese of Chicago
AAG	Archivo Histórico de la Arquidiócesis de Guadalajara
ADLA	Archival Center, Archdiocese of Los Angeles
BHNC	Bethlehem-Howell Neighborhood Center Papers, in UIC
CAP	Chicago Area Project Papers, in CHM
CCSS	Cardinal's Committee on the Spanish Speaking
CFLPS	Chicago Foreign Language Press Survey
CHM	Chicago History Museum
CMA	Claretian Missionaries Archive USA-Canada
CMF	Claretian Missionary Fathers
CPL	Chicago Public Library, Special Collections
CSAGSI	Czech & Slovak American Genealogy Society of Illinois
CT	*Chicago Tribune*
CYO	Catholic Youth Organization
DPA	Dominican Provincial Archives, Province of St. Albert the Great, Chicago
IAF	Industrial Areas Foundation Records, in UIC
JEG	John J. Egan Papers, in UNDA
LWSCC	Lower West Side Community Collection, in CPL
MNA	Marcy-Newberry Association Papers, in UIC
MWC	Mexican Welfare Center
NL	Newberry Library
NWSCC	Near West Side Community Council Papers, in UIC

NYT *New York Times*
PMA Polish Museum of America
PMP Peter Mizera Papers, in SPAA
PNCC Pilsen Neighbors Community Council
SFC *St. Francis Crier*
SSC Sisters of St. Casimir Archive, Chicago
SSF Annals, St. Francis Assisi Mission, Archive of the Sisters of Saint Francis of Mary Immaculate, Joliet, IL
SPAA St. Procopius Abbey Archives, Lisle, IL
UC Special Collections, Regenstein Library, University of Chicago
UIC Special Collections and University Archives, University of Illinois at Chicago
UNDA University of Notre Dame Archives, Notre Dame, IN
WCMC Welfare Council of Metropolitan Chicago Papers, in CHM
WSCC West [Near West] Side Community Collection, in CPL

Interviews

Unless otherwise noted, interviews were conducted by the author.

Almendarez, Lisa, Lupe Almendarez, and Matías Almendarez, July 7, 2003, Chicago, IL
Belman, Irene, May 15, 2002, Lockport, IL
Belmares, Ben, July 10, 2004, Chicago, IL
Cabrera, Alice, and Wally Cabrera, July 15, 2004, Naperville, IL
Calderón, Clemencia, July 16, 2004, Chicago, IL
Castillo, Rubén, May 21, 2002, Chicago, IL
Durán, Elena, May 21, 2002, Chicago, IL
Duran, Jobita, and Frank Duran, May 25, 2002, Chicago, IL
Espinoza, Frances, May 21, 2002, Chicago, IL
Fitzmaurice, Fr. Terence, OSB, July 1, 2003, Lisle, IL
Galvan, Alfred, May 17, 2002, Lombard, IL
González, Grace, July 6, 2003, Chicago, IL
Jaimes, Loretta, May 14, 2002, and July 9, 2003, Chicago, IL
Kaspar, Alex, July 9, 2004, Chicago, IL
López, Ruth, July 8, 2003, Chicago, IL
Mahon, Fr. Leo, interview with Fr. Mark Servillo, July 9, 1999, Museum Oral History Project, AAC
Márquez, Guadalupe, and Livier Márquez, July 9, 2004, Summit, IL
Martínez, Jose L., May 22, 2002, Chicago, IL
McPolin, Fr. Patrick, CMF, November 25, 2002, Rancho Dominguez, CA
Pérez, Blaze, July 4, 2003, Chicago, IL
Reindl, Edward, July 8, 2004, Norridge, IL
Rodríguez, Julia, July 7, 2004, Chicago, IL

Santos, August, July 2, 2003, Chicago, IL
Saucedo, Esperanza, May 23, 2002, Aurora, IL
Skowronski, Evangelina, July 7, 2003, LaGrange Park, IL
Todd, Fr. Richard, CMF, July 2, 2003, Chicago, IL
Valdes, Margarita, May 24, 2002, Chicago, IL
Zuñiga, Amelia, and Vicente Zuñiga, July 13, 2004, Chicago, IL

Published Works

Acuña, Rodolfo. *Occupied America: A History of Chicanos*. 4th ed. New York: Longman, 2000.

Alanis, Jaime. "The Harrison High School Walkouts of 1968: Struggle for Equal Schools and Chicanismo in Chicago." PhD diss., University of Illinois at Urbana-Champaign, 2010.

Aldrich, Rowena Atwood. *An Open Door to the Marcy Center, 1883–1963*. Chicago: Marcy Center Board, 1964.

Alvarez, Luis. *The Power of the Zoot: Youth Culture and Resistance during World War II*. Berkeley: University of California Press, 2008.

Alvarez, René Luis. "Minority Education in the Urban Midwest: Culture, Identity, and Mexican Americans in Chicago, 1910–1977." PhD diss., University of Pennsylvania, 2008.

Álvarez Curbelo, Silvia. "The Color of War: Puerto Rican Soldiers and Discrimination during World War II." In *Beyond the Latino World War II Hero: The Social and Political Legacy of a Generation*, edited by Maggie Rivas-Rodriguez. Austin: University of Texas Press, 2009.

Amezcua, Mike. "The Second City Anew: Mexicans, Urban Culture, and Migration in the Transformation of Chicago, 1940–1965." PhD diss., Yale University, 2011.

Appleby, R. Scott, and Kathleen Sprow Cummings, eds. *Catholics in the American Century: Recasting Narratives of U.S. History*. Ithaca, NY: Cornell University Press, 2012.

Arredondo, Gabriela F. *Mexican Chicago: Race, Identity, and Nation, 1916–39*. Urbana: University of Illinois Press, 2008.

Avella, Steven M. *This Confident Church: Catholic Leadership and Life in Chicago, 1940–1965*. Notre Dame, IN: University of Notre Dame Press, 1992.

Bada, Xóchitl. *Mexican Hometown Associations in Chicago: From Local to Transnational Civic Engagement*. New Brunswick, NJ: Rutgers University Press, 2014.

Badillo, David. "The Catholic Church and the Making of Mexican-American Parish Communities in the Midwest." In *Mexican Americans and the Catholic Church 1900–1965*, edited by Jay P. Dolan and Gilberto M. Hinojosa. Notre Dame, IN: University of Notre Dame Press, 1994.

———. *Latinos and the New Immigrant Church*. Baltimore, MD: Johns Hopkins University Press, 2006.

Balderrama, Francisco E., and Raymond Rodríguez. *Decade of Betrayal: Mexican Repatriation in the 1930s*. Rev. ed. Albuquerque: University of New Mexico Press, 2006.

Barber, Llana. *Latino City: Immigration and Urban Crisis in Lawrence, Massachusetts, 1945–2000*. Chapel Hill: University of North Carolina Press, 2017.

Barrett, James R. *The Irish Way: Becoming American in the Multiethnic City*. New York: Penguin Press, 2012.

Barton, Josef J. "Religion and Cultural Change in Czech Immigrant Communities, 1850–1920." In *Immigrants and Religion in Urban America*, edited by Randall M. Miller and Thomas D. Marzik. Philadelphia: Temple University Press, 1977.

Bautista, Adrian A. "Vatos Sagrados: Exploring Northern Ohio's Religious Borderlands." PhD diss., Bowling Green State University, 2013.

Berkow, Ira. *Maxwell Street: Survival in a Bazaar*. Garden City, NY: Doubleday, 1977.

Bigott, Joseph. "Form Followed Culture: Roman Catholic Parish Architecture in Chicagoland, 1900–1970." Paper presented at the American Historical Association, Chicago, January 5–8, 2012.

Bukowczyk, John J. *A History of the Polish Americans*. New Brunswick, NJ: Transaction Publishers, 2008.

Bukowski, Douglas. *Pictures of Home: A Memoir of Family and City*. Chicago: Ivan R. Dee, 2004.

Burns, Jeffrey M. "The Mexican Catholic Community in California." In *Mexican Americans and the Catholic Church, 1900–1964*, edited by Jay P. Dolan and Gilberto M. Hinojosa. Notre Dame, IN: University of Notre Dame Press, 1994.

Butler, Matthew. *Popular Piety and Political Identity in Mexico's Cristero Rebellion: Michoacán, 1927–29*. New York: Oxford University Press, 2004.

Byrne, Julie. *O God of Players: The Story of the Immaculata Mighty Macs*. New York: Columbia University Press, 2003.

Chowning, Margaret. "The Catholic Church and the Ladies of the Vela Perpetua: Gender and Devotional Change in Nineteenth-Century Mexico." *Past & Present* 221, no. 1 (November 2013): 197–237.

Chupungco, Anscar J., OSB. "Inculturation of Worship: Forty Years of Progress and Tradition." http://www.valpo.edu/ils/assets/pdfs/chupungco1.pdf 2003.

Cisneros, Sandra. *Caramelo*. New York: Vintage Books, 2002.

———. *A House of My Own: Stories from My Life*. New York: Vintage Books, 2016.

———. *Woman Hollering Creek and Other Stories*. New York: Vintage Books, 1991.

Claretians in America: A Pictorial History 1902–2012. Chicago: Claretian Missionaries U.S., 2015.

Cohen, Deborah. *Braceros: Migrant Citizens and Transnational Subjects in the Postwar United States and Mexico*. Chapel Hill: University of North Carolina Press, 2011.

Cohen, Lizabeth. *A Consumers' Republic: The Politics of Mass Consumption in Postwar America*. New York: Vintage Books, 2003.

———. *Making a New Deal: Industrial Workers in Chicago, 1919–1939*. Cambridge: Cambridge University Press, 1990.

Dahm, Charles W., OP. *Parish Ministry in a Hispanic Community*. Mahwah, NJ: Paulist Press, 2004.

Davalos, Karen Mary. "'The Real Way of Praying': The Via Crucis, *Mexicano* Sacred

Space, and the Architecture of Domination." In *Horizons of the Sacred: Mexican Traditions in U.S. Catholicism*, edited by Timothy Matovina and Gary Riebe-Estrella, SVD. Ithaca, NY: Cornell University Press, 2002.

Deck, Allan Figueroa. *The Second Wave: Hispanic Ministry and the Evangelization of Cultures in the United States*. Mahwah, NJ: Paulist Press, 1989.

DeGenova, Nicholas. *Working the Boundaries: Race, Space, and "Illegality" in Mexican Chicago*. Durham, NC: Duke University Press, 2005.

Diamond, Andrew. *Mean Streets: Chicago Youths and the Everyday Struggle for Empowerment in the Multiracial City, 1908–1969*. Berkeley: University of California Press, 2009.

Díaz-Stevens, Ana María. *Oxcart Catholicism on Fifth Avenue: The Impact of the Puerto Rican Migration upon the Archdiocese of New York*. Notre Dame, IN: University of Notre Dame Press, 1993.

Dobie, J. Frank, ed. *Puro Mexicano*. Austin: Texas Folk-Lore Society, 1935.

Dolan, Jay P. *In Search of an American Catholicism: A History of Religion and Culture in Tension*. New York: Oxford University Press, 2002.

Dolan, Jay P., and Allan Figueroa Deck, SJ, eds. *Hispanic Catholic Culture in the U.S.: Issues and Concerns*. Notre Dame, IN: University of Notre Dame Press, 1994.

Dolan, Jay P., and Gilberto M. Hinojosa, eds. *Mexican Americans and the Catholic Church, 1900–1964*. Notre Dame, IN: University of Notre Dame Press, 1994.

Driscoll, Barbara A. *The Tracks North: The Railroad Bracero Program of World War II*. Austin, TX: CMAS Books, 1999.

Durand, Jorge, and Douglas S. Massey. *Miracles on the Border: Retablos of Mexican Migrants to the United States*. Tucson: University of Arizona Press, 1995.

Dybek, Stuart. *Childhood and Other Neighborhoods*. Chicago: University of Chicago Press, 2003.

Dyja, Thomas. *The Third Coast: When Chicago Built the American Dream*. New York: Penguin, 2014.

Eastwood, Carolyn. *Near West Side Stories: Struggles for Community in Chicago's Maxwell Street Neighborhood*. Chicago: Lake Claremont Press, 2002.

Ehrenhalt, Alan. *The Lost City: Discovering the Forgotten Virtues of Community in the Chicago of the 1950s*. New York: Basic Books, 1995.

Enright, Michael P. *Diary of a Barrio Priest*. Maryknoll, NY: Orbis Books, 1994.

Escobedo, Elizabeth R. *From Coveralls to Zootsuits: The Lives of Mexican American Women on the World War II Home Front*. Chapel Hill: University of North Carolina Press, 2013.

Espinosa, Gastón. "History and Theory in the Study of Mexican American Religions." In *Mexican American Religions: Spirituality, Activism, and Culture*, edited by Gastón Espinosa and Mario T. García. Durham, NC: Duke University Press, 2008.

Espinosa, Gastón, and Mario T. García, eds. *Mexican American Religions: Spirituality, Activism, and Culture*. Durham, NC: Duke University Press, 2008.

Felter, Eunice. "The Social Adaptations of the Mexican Churches in the Chicago Area." MA thesis, University of Chicago, 1941.

Fernández, Delia. "Becoming Latino: Mexican and Puerto Rican Community Formation in Grand Rapids, Michigan, 1926–1964." *Michigan Historical Review* 39, no. 1 (Spring 2013): 71–100.

Fernandez, Lilia. *Brown in the Windy City: Mexicans and Puerto Ricans in Postwar Chicago.* Chicago: University of Chicago Press, 2012.

Flores, John H. "Deporting Dissidence: Examining Transnational Mexican Politics, US Naturalization, and American Unions through the Life of a Mexican Immigrant, 1920–1954." *Aztlán: A Journal of Chicano Studies* 38, no. 1 (2013): 95–123.

———. *The Mexican Revolution in Chicago: Immigration Politics from the Early Twentieth Century to the Cold War.* Urbana: University of Illinois Press, 2018.

Flores, Lori A. *Grounds for Dreaming: Mexican Americans, Mexican Immigrants, and the California Farmworker Movement.* New Haven, CT: Yale University Press, 2016.

Foley, Neil. *Mexicans in the Making of America.* Cambridge, MA: Harvard University Press, 2014.

Foner, Nancy, and George Fredrickson, eds. *Not Just Black and White: Historical and Contemporary Perspectives on Immigration, Race, and Ethnicity in the United States.* New York: Russell Sage, 2004.

Ford, Liam T. A. *Soldier Field: A Stadium and Its City.* Chicago: University of Chicago Press, 2009.

Frisbie, Margery. *An Alley in Chicago: The Life and Legacy of Monsignor John Egan.* Franklin, WI: Sheed and Ward, 2002.

Gamio, Manuel. *The Mexican Immigrant: His Life-Story.* Chicago: University of Chicago Press, 1931.

———. *Mexican Immigration to the United States: A Study of Human Migration and Adjustment.* Chicago: University of Chicago Press, 1930.

Ganz, Cheryl R. *The 1933 Chicago World's Fair: A Century of Progress.* Urbana: University of Illinois Press, 2008.

Ganz, Cheryl R., and Margaret Strobel, eds. *Pots of Promise: Mexicans and Pottery at Hull House, 1920–40.* Urbana: University of Illinois Press, 2004.

García, Juan R. *Mexicans in the Midwest, 1900–1932.* Tucson: University of Arizona Press, 1996.

García, Mario T. *Católicos: Resistance and Affirmation in Chicano Catholic History.* Austin: University of Texas Press, 2010.

———. *Luis Leal: An Auto/biography.* Austin: University of Texas Press, 2000.

———. *Mexican Americans: Leadership, Ideology, & Identity, 1930–1960.* New Haven, CT: Yale University Press, 1989.

Garcilazo, Jeffrey Marcos. *Traqueros: Mexican Railroad Workers in the United States 1870 to 1930.* Denton: University of North Texas Press, 2012.

Godínez, Esperanza Delgado. "Mexicanidad: An Oral History." MA thesis, Catholic Theological Union, 2003.

Goizueta, Roberto S. *Caminemos con Jesús: Toward a Hispanic/Latino Theology of Accompaniment.* Maryknoll, NY: Orbis Books, 1995.

González, Luis. *San José de Gracia: Mexican Village in Transition.* Translated by John Upton. Austin: University of Texas Press, 1974.

González, Sergio M. "Interethnic Catholicism and Transnational Religious Connections: Milwaukee's Mexican Mission Chapel of Our Lady of Guadalupe, 1924–1929." *Journal of American Ethnic History* 36, no. 1 (Fall 2016): 5–30.

———. "'I Was a Stranger and You Welcomed Me': Latino Immigration, Religion, and Community Formation in Milwaukee, 1920–1990." PhD diss., University of Wisconsin, 2018.

Grande, Reyna. *The Distance Between Us: A Memoir*. New York: Atria Books, 2012.

Grove, Lori, and Laura Kamedulski. *Chicago's Maxwell Street*. Chicago: Arcadia, 2002.

Guglielmo, Thomas A. "Fighting for Caucasian Rights: Mexicans, Mexican Americans, and the Transnational Struggle for Civil Rights in World War II Texas." *Journal of American History* 92, no. 4 (2006): 1212–37.

———. *White on Arrival: Italians, Race, Color, and Power in Chicago, 1890–1945*. New York: Oxford University Press, 2003.

Gunckel, Colin. *Mexico on Main Street: Transnational Film Culture in Los Angeles before World War II*. New Brunswick, NJ: Rutgers University Press, 2015.

Gutiérrez, David G. "The New Turn in Chicano/Mexicano History: Integrating Religious Belief and Practice." In *Catholics in the American Century: Recasting Narratives of U.S. History*, edited by R. Scott Appleby and Kathleen Sprow Cummings. Ithaca, NY: Cornell University Press, 2012.

———. *Walls and Mirrors: Mexican Americans, Mexican Immigrants, and the Politics of Ethnicity*. Berkeley: University of California Press, 1995.

Hall, David D., ed. *Lived Religion in America: Toward a History of Practice*. Princeton, NJ: Princeton University Press, 1997.

Harrison, Carlos. *The Ghosts of Hero Street: How One Small Mexican-American Community Gave So Much in World War II and Korea*. New York: Penguin Books, 2014.

Heisser, Christina. "Thanks to the Virgin of San Juan: Migration and Transnational Devotion during the 'Mexican Miracle', 1940–1970." PhD diss., Indiana University, 2012.

Hernandez, Tim Z. *All They Will Call You: The Telling of the Plane Wreck at Los Gatos Canyon*. Tucson: University of Arizona Press, 2017.

Hinojosa, Felipe. *Latino Mennonites: Civil Rights, Faith, and Evangelical Culture*. Baltimore, MD: Johns Hopkins University Press, 2014.

Hinojosa, Gilberto M. "Mexican-American Faith Communities in Texas and the Southwest." In *Mexican Americans and the Catholic Church, 1900–1964*, edited by Jay P. Dolan and Gilberto M. Hinojosa. Notre Dame, IN: University of Notre Dame Press, 1994.

Hirsch, Arnold. *Making the Second Ghetto: Race and Housing in Chicago 1940–1960*. Chicago: University of Chicago Press, 1998.

Horowitz, Ruth. *Honor and the American Dream: Culture and Identity in a Chicano Community*. New Brunswick, NJ: Rutgers University Press, 1983.

Horwitt, Sanford D. *Let Them Call Me Rebel: Saul Alinsky—His Life and Legacy*. New York: Knopf, 1989.

Hoy, Suellen. *Good Hearts: Catholic Sisters in Chicago's Past*. Urbana: University of Illinois Press, 2006.

Hughes, Jennifer Scheper. *Biography of a Mexican Crucifix: Lived Religion and Local Faith from the Conquest to the Present*. New York: Oxford University Press, 2010.

Hurtig, Janise D. "Hispanic Immigrant Churches and the Construction of Ethnicity." In *Public Religion and Urban Transformation: Faith in the City*, edited by Lowell W. Livezey. New York: New York University Press, 2000.

Innis-Jiménez, Michael. *Steel Barrio: The Great Mexican Migration to South Chicago, 1915–1940*. New York: New York University Press, 2013.

Jirasek, Rita Arias, and Carlos Tortolero. *Mexican Chicago*. Chicago: Arcadia, 2001.

Jones, Anita Edgar. "Conditions Surrounding Mexicans in Chicago." PhD diss., University of Chicago, 1928.

Jones, Robert C., and Louis R. Wilson. *The Mexican in Chicago*. Chicago: Chicago Comity Commission of the Chicago Church Federation, 1931.

Kane, Paula M. "Marian Devotion since 1940: Continuity or Casualty?" In *Habits of Devotion: Catholic Religious Practice in Twentieth-Century America*, edited by James M. O'Toole. Ithaca, NY: Cornell University Press, 2004.

Kanter, Deborah. "Faith and Family for Early Mexican Immigrants to Chicago: The Diary of Elidia Barroso." *Diálogo* 16, no. 1 (Spring 2013): 21–34.

———. *Hijos del Pueblo: Gender, Family and Community in Rural Mexico, 1730–1850*. Austin: University of Texas Press, 2009.

———. "Making Mexican Parishes: Ethnic Succession in Chicago Churches, 1947–77." *U.S. Catholic Historian* 30, no. 1 (2012): 35–58.

Kelliher, Thomas G. "Hispanic Catholics and the Archdiocese of Chicago, 1923–1970." PhD diss., University of Notre Dame, 1996.

Koenig, Rev. Harry C. *A History of Parishes of the Archdiocese of Chicago*. Chicago: Archdiocese of Chicago, 1980.

Kolin, Philip C. *Pilsen Snow: Poems*. Georgetown, KY: Finishing Line Press, 2015.

Kselman, Thomas A., and Steven Avella. "Marian Piety and the Cold War in the United States." *Catholic Historical Review* 72 (1986): 403–24.

Lara, Jaime. *Christian Texts for Aztecs: Art and Liturgy in Colonial Mexico*. Notre Dame, IN: University of Notre Dame Press, 2008.

León, Luis D. *La Llorona's Children: Religion, Life, and Death in the U.S.-Mexican Borderlands*. Berkeley: University of California Press, 2004.

Levitt, Peggy. *God Needs No Passport: Immigrants and the Changing Religious Landscape*. New York: New Press, 2007.

Limón, José. "*Al Norte*: Toward Home; Texas, the Midwest, and Mexican American Critical Regionalism." In *The Latina/o Midwest Reader*, edited by Omar Valerio-Jiménez, Santiago Vaquera-Vásquez, and Claire F. Fox. Urbana: University of Illinois Press, 2017.

Livezey, Lowell W., ed. *Public Religion and Urban Transformation: Faith in the City*. New York: New York University Press, 2000.

López, José. "The Liturgical Year and Hispanic Customs." In *Misa, Mesa, y Musa: Liturgy in the U.S. Hispanic Church*, edited by Kenneth G. Davis, OFM. Schiller Park, IL: World Library Publications, 1997.

Lopez, Peter E. *Edward O'Brien, Mural Artist 1910–1975*. Santa Fe, NM: Sunstone Press, 2013.

Lopez, Sarah Lynn. *The Remittance Landscape: Spaces of Migration in Rural Mexico and Urban USA*. Chicago: University of Chicago Press, 2015.

Lopez, Severino, CMF. *El Poche: Memoirs of a Mexican American Padre*. Chicago: Claretian Publications, 2004.

Loza, Mireya. *Defiant Braceros: How Migrant Workers Fought for Racial, Sexual, and Political Freedom*. Chapel Hill: University of North Carolina Press, 2016.

Macías, Anthony. *Mexican American Mojo: Popular Music, Dance, and Urban Culture in Los Angeles, 1935–1968*. Durham, NC: Duke University Press, 2008.

Manning, Molly Guptill. *When Books Went to War: The Stories That Helped Us Win World War II*. Boston: Houghton-Mifflin Harcourt, 2014.

Mapes, Kathleen. *Sweet Tyranny: Migrant Labor, Industrial Agriculture, and Imperial Politics*. Urbana: University of Illinois Press, 2009.

Marling, Karal Ann, and John Wetenhall. *Iwo Jima: Monuments, Memories, and the American Hero*. Cambridge, MA: Harvard University Press, 1991.

Martínez-Serros, Hugo. *The Last Laugh and Other Stories*. Houston, TX: Arte Público Press, 1988.

Matin, Thomas, CMF. *The Mystery of Konnersreuth*. St. Meinrad, IN: Abbey Press, 1961.

Matovina, Timothy. *Guadalupe and Her Faithful: Latino Catholics in San Antonio, from Colonial Origins to the Present*. Baltimore, MD: Johns Hopkins University Press, 2005.

———. *Latino Catholicism: Transformation in America's Largest Church*. Princeton, NJ: Princeton University Press, 2012.

Matovina, Timothy, and Gerald E. Poyo, eds. *¡Presente! U.S. Latino Catholics from Colonial Origins to the Present*. Maryknoll, NY: Orbis Books, 2005.

Matovina, Timothy, and Gary Riebe-Estrella, SVD, eds. *Horizons of the Sacred: Mexican Traditions in U.S. Catholicism*. Ithaca, NY: Cornell University Press, 2002.

McCarthy, Malachy Richard. "Which Christ Came to Chicago: Catholic and Protestant Programs to Evangelize, Socialize and Americanize the Mexican Immigrant, 1900–1940." PhD diss., Loyola University, 2002.

McCoyer, Michael. "Darkness of a Different Color: Mexicans and Racial Formation in Greater Chicago, 1916–1960." PhD diss., Northwestern University, 2007.

McDannell, Colleen. *The Spirit of Vatican II: A History of Catholic Reform in America*. New York: Basic Books, 2011.

McGreevy, John T. "The American Catholic Century." In *Catholics in the American Century: Recasting Narratives of U.S. History*, edited by R. Scott Appleby and Kathleen Sprow Cummings. Ithaca, NY: Cornell University Press, 2012.

———. *Parish Boundaries: The Catholic Encounter with Race in the Twentieth-Century Urban North*. Chicago: University of Chicago Press, 1996.

McGurn, Barrett. *Yank, the Army Weekly: Reporting the Greatest Generation*. Golden, CO: Fulcrum Publishing, 2004.

McMahon, Eileen M. *What Parish Are You From? A Chicago Irish Community & Race Relations*. Lexington: University Press of Kentucky, 1995.

Menchaca, Martha. *The Mexican Outsiders: A Community History of Marginalization and Discrimination in California*. Austin: University of Texas Press, 1995.

Miller, Randall M., and Thomas D. Marzik, eds. *Immigrants and Religion in Urban America*. Philadelphia: Temple University Press, 1977.

Murillo, Luis. "La Vela Perpetua en Michoacán: Fe eucarística, patria chica y poder de mujeres." In *Experiencia religiosa e identidades en América Latina*. San José, Costa Rica: DEI y CEHILA, 2013.

Nabhan-Warren, Kristy. "'Blooming Where We're Planted': Mexican-Descent Catholics Living Out Cursillo de Cristianidad." *U.S. Catholic Historian* 28, no. 4 (Fall 2010): 99–125.

———. *The Cursillo Movement in America: Catholics, Protestants, and Fourth-Day Spirituality*. Chapel Hill: University of North Carolina Press, 2013.

Neary, Timothy B. *Crossing Parish Boundaries: Race, Sports, and Catholic Youth in Chicago, 1914–1954*. Chicago: University of Chicago Press, 2016.

Necoechea Gracia, Gerardo. *Parentesco, comunidad y clase: Mexicanos en Chicago, 1916–1950*. Mexico City: INAH, 2015.

Nemecek, Paul. "History of Dvorak Park, Pilsen Neighborhood Chicago." *KORENY* 9, no. 3 (June 2005): 13–15.

Noboa, Julio. "On the West Side: A Portrait of Lanier High School during World War II." In *Mexican Americans & World War II*, edited by Maggie Rivas-Rodriguez. Austin: University of Texas Press, 2005.

Orsi, Robert Anthony. *Between Heaven and Earth: The Religious Worlds People Make and the Scholars Who Study Them*. Princeton, NJ: Princeton University Press, 2005.

———. "Everyday Miracles: The Study of Lived Religion." In *Lived Religion in America: Toward a History of Practice*, edited by David D. Hall. Princeton, NJ: Princeton University Press, 1997.

———. *The Madonna of 115th Street: Faith and Community in Italian Harlem, 1880–1950*. New Haven, CT: Yale University Press, 1985.

———. *Thank You, St. Jude: Women's Devotion to the Patron Saint of Hopeless Causes*. New Haven, CT: Yale University Press, 1996.

O'Toole, James M. *The Faithful: A History of Catholics in America*. Cambridge, MA: Harvard University Press, 2008.

——— ed. *Habits of Devotion: Catholic Religious Practice in Twentieth-Century America*. Ithaca, NY: Cornell University Press, 2004.

Pacyga, Dominic A. *Chicago: A Biography*. Chicago: University of Chicago Press, 2009.

Padilla, Felix M. *Latino Ethnic Consciousness: The Case of Mexican Americans and Puerto Ricans in Chicago*. Notre Dame, IN: University of Notre Dame Press, 1985.

Peña, Elaine A. *Performing Piety: Making Space Sacred with the Virgin of Guadalupe*. Berkeley: University of California Press, 2011.

Perales, Monica. *Smeltertown: Making and Remembering a Southwest Border Community*. Chapel Hill: University of North Carolina Press, 2010.

Perez, Mario. "The Color of Youth: Mexicans and the Power of Schooling in Chicago, 1917–1939." PhD diss., University of Illinois, 2012.

Pérez-Rodríguez, Arturo J. "Toward a Hispanic Rite, *Quizas*." In *Misa, Mesa, y Musa: Liturgy in the U.S. Hispanic Church*, edited by Kenneth G. Davis, OFM. Schiller Park, IL: World Library Publications, 1997.

Pero, Peter N. *Chicago's Pilsen Neighborhood*. Charleston, SC: Arcadia Books, 2011.

Pescador, Juan Javier. *Crossing Borders with the Santa Niño de Atocha*. Albuquerque: University of New Mexico Press, 2009.

———. "Los Héroes del Domingo: Soccer, Border and Social Spaces in the Great Lakes Mexican Communities, 1940–1970." In *Mexican Americans and Sports: A Reader on Athletics and Barrio Life*, edited by Jorge Iber and Samuel Regalado. College Station: Texas A&M University Press, 2007.

Pitti, Gina Marie. "To 'Hear about God in Spanish': Ethnicity, Church, and Community Activism in the San Francisco Archdiocese's Mexican American Colonias, 1942–1965." PhD diss., Stanford University, 2003.

Prieto, Jorge. *Harvest of Hope: The Pilgrimage of a Mexican-American Physician*. Notre Dame, IN: University of Notre Dame Press, 1989.

Ramírez, Daniel. *Migrating Faith: Pentecostalism in the United States and Mexico in the Twentieth Century*. Chapel Hill: University of North Carolina Press, 2015.

Ramírez, Leonard G. *Chicanas of 18th Street: Narratives of a Movement from Latino Chicago*. Urbana: University of Illinois Press, 2011.

Reardon, Patrick T. "The Americanization of the Lunas." *Chicago Tribune Magazine*, March 4, 2001.

Rivas-Rodriguez, Maggie, ed. *Beyond the Latino World War II Hero: The Social and Political Legacy of a Generation*. Austin: University of Texas Press, 2009.

———. *A Legacy Greater Than Words: Stories of U.S. Latinos and Latinas of the WWII Generation*. Austin: University of Texas Press, 2006.

———, ed. *Mexican Americans & World War II*. Austin: University of Texas Press, 2005.

Rivera, Angelica. "Re-inserting Mexican-American Women's Voices into 1950s Chicago Educational History." PhD diss., University of Illinois, 2008.

Roediger, David R. *Working Toward Whiteness: How America's Immigrants Became White*. New York: Basic Books, 2005.

Roediger, David, and James Barrett. "Making New Immigrants 'Inbetween': Irish Hosts and White Panethnicity, 1890 to 1930." In *Not Just Black and White: Historical and Contemporary Perspectives on Immigration, Race, and Ethnicity in the United States*, edited by Nancy Foner and George Fredrickson. New York: Russell Sage, 2004.

Rosas, Ana Elizabeth. *Abrazando el Espíritu: Bracero Families Confront the US-Mexico Border*. Berkeley: University of California Press, 2014.

Rosen, George. *Decision-Making Chicago-Style: The Genesis of a University of Illinois Campus*. Urbana: University of Illinois Press, 1980.

Rúa, Mérida M. *A Grounded Identidad: Making New Lives in Chicago's Puerto Rican Neighborhoods*. New York: Oxford University Press, 2012.

Rudy Lozano: His Life, His People. Chicago: Taller de Estudios Comunitarios, 1991.

Ruiz, Vicki L. *From Out of the Shadows: Mexican Women in Twentieth-Century America*. New York: Oxford University Press, 1998.

Samors, Neal, and Michael Williams. *The Old Chicago Neighborhood: Remembering Life in the 1940s*. Chicago: Chicago's Neighborhoods, Inc., 2003.

Sánchez, George. *Becoming Mexican American: Ethnicity, Culture, and Identity in Chicano Los Angeles, 1900–1945*. New York: Oxford University Press, 1993.

Sandoval-Strausz, A. K. "Latino Landscapes: Postwar Cities and the Transnational Origins of a New Urban America." *Journal of American History*, December 2014, 804–31.

Sanguino, Laurencio, and Mauricio Tenorio. "Orígenes de una ciudad mexicana: Chicago y la ciencia del Mexican Problem (1900–1930)." Mexico City: CIDE, 2007.

Seitz, John C. *No Closure: Catholic Practice and Boston's Parish Shutdowns*. Cambridge, MA: Harvard University Press, 2011.

Seligman, Amanda I. *Block by Block: Neighborhoods and Public Policy on Chicago's West Side*. Chicago: University of Chicago Press, 2005.

Shanabruch, Charles. *Chicago's Catholics: The Evolution of an American Identity*. Notre Dame, IN: University of Notre Dame Press, 1981.

Sinnott, John Francis. "The West Side Community Center." Master's thesis, Loyola University Chicago, 1949.

Skerrett, Ellen. "Documenting the Immigrant Experience through Catholic Records." In *Documenting Diversity: The American Catholic Experience; Proceedings of the 1992 Conference Sponsored by the Association of Catholic Diocesan Archivists in Conjunction with the Catholic University of America and the Archdiocese of Chicago*, edited by George C. Michalek, Nancy Sandleback, and John J. Treanor. Chicago: Archdiocese of Chicago, Archives and Records Center, 1994.

———. "Sacred Space: Parish and Neighborhood in Chicago." In *Catholicism, Chicago Style*, by Ellen Skerrett, Edward R. Kantowicz, and Steven M. Avella. Chicago: Loyola University Press, 1993.

Skerrett, Ellen, Edward R. Kantowicz, and Steven M. Avella. *Catholicism, Chicago Style*. Chicago: Loyola University Press, 1993.

Smith, Robert Courtney. *Mexican New York: Transnational Lives of New Immigrants*. Berkeley: University of California Press, 2006.

Sommers, Laurie Kay. *Fiesta, Fe y Cultura: Celebrations of Faith and Culture in Detroit's Colonia Mexicana*. Detroit: Casa de Unidad; and East Lansing: Michigan State University Museum, 1995.

Stark, Robert H. "Religious Ritual and Class Formation: The Story of Pilsen, St. Vitus Parish, and the 1977 *Via Crucis*." PhD diss., University of Chicago, 1981.

Stern, Gwen Louise. "Ethnic Identity and Community Action in El Barrio." PhD diss., Northwestern University, 1976.

Sternstein, Malynne. *Czechs of Chicagoland*. Charleston, SC: Arcadia Books, 2008.

St. Procopius Church 1875–2000 125th Anniversary souvenir book. Private printing, n.d.

Taylor, Paul S. *Mexican Labor in the United States Chicago and the Calumet Region.* Berkeley: University of California Press, 1932.

———. "Songs of the Mexican Migration." In *Puro Mexicano*, edited by J. Frank Dobie. Austin: Texas Folk-Lore Society, 1935.

Taylor, William B. *Shrines & Miraculous Images: Religious Life in Mexico before the Reforma.* Albuquerque: University of New Mexico Press, 2010.

Tentler, Leslie Woodcock. "Beyond the Margins." *American Catholic Studies Newsletter* 38, no. 1 (Spring 2011): 8–11.

———. *Seasons of Grace: A History of the Catholic Archdiocese of Detroit.* Detroit, MI: Wayne State University Press, 1990.

Tregaskis, Richard. *Guadalcanal Diary.* New York: Random House, 1943.

Treviño, Roberto R. *The Church in the Barrio: Mexican American Ethno-Catholicism in Houston.* Chapel Hill: University of North Carolina Press, 2006.

Trexler, Richard C. *Reliving Golgotha: The Passion Play of Iztapalapa.* Cambridge, MA: Harvard University Press, 2003.

Tweed, Thomas A. *Our Lady of the Exile: Diasporic Religion at a Cuban Catholic Shrine in Miami.* New York: Oxford University Press, 1997.

Valdes, Dionicio Nodín. *Al Norte: Agricultural Workers in the Great Lakes Region, 1917–1970.* Austin: University of Texas Press, 1991.

———. *Barrios Norteños: St. Paul and Midwestern Mexican Communities in the Twentieth Century.* Austin: University of Texas Press, 2000.

Valerio-Jiménez, Omar, Santiago Vaquera-Vásquez, and Claire F. Fox, eds. *The Latina/o Midwest Reader.* Urbana: University of Illinois Press, 2017.

Vargas, Zaragoza. *Proletarians of the North: A History of Mexican Industrial Workers in Detroit and the Midwest, 1917–1933.* Berkeley: University of California Press, 1993.

Wilson, Catherine E. *The Politics of Latino Faith: Religion, Identity, and Urban Community.* New York: New York University Press, 2008.

Wright-Rios, Edward. *Revolutions in Mexican Catholicism: Reform and Revelation in Oaxaca, 1887–1934.* Durham, NC: Duke University Press, 2009.

Wrobel, Paul. *Our Way: Family, Parish, and Neighborhood in a Polish-American Community.* Notre Dame, IN: University of Notre Dame Press, 1979.

Young, Julia G. *Mexican Exodus: Emigrants, Exiles, and Refugees of the Cristero War.* New York: Oxford University Press, 2015.

Zárate Hernández, José Eduardo. *La celebración de la infancia: El culto al Niño Jesús en el área purhépecha.* Zamora, Michoacán: El Colegio de Michoacán, 2017.

Zimdars-Swartz, Sandra. *Encountering Mary: From LaSallette to Medjugore.* Princeton, NJ: Princeton University Press, 1991.

Index

Note: Page numbers in italics indicate figures; page numbers followed by "t" indicate tables.

DEBORAH E. KANTER is John S. Ludington Endowed Professor of History at Albion College. She is the author of *Hijos del Pueblo: Gender, Family, and Community in Rural Mexico, 1730–1850.*

Latinos in Chicago and the Midwest

Pots of Promise: Mexicans and Pottery at Hull-House, 1920–40
Edited by Cheryl R. Ganz and Margaret Strobel
Moving Beyond Borders: Julian Samora and the Establishment of Latino Studies
Edited by Alberto López Pulido, Barbara Driscoll de Alvarado, and Carmen Samora
¡Marcha! Latino Chicago and the Immigrant Rights Movement
Edited by Amalia Pallares and Nilda Flores-González
Bringing Aztlán to Chicago: My Life, My Work, My Art *José Gamaliel González, edited and with an Introduction by Marc Zimmerman*
Latino Urban Ethnography and the Work of Elena Padilla
Edited by Mérida M. Rúa
Defending Their Own in the Cold: The Cultural Turns of U.S. Puerto Ricans
Marc Zimmerman
Chicanas of 18th Street: Narratives of a Movement from Latino Chicago
Leonard G. Ramírez with Yenelli Flores, María Gamboa, Isaura González, Victoria Pérez, Magda Ramírez-Castañeda, and Cristina Vital
Compañeros: Latino Activists in the Face of AIDS *Jesus Ramirez-Valles*
Illegal: Reflections of an Undocumented Immigrant *José Ángel N.*
Latina Lives in Milwaukee *Theresa Delgadillo*
The Latina/o Midwest Reader *Edited by Omar Valerio-Jiménez, Santiago Vaquera-Vásquez, and Claire F. Fox*
In Search of Belonging: Latinas, Media, and Citizenship *Jillian M. Báez*
The Mexican Revolution in Chicago: Immigration Politics from the Early Twentieth Century to the Cold War *John H. Flores*
Ilegal: Reflexiones de un inmigrante indocumentado *José Ángel N.*
Negotiating Latinidad: Intralatina/o Lives in Chicago *Frances R. Aparicio*
Chicago Católico: Making Catholic Parishes Mexican *Deborah E. Kanter*

The University of Illinois Press
is a founding member of the
Association of University Presses.

University of Illinois Press
1325 South Oak Street
Champaign, IL 61820-6903
www.press.uillinois.edu